# Contract Law in South Korea

# Contract Law in South Korea

**Won-Lim Jee**
**Jung Won (Jamie) Jun**

This book was originally published as a monograph in the International Encyclopaedia of Laws/Contracts.

Founding Editor: Roger Blanpain
General Editor: Frank Hendrickx
Volume Editor: Jacques Herbots

Wolters Kluwer

*Published by:*
Kluwer Law International B.V.
PO Box 316
2400 AH Alphen aan den Rijn
The Netherlands
E-mail: international-sales@wolterskluwer.com
Website: lrus.wolterskluwer.com

*Sold and distributed in North, Central and South America by:*
Wolters Kluwer Legal & Regulatory U.S.
7201 McKinney Circle
Frederick, MD 21704
United States of America
Email: customer.service@wolterskluwer.com

*Sold and distributed in all other countries by:*
Air Business Subscriptions
Rockwood House
Haywards Heath
West Sussex
RH16 3DH
United Kingdom
Email: international-customerservice@wolterskluwer.com



ISBN 978-94-035-1143-6

e-Book: ISBN 978-94-035-1181-8
web-PDF: ISBN 978-94-035-1182-5

# The Authors

Won-Lim Jee (1958) is professor of Law at Korea University School of Law, Seoul, where he teaches Civil Law. He began his professorship in 1989 and has authored numerous books and articles. He has served as the president of the Korean Association of Civil Law and the Korean Association of Comparative Private Law. He received his LL.B. (1981), LL.M. (1984), and Ph.D. (1993) degrees from Seoul National University. He was a visiting scholar (1996–1998) at the Institute for International and Comparative Law at the University of Cologne, sponsored by the Alexander von Humboldt Foundation.

Jung Won (Jamie) Jun (1984) is assistant professor in the College of Law at Kookmin University, Seoul. Prior to joining Kookmin in 2014, she served as a judicial clerk at the Superior Court in the State of Connecticut in its civil division, as well as on the complex litigation docket (2010–2013). She obtained her B.S. degree (2007) from Cornell University and J.D. degree (2010) from the University of Georgia School of Law. She is licensed to practice Law in Georgia, New York, and New Jersey.

**The Authors**

# Table of Contents

# General Introduction

## §1. General Background of the Korean Private Law

*1.* Up to the early twentieth century, Korea, as a Confucian State, had remained in an isolated and premodern agrarian society, and most disputes surrounding private affairs were settled by means of the conventional institutions mainly based on courtesy and common interests of society.

Under the Japanese colonial rule from 1910 to 1945, the Japanese Governor attempted to transplant Japanese law into Korea. As a result, the Japanese Civil Code, except parts on the family law and the law of inheritance, was enforced in Korea, which means that the modern (private) law was introduced for the first time into Korea. Soon after the restoration of national independence (National Liberation) in 1948, the Korean government started to draft a new Civil Code as a matter of course. The Civil Code was promulgated in 1958 and came into force on January 1, 1960 (as to the Commercial Code, *see infra* paragraph 14).

On account of the short preparatory period and poor manpower, the drafters had to rely largely on the Japanese Civil Code (usually referred to in Korea as "old Civil Code"), and therefore the Civil Code resembles the Japanese Civil Code in some respects. However, there are several significant differences. For instance, under the Korean Civil Code, the registration is a requirement for changes in real rights over immovable properties to take effect (Article 186). By contrast the Japanese Civil Code requires the registration of title in order to assert real rights concerning immovables against third parties (i.e., the creation and transfer of real rights shall take effect solely by a declaration of intention of the relevant parties; however, acquisitions of, losses of and changes in real rights over immovable properties may not be asserted against third parties without registration. Articles 176 and 177, the Japanese Civil Code). In addition, it should be pointed out that the Japanese Civil Code itself is not an original work with regard to its contents as well as system in that it is largely based on European Civil Codes.

On the other hand, the Civil Code had remained unchanged until recently in essence, with some exceptions mainly for parts on the family law and the law of inheritance. However, in the 2010s, there were remarkable revisions (e.g., with regard to adult guardianship, suretyship and package tour contract), which will be discussed later.

§2. To What Legal Family Does Korean Law Belong?

*2.* The Korean private law belongs to that family of the legal system which is referred to as the Civil law system. More precisely, the Civil Code is derived mainly from Germany (and partly from France) via Japan.

The system of the Civil Code resembles that of the German Civil Code (*Bürgerliches Gesetzbuch*, hereafter "BGB" for short), i.e., is organized in line with the Pandekten system which starts with General Part, although the order of Part concerning Real Rights and Part of Claims is reversed. In addition, many key concepts originated from BGB. For instance, the juristic act is equivalent to the German term "*Rechtsgeschäft*," and the declaration of intention tantamount to "*Willenserklärung*" (*see infra* paragraphs 17 and 104). Moreover, regarding changes in real rights, the Civil Code adopted the German model (*see infra* paragraph 347) instead of the French model adopted into the so-called old Civil Code.

§3. Primacy of Legislation

## I. Overview

*3.* In conformity with the characteristics of the Civil law system, the positive law (*lex scripta*) is the primary source of law in Korea too. (*Lex scripta* is general in that it is applicable to every person and abstract in that it shall apply in most cases). The private law is contained mainly in the Codes which are systematic and comprehensive statements of a body of law (i.e., the Civil Code and the Commercial Code), and in many other statutes which modify or supplement the Codes.

## II. Statute

*4.* For a layman, the positive law is hardly comprehensible especially because of highly technical terms used therein and the complicated system of statutes owing to the necessity of detailed regulation in modern society. Nevertheless, *lex scripta* is the main source of most fields of law in Korea. In the public sphere, the positive law is in principle an indispensable condition for the justifiable exercise of public authority. In the private field, in contrast, *lex scripta* is an essential basis to promote transactions and to secure the freedom and equality of the parties thereto.

The raw material for statutes of the Republic of Korea in English (in my opinion: some translations may not be correct) may be retrieved at http://elaw.klri.re.kr/eng_service/lawTotalSearch.do.

## III. Decisions of the Court

*5.* Pursuant to the principle of the separation of powers, the competence of the court shall be confined to the judicial function of applying the law(s) to the case in question, and the power to lay down general rules is, in principle, not delegated to the court. In this context, Article 103 of the Constitution of the Republic of Korea provides that "Judges shall rule independently according to their conscience and in conformity with the Constitution and laws."

On the other hand, any decision made in a judgment of a higher court shall bind the court of lower instance with respect to the very case (Article 8, the Court Organization Act). In other words, the idea that decisions of a higher court (precedent) shall bind the court is not adopted into the Korean judiciary system. In this sense, the decisions of the court are not a source of law, and there is no doctrine equivalent to the Anglo-American doctrine of stare decisis. Nevertheless, in practice, decisions of a higher court, especially those of the Supreme Court, have a decisive influence, i.e., a strong de facto binding force.

*6.* Notwithstanding the above mentioned, some legal institutions have been concretized and/or developed by way of the court decisions. First, the court of the suit must give reasons for its decisions and the reason should, as a rule, be derived from *lex scripta*. In this context, in order to interpret and concretize provisions of *lex scripta* as indispensable premises for judgments, the court may exercise the creative power of the judiciary. Second and more importantly, some significant developments of law have taken place through decisions of the court, because the codification cannot cover all the eventualities which might arise (what is more, in some exceptional cases the legislators themselves leave knowingly the development of law to the court), and changes in social environments often require a new legal concept or new content(s) of a legal concept in existence. In this sense, a specific legal institution which is not explicitly provided for by *lex scripta* may be created and approved by the court (e.g., the return of reimbursement (derived from section 285, BGB). *See infra* paragraph 252).

In short, under the Korean legal system *lex scripta* is the primary source of law, while the judge-made law is also of some importance.

## §4. The Position of the Judiciary

*7.* Now, the Korean judiciary and court system will be introduced briefly.

Similar to other Civil law countries, Korea has a career judiciary system. In the past, persons who had passed the national bar examination (including even those who did not major in law) had been admitted to the Judicial Research and Training Institute for two years of practical training. Thereafter, they became lawyers, and judges and prosecutors were appointed among them. However, in 2007, the Act on the Establishment and Management of Professional Law Schools was promulgated, and thereby the system of legal education and qualification of lawyer has been changed radically. Now, a person who intends to apply for the new national bar examination have to get a *juris doctorate* degree from a professional law school, and successful applicants shall become lawyers, and judges and prosecutors shall be appointed among them. The new law school system was launched in 2009.

*8.* In Korea, the court shall be classified into six categories: Supreme Court, High Court, Patent Court, District Court, Family Court and Administrative Court

(Article 3, the Court Organization Act). The Korean judiciary system is based on the three instance trial system; i.e., it is composed of district courts as the first tier court, high courts which shall judge generally cases of the appeal against, e.g., judgment(s) made in the first instance and the Supreme Court as the highest court. (The Patent Court, the Family Court and the Administrative Court carry out specialized functions.) The court of the second instance (usually a high court, but on occasion a district court) can substitute its view regarding facts as well as law for that of the first instance. The Supreme Court, as the court in the last instance, shall rule cases of the final appeal against judgment(s) of the second instance, on the basis of whether a judgment of the court below is in conformity with law or not. In cases where the final appeal is justifiable, the Supreme Court usually quashes the decision and returns it for further consideration to another court equivalent to the original court (it may substitute its own judgment as a final decision. Articles 436 and 437, the Civil Procedure Act).

## §5. Distinction Between Public Law and Private Law

*9.* In Korea, similar to other jurisdictions, it is generally accepted that law is divided into private law and public law. (Since the State exclusively exercises the authority to prosecute, criminal law is regarded as part of public law.)

Many theories have been suggested to draw a line between public law and private law. The dominant theory defines public law as rules which confer power and impose obligation only on the holder of public authority. In the public sphere, in order to guarantee the development of capabilities of individuals in all the fields by further strengthening the free and democratic order conducive to the private initiative and public harmony, the public authority should be exercised in strict compliance with law (the principle of the rule of law), and the exercise of such authority needs special justification therefor. By contrast, private law is applicable to any legal subject. Private law, based on the principle of the party autonomy (*infra* paragraph 22), regards the individual as a free and equal legal subject and furnishes legal institutions to facilitate the free development of the personality (e.g., contract, ownership, will/testament and company).

*10.* On the other hand, in recent legislations it is not seldom that concerning certain matters, public law provisions and private law provisions are integrated into one single Act. For instance, the Unfair Competition Prevention and Trade Secret Protection Act aims primarily to maintain orderly trade by preventing acts of unfair competition such as improper use of domestically well-known trademarks and trade names, and by preventing infringement of trade secrets. In this sense, this Act is public law in nature. However, this Act provides also for the liability to compensate losses caused by acts of unfair competition and so on. In this regard, this Act belongs to private law. The Framework Act on Consumers, which aims to protect consumers' rights and interests, also contains private law provisions as well as public law provisions.

*11.* The administrative litigations shall in principle be governed by the Administrative Litigation Act. An administrative lawsuit may be filed without previously resorting to the administrative adjudication, unless otherwise provided for by law. (In the past, the exhaustion of administrative adjudication was a premise to file an administrative lawsuit with the court.) On the other hand, all the ordinary courts have jurisdiction over acts of administration, although there is Administrative Court as a specialized court.

## §6. Distinction Between Civil Law and Commercial Law

### I. Overview

*12.* In contrast to several other countries' legal systems, in which commercial law is incorporated into the Civil Code, in Korea the Civil Code and the Commercial Code are the two separate pillars of private law. To commercial transactions, as a result, special provisions in the Commercial Code and related legislations shall apply prior to those of the Civil Code.

### II. The Civil Code

*13.* The Civil Code is organized on the lines of the (German) Pandekten system, and it is a prominent characteristic of the Pandekten system that general principles and basic rules are singled out and put at the beginning of the Code.

The Civil Code is divided into five Parts. Part One entitled "General Provisions" contains provisions which are applicable to all the following Parts. This part provides for basic rules of civil law (i.e., the source of law and the doctrine of trust and good faith), legal capacities of natural and juristic persons, juristic act and declaration of intention, agency and extinctive prescription (limitation). Part Two headed "Real Rights" is the law of things and regulates legal relations between persons and things, i.e., possession, ownership and other real rights such as mortgage. Part Three under the heading of "Claims" is the law of obligation and deals with legal relations between (specific) persons. Contract which is the concern of this monograph is the most important source of obligation; however, for instance, tort as one of the sources of obligation is also laid down in this part. Part Four headed "Relatives" is the law of family and regulates marriage, divorce and legal relations between parents and children. Part Five is entitled "Inheritance" and deals with succession and will (testament).

On the other hand, there are special statutes which modify and/or supplement the Civil Code. Among these statutes, some important statutes related to the contract law will be introduced later in this monograph.

Hereinafter, provisions of the Civil Code will in principle be cited without the specific name of the Code.

## III. The Commercial Code

*14.* The Commercial Code was enacted in 1962 and came into force on January 1, 1963. This Code consists of six Parts: General Provisions, Commercial Activities, Company, Insurance, Marine Commerce and Carriage by Air (the last Part was inserted in 2011). This Code is modified and/or supplemented by various statutes such as the Check Act, the Bills of Exchange and Promissory Notes Act, the Commercial Registration Act and, what is more concerning company, the Financial Investment Services and Capital Markets Act.

In cases where both provisions of the Civil Code and those of the Commercial Code may apply, the latter, as the special rule, take priority: Where the Commercial Code does not provide for a particular commercial matter, commercial customary law shall apply, and if no such law exists, the Civil Code shall apply (Article 1, the Commercial Code. *See* also *infra* paragraph 51).

# Introduction to the Law of Contract

§1. DEFINITION OF CONTRACT

## I. Introduction

*15.* The Civil Code does not provide for a definition of contract. However, a definition which is generally accepted in Korea does not differ in essence from that of other legal systems:

> A contract is a juristic act, established by the coinciding declarations of intention of more than two persons, aimed to give rise to a binding legal relation.

The creation, modification or extinction of obligation(s) is the principal effect of a contract.

*16.* The indispensable element of contract is the coinciding/corresponding declarations of intention of the parties thereto, which will be discussed later.

In addition, the intentions of the parties must be directed toward producing certain "legal" effects. There are some agreements which do not aim to produce legal effects but lead merely to social or moral burdens. For instance, a promise to give a ride somewhere does not create legal effects in general. Nevertheless, such promise may produce legal effects, if there is an intention of the promisor to be bound legally.

## II. Juristic Act

*17.* A contract is a species of the genus "juristic act." The concept of juristic act stemmed from the German term "*Rechtsgeschäft*," which plays a central and important role in the German civil law. This term, as a unique fruit of the Pandekten jurisprudence, is an overall concept extracted from common characteristics of contract, will/testament and act of incorporation (a majority of scholars in Korea are of the opinion that it is not a contract, but a so-called joint act; however, both are not different in substance). The Civil Code has followed this model. (In recent years, some scholars raise doubts about the usefulness and desirableness of this model.)

As one of the key concepts of private law as a whole, a juristic act shall be defined as a voluntary act aimed to produce certain legal effects based on the intentions of the parties, which can be enforced through the judicial system. Legal relations not merely between subjects but also between subject(s) and object(s) take place in principle by a juristic act under the economic order based on a respect for the freedom and creative initiative of enterprises and individuals (Article 119, paragraph 1, the Constitution of the Republic of Korea.) In this regard, a juristic act is the most important legal means by which individuals may manage their private affairs on their own initiative, i.e., a means to realize the party autonomy.

*18.* Legal effects of a juristic act arise from an intention of the party. In this sense, an indispensable element of a juristic act is the declaration/manifestation of intention ("*Willenserklärung*") directed at certain legal effects. However, a juristic act and a declaration of intention should be distinguished. The latter is a constructive element of the former, nevertheless it is not a juristic act itself, because a juristic act may require element(s) other than a mere declaration of intention (*See infra* paragraph 104.)

On the other hand, the purpose and consequence (i.e., legal effects) of a juristic act must comply with law (not merely mandatory provisions but also social order (Article 103. Hereafter, social order includes good moral under this Article. *See* also *infra* paragraph 130.) Both set limits to the principle of the freedom of contract). If a juristic act cannot be recognized by law, the act shall be void or voidable (i.e., unenforceable through the judicial system). As to conditions of the substantive validity of a contract, *see infra* paragraphs 85 ff.

*19.* Similar to German law, the relation between "act/transaction of obligation" (*Verpflichtungsgeschäft*) and "act/transaction of disposition" (*Verfüngsgeschäft*) is one of the most controversial issues under the Korean civil law. (In the French legal family, since contract itself effects changes in real rights, the concept of act of disposition is unnecessary, and therefore this question does not arise. In recent years, a few Korean scholars raise doubts about the usefulness and desirableness of these concepts.) The former is a juristic act by which merely obligation(s), i.e., right(s) in personam, shall be created. This act is normally a contract. The real rights themselves (e.g., ownership of the thing sold) shall not be affected by this act. The act of disposition, in contrast, is a juristic act which transfers, burdens, alters or terminates rights in rem (or rights in personam themselves) directly. An act of disposition is also usually a contract (referred to in Korea usually as "agreement").

*20.* An act of obligation forms usually the legal cause for an act of disposition. However, a line should be drawn between both acts (the principle of division: *Trennungsprinzip*), because both acts have different requirements as well as effects. As legal effects of an act of obligation, e.g., a contract of sale, merely obligations to transfer ownership of the thing sold and to pay the purchase-money are produced. By contrast, the ownership passes to the buyer upon completion of an act of disposition. In addition, an act of disposition requires an authority to dispose of, and this authority belongs usually to the person whose rights are being disposed of, e.g., the owner of a thing sold. On the contrary, an act of obligation does not require such authority. Under Article 569, a sale of the right belonging to another person shall be valid, even if the buyer may not acquire the very right. (If the seller is unable to transfer the ownership, the Civil Code imposes the liability for warranty on the seller. Article 570, *infra* paragraph 263) Taking into consideration this Article and the retention of ownership, which aims to secure the payment of the purchase-money in case of a sale of goods via installment, this division is supported by most civil law experts.

In reality, however, an act of disposition is usually contained in and confused with fulfillment of the act of obligation, with the result that in general, the former is not done consciously and separately.

*21.* There is a more crucial and long-pending controversy surrounding the principle of abstraction (*Abstraktionsprinzip*). Pursuant to this principle, even if an act of obligation, e.g. a contract of sale, is invalid, an act of disposition, e.g., the transfer of an ownership, in compliance with conditions of the substantive validity shall remain valid, and an obligation to reverse the act of disposition by making restitution may arise.

However, in contrast to German law, the Supreme Court did not accept this principle (75Da1394. *See* also 81DaKa1110). Therefore, the validity of the transfer of ownership is dependent upon the validity of a contract creating an obligation to transfer ownership. In other words, an act of disposition is "causal." If a contract of sale is invalid, the transfer of ownership is also invalid, and the seller (S), as an owner, may demand the return of the article sold from the buyer (B) (*rei vindicatio*. Article 213). In case of a resale between B and T, S has an overtaking right and may demand return of the article from T. However, if T has another ground for acquisition of the ownership (e.g., bona fide acquisition. Article 249), S may not exercise *rei vindicatio* against T. In addition, in a case where the contract between S and B is void or voided, T may be protected as a third person acting in good faith (Article 107, paragraph 2; Article 108, paragraph 2; Article 109, paragraph 2; Article 110, paragraph 3. *See infra* paragraph 142), and in case of the rescission of contract between S and B, T shall not be prejudiced thereby (Article 548, paragraph 1. *See infra* paragraph 285).

## III. The Principle of the Freedom of Contract and Its Modifications

*22.* All individuals shall be assured of human worth and dignity and have the right to pursue happiness. It shall be a duty of the State to confirm and guarantee the fundamental and inviolable human rights of individuals (Article 10, the Constitution of the Republic of Korea). In this regard, although there is no explicit provision in *lex scripta*, the foundation stone of the Korean private law is the principle of the party autonomy (*Privatautonomie*), which is based on the freedom of individuals. This principle governs all the aspects of contract, i.e., from the formation to the extinction of contract.

As an expression of the party autonomy concerning contract, the principle of the freedom of contract is the basic and indispensable element of the Korean contract law. As a rule, a contractual obligation can be derived solely from the free intentions of the persons bound to the contract. In this sense, anyone is free to enter into a contract with someone at his/her choice, to decide the contents of contract (including the possibility to develop a new type of contract or to conclude a named contract with new/modified contents), and to impose any requirements regarding its form.

*23.* Nevertheless, this principle, which is based on a liberal approach of the nineteenth century (*laissez-faire*), cannot survive without any modification in modern society. First, this principle assumes that every person as a separate and independent individual would be capable of watching out for his/her own interest in compliance with his/her intention/will in the struggle for survival. However, the equality of ability between individuals is indeed a myth or fiction. Second, to an ever-increasing extent every person had become a member of various social groups (e.g., as a worker or consumer), in line with the tendency in social structures and relations toward organization and collectivization. The power of these groups leads to restrictions on the "substantial" (not formal) freedom of contract. Third, owing to the disparity of bargaining power of the parties, especially in employment agreements or leases of immovables (e.g., a housing lease), the principle of the freedom of contract, in particular with regard to determination of its contents (also due to standard terms), may give rise to unfairness and injustice to the weaker party.

*24.* Under such circumstances, in order to protect the weaker member of society against exploitation by the stronger and thereby to promote more of a balance of the interests between the parties, modifications shall be made to that principle. Modification takes place usually in the form of public intervention in the contents of contract. As a rule, a juristic act contrary to social order, including an unfair juristic act, shall be null and void (Articles 103 and 104. *See infra* paragraphs 131 ff. and 122). In addition, public intervention by way of mandatory provisions is ever increasing, in order to protect those who are in socially or economically weak positions as well as to promote common interests of society. For instance, concerning a lease of immovables, some provisions (e.g., provision on the right to demand increase of the rent, or on the lessee's right to demand renewal of the contract or to demand purchase of the building. *See infra* paragraphs 376, 382 and 388) are mandatory, i.e., any agreement entered into by the parties in contravention thereof, which is unfavorable to the lessee, shall be null and void (Article 652). On the other hand, employment agreements are subject to strict control under the Labor Standards Act. Furthermore, owing to the growing necessity to protect the interest of consumers, the so-called consumer law, which imposes some restrictions on the freedom of contract, has been enacted (*see infra* paragraphs 352 ff.).

*25.* In short, the freedom to contract or not may be restricted pursuant to *lex scripta* (e.g., compulsory third-party insurance of motorists) or on account of economic circumstances (e.g., monopolies). The freedom to determine the contents of contract may also be affected by the great expansion in the number and scope of mandatory provisions, aimed primarily to correct the consequences of inequality of bargaining power. For instance, Article 6, paragraph 1 of the Act on the Regulation of Terms and Conditions provides that any clause in standard terms, which is contrary to the doctrine of bona fides and is not fair, shall be null and void (*see infra* paragraph 156).

In spite of various restrictions on the freedom of contract just referred to, in the absence of such restrictions, the principle of the party autonomy still operates and shall operate.

## IV. The Basis of Contractual Liability

*26.* The parties to a contract shall be bound to perform obligations arising from the contract they have entered into. The binding force of a contract is not expressly laid down by the Civil Code; however, it is implied in Article 389, paragraph 1, which states that in a case where an obligor does not perform his/her obligation voluntarily, the obligee may apply to the court for the compulsory execution thereof (*see infra* paragraphs 273 ff.).

*27.* There is a controversy surrounding the basis of contractual liability. According to the will theory, it is coinciding intentions of the parties to a contract (primarily: the obligor's free intention) which bind them. By contrast, the theory of reliance lays stress upon the fact that the obligor induces the obligee to rely on the obligor's promise.

In my opinion, the Civil Code takes both factors into consideration. On the one hand, as mentioned above, the principle of the freedom of contract is the foundation stone of the Korean contract law, although this principle is restricted in various ways. Pursuant to this principle, only a contract based on free intentions of the parties may be binding. Therefore, as a rule, a contract requires, as an indispensable premise of self-binding, coinciding intentions of parties thereto to produce certain legal effects. Without intention of any party, there is no contract. On the other hand, the reliance of one party on the appearance, which looks as if the other party has the intention to produce certain legal effects, shall on occasion be protected in various ways even in the absence of such intention. For example, a declaration of "untrue" intention shall be valid in principle (Article 107). In these exceptional cases, a party may be bound to such an appearance and a valid contract takes effect, irrespective of his/her actual intention, or he/she may be liable for damages. However, even in these cases, since the reliance should aim toward and may be justified by the "putative" intention of the other party, the intention of the party is of great importance. As to the protection of the bona fide third person, *see infra* paragraphs 141 f.

## V. The Role of Contracts in Korea

*28.* Up to the middle of the twentieth century, in Korea, as a premodern agrarian society, a mutually beneficial and cooperative relationship between people based on the confucian tradition, was of importance. Conventionally, courtesy and general/common interests of society were regarded highly. In this kind of society, insistence on individual interests and/or resort to law to resolve a dispute caused on occasion alienation from society. On the other hand, since modern law was implanted by the Japanese Governor, the antipathy toward Japan, as the occupying nation, led to some extent to the negative perspective on law itself and contract. In this regard, a "social" way to settle a dispute was preferred to law.

In recent decades, however, social and economic circumstances have changed significantly. Not only companies, but also people at large have recognized contracts as one of the essential conditions for social order("*contrat social*"), and have accepted the binding force of contracts and the necessity of contracts to be made in writing, especially to avoid a dispute therefrom and/or to mitigate the burden of proof. Although the conventional attitude toward law remains still in part and the role of contracts is limited to some extent, the binding force of contracts is for the present as strict as in Europe or the United States in some respects.

## §2. Classification of Contract

### I. Classification of Contract as a Whole

*29.* Contract may be classified in line with the branch of civil law to which they relate:

(1) Contract concerning the family law (e.g., marriage or adoption).
(2) Contract regarding real rights (referred to usually as "agreement"). It is a contract directed at changes of (i.e., acquisition of, loss of or alteration in) real rights. This kind of contract is closely related to an obligatory contract and, as mentioned above, the Supreme Court found that the validity of the former depends upon that of the latter (*see supra* paragraph 21). For instance, the transfer of ownership of the thing sold shall be invalidated as a rule, if the contract of sale is void or voided. On the other hand, any change in real rights over immovables by a juristic act takes effect upon its registration (Article 186: the proclamation system. As to the transfer of real rights over movables, *see* at first Article 188, paragraph 1).
(3) Obligatory contract. The Civil Code contains special provisions on obligatory contract in section 1, Chapter 2 of Part Three. Further distinctions shall be drawn within this class.

### II. The Distinctions Within the Class of Obligatory Contracts

*30.* The usual and meaningful classifications are as follows:

(1) *Contractus nominati*, *contractus innominati* and mixed contract

A contract is "named" (*contractus nominati*) if there are provisions on the contract concerned in *lex scripta* (including the Commercial Code), or "unnamed" (*contractus innominati*) if there is no provision on the contract in question. On the other hand, a mixed contract is one which combines elements of more than two named contracts.

All the contracts are subject to general principles thereof, especially the principle of party autonomy. In this respect, provisions on certain contract in *lex scripta* are at first intended to furnish an appropriate standard for the equilibrium and balance between the interests of both parties to the relevant contract, and these provisions are normally at the disposition of the parties. Therefore, requirements and legal effects of the named contract shall be derived, unless otherwise agreed upon between the parties, from provisions in *lex scripta*. By contrast, those of the unnamed contract shall be derived in principle from coinciding intentions of the parties (however, there is a possibility of analogy.)

*31.* (2) Consensual, real and formal contracts

Pursuant to the principle of the freedom of contract, an obligatory contract is, as a rule, made by a mere agreement between the contracting parties (a consensual contract). However, there are some exceptions to this rule.

At first, *lex scripta* lays down a few contracts in which, besides consensus of the parties, transfer of a thing or accomplishment of an act is necessary to create obligation(s). These contracts are referred to as real contracts. An example is advertisement offering prizes (Articles 675 ff. A few scholars are of the opinion that it is not a contract, but a unilateral act.) (In addition, most scholars are of the opinion that an accord (Article 466. *See infra* paragraph 223) is also a real contract.) A real contract comes into existence when the thing is transferred or the act is accomplished. On the other hand, in contrast to the French legal family, a loan for consumption and a bailment are consensual contracts in Korea (Articles 609 and 693).

Second, *lex scripta* requires regarding some contracts that consensus of the parties shall be expressed in a certain form (usually in writing) or be accompanied by a certain specific formality. These contracts are called formal contracts. An archetype is suretyship (Article 428-2). As to the formal contract, *see infra* paragraphs 69 ff.

*32.* (3) Synallagmatic and unilateral contracts

A synallagmatic (referred to also as reciprocal or bilateral) contract is one which creates reciprocal obligations, each obligation being the counterpart of the other (*do ut des*). In other words, a contract is synallagmatic if both contracting parties are bound to perform obligations reciprocally toward each other. The requirement of reciprocity is complied with if the obligations are interdependent; it is not necessary that one should be the price of the other. Examples of synallagmatic contracts are sale, lease, contract for work, and do on. In a contract of sale, for instance, the buyer assumes his/her obligation(s) in order to impose obligation(s) on the seller, and vice versa. The Civil Code contains provisions on special effects of the synallagmatic contract in subsection 2, section 1, Chapter 2 of Part Three (Articles 536 ff.). As a rule, in synallagmatic contracts (in reality: in most, but not all, contracts), nonperformance of one party may give rise to *exceptio non adimpleti contractus* (defense for simultaneous performance) of the opposing party, and the subsequent impossibility of performance by any cause for which neither of the parties is responsible may lead to the discharge of the obligee from the counter-performance (*see infra* paragraphs 288 ff. and 253 f.). In a synallagmatic contract, obligations of the parties must be not merely reciprocal but also in principle concurrent. In this context, the so-called imperfectly synallagmatic contract should be regarded as unilateral. For instance, in case of a loan for use (Article 609), both parties assume obligations. However, the borrower's obligation to return the object borrowed is not concurrent with the lender's obligation to deliver the object for use, and therefore, the effects mentioned above shall not arise therefrom.

A contract is, in contrast, unilateral, if one or each of the parties undertakes to perform obligation(s), without receiving in return any promise of performance from the other party. An example of a unilateral contract is a gift or suretyship.

*33.* (4) Onerous and gratuitous contracts

An onerous contract (a contract for value) is one in which each party makes a contribution to the other party with the intention of obtaining a reciprocal contribution from him/her (i.e., gives or promises something or some service to which the opposing party, in exchange, gives or promises), although unequal in value. In contrast to a synallagmatic contract in which each party "obliges" himself/herself toward the opposing party, each party to an onerous contract makes "contribution" reciprocally. An archetype of onerous contracts is a contract of sale, and provisions on sale (especially on the seller's liability for warranty) shall apply *mutatis mutandis* to onerous contracts other than contracts of sale (Article 567).

A contract is, by contrast, gratuitous if one or each of the parties gives or promises something or some service without any contribution from the other party in exchange. An example of a gratuitous contract is gift or suretyship. With regard to the gratuitous contract, the standard of care is on occasion lightened (e.g., Article 695 on the gratuitous bailment. A gratuitous mandatary, nevertheless, shall manage the entrusted affairs with the care of a good manager under Article 681.) and the binding force of contract is much weaker (e.g., rescission of a gift set forth in Articles 555 ff.).

The distinction between synallagmatic and unilateral contracts and the present distinction largely coincide. All synallagmatic contracts are onerous, and most unilateral contracts are gratuitous; however, this is not always the case. For instance, an advertisement offering prizes is a unilateral contract for value (Articles 675 ff.), and a gift with burden is a gratuitous contract, to which provisions on synallagmatic contract shall apply (Article 561).

*34.* (5) Principal and accessory contracts

A principal/main contract is one entered into by one or each of the parties on his/her own account, and thereby has an independent reason for existence. On the contrary, the characteristics of accessory/auxiliary contract are that they depend upon an external legal relationship. For instance, a contract of surety as an accessory contract is made for assuring performance of the principal contract, and is of appendant nature.

## §3. Contract and Torts

*35.* Contractual obligations come into existence by a juristic act, i.e., a contract (pursuant to the principle of party autonomy), but obligations may arise also from other sources (i.e., tort, management of affairs of another without mandate and unjust enrichment. *See* at first *infra* paragraph 38). Therefore, the Civil Code brings not merely contract but also other sources under the heading of claims, and in line with the Pandekten system (*supra* paragraph 13) some common matters (e.g., extinction and assignment of the claim) are treated under general provisions on claims (Chapter 1, Part Three of the Civil Code).

*36.* An unlawful act (tort) and a failure to perform obligation(s) resemble each other, in that both are unlawful and lead to a claim for damages. Therefore, the Civil Code provides for damages with regard to the failure to perform (Articles 390 ff.), and some provisions thereof shall apply *mutatis mutandis* to a claim for damages in tort (Article 763). It is worthy of being mentioned that both a contractual liability and a liability in tort require fault, i.e., intention or negligence, in Korea (Articles 390 and 750).

*37.* There are cases in which a failure to perform an obligation may at the same time constitute a tort. For instance, a party leases a thing from a person who owns the thing and then breaks up the thing at the former's fault: the loss caused to the latter's property may in principle lead to a failure to perform the obligation to return the thing leased as well as an unlawful act (tort). Since, in this case, e.g., there is a difference in particular with regard to the period of extinctive prescription (*see* Articles 162 and 766), the question about whether the lessor-owner may exercise both the claim for damages based on the failure in performance and the claim in tort or not, is of great importance in practice. Moreover, the burden of proof of the wrongdoer's fault lies with the obligor in the former claim (Article 390), while with the obligee in the latter claim (Article 750. As to the burden of proof in general, *see infra* paragraphs 145 f.).

Despite a crucial controversy over the relation between both claims, the Supreme Court is of the opinion that the obligee (victim) may choose any of the claims (82DaKa1533).

## §4. Contract and Quasi-Contract

*38.* Although, similar to other Civil law countries, the Civil Code draws a line between an obligation which arises from a contract/agreement and one which does not, the French traditional classification of the sources of obligation in "*contrats, quasi-contrats, delits, quasi-delits, loi*" is unknown in Korean law.

However, there are categories equivalent to the quasi-contract: the Civil Code contains provisions on, in addition to contract and torts, two other sources of obligations, i.e., management of affairs of another without mandate (*negotiorum gestio*) and unjust enrichment (*condictio*).

§5. CONTRACT AND THE LAW OF PROPERTY

## I. Relative Right and Absolute Right

*39.* The Civil Code divides the law of property into the law of obligation (Part Three headed Claims) and the law of real property (Part Two entitled Real Rights). The criterion for this division is the legal nature of the right concerned, i.e., the latter regulates absolute rights (rights in rem), while the former deals with relative rights (rights in personam).

A relative right is aimed at performance by a specific person and can be asserted as a rule solely against the very person (referred to as obligor or debtor). As to the principle of relative effect, *see infra* paragraph 177. By contrast, an absolute right is enforceable against the whole world and therefore can be asserted against everyone. For instance, an owner may demand cessation of the disturbance, including return of the article owned, from any person who disturbs the ownership (Articles 213 and 214. *rei vindicatio*).

In this context, no real right can be created at will other than those prescribed by law or customary law (Article 185: *numerus clausus* of real rights), while obligation(s) can in principle be produced at will of the parties with regard to requirements as well as legal effects (the principle of the freedom of contract. *See supra* paragraph 25).

## II. Relative Right with Absolute Character

*40.* Exceptionally, a right arising from an obligatory contract may have an absolute character.

An example is a right of the lessee registered (*see infra* paragraph 379): The lease takes effect in principle only between the parties thereto and not against a third person; however, a lease of an immovable property, if registered, shall be effective against third persons from the time registration has been effected (Article 621).

In addition, even if not registered, a lease shall become effective against third persons on the day following the date on which the lessee has completed delivery of the object of lease and residents registration (Article 3, paragraph 1, the Housing Lease Protection Act and Article 3, paragraph 1, the Commercial Building Lease Protection Act. *See infra* paragraphs 386 and 389). In such cases, the transferee of the immovable shall be deemed to have succeeded to the status of the lessor (Article 3, paragraph 4, the Housing Lease Protection Act and Article 3, paragraph 2, the Commercial Building Lease Protection Act). As to the preferential repayment right of the lessee just mentioned, *see infra* paragraph 387.

§6. CONTRACT AND TRUST

*41.* In Korea, there is a separate Act regulating the trust, called the Trust Act.

This Act defines trust as a legal relation that a person who creates a trust (truster) transfers a specific piece of property (including part of a business or an intellectual property right), establishes a security right or makes any other disposition to a person who accepts the trust (trustee), and requires the trustee to manage, dispose of, operate or develop such property or engage in other necessary conduct to fulfill the purpose of the trust, for the benefit of a specific person (beneficiary) or for a specific purpose, based on a confidence relation between the truster and the trustee (Article 2). A trust may be created by way of (i) a contract between the truster and the trustee, (ii) the will/testament of the truster or (iii) a declaration of the truster in which he/she has specified the purpose of the trust, trust property, beneficiary, etc., and has designated himself/herself as the trustee (Article 3).

The trust property as a special/separate property shall be protected in various ways. For instance, no compulsory execution or auction for exercise, etc. of security rights, conservative measure or disposition of default on national taxes, etc. may as a rule be made against any trust property (Article 22, paragraph 1), and a claim belonging to the trust property and a debt not belonging to the trust property shall not offset each other (Article 25, paragraph 1).

*42.* There is another type of trust unique to Korean law. For a long time, the Supreme Court has approved the validity of so-called title trust. The term "title trust" means a legal relationship between a person (title-truster) who holds, has actually acquired, or is to acquire an ownership of or other real rights to any real estate (real rights to real estate) and another person (title-trustee), to the effect that the title-truster having the actual right holds or is to hold real right to real estate internally and the title-trustee registers the ownership under his/her name (including a provisional registration), and thereby the title-trustee becomes the holder of real right to real estate externally.

However, since the title trust has been frequently misused as a means to the speculative investment in real estate, the Act on the Registration of Real Estate under Actual Titleholder's Name (enacted in 1995) prohibits the title trust (with a few exceptions thereto): Any title trust agreement shall be null and void, and any change in real rights to any real estate by a registration made under the title trust agreement shall be null and void. However, this shall not apply where the title-trustee is one of the parties to the contract to acquire real right to real estate, and the other party thereto does not know the fact that the title trust agreement (as contract of nominal trust) exists. On the other hand, invalidity of the title trust shall not be effective in respect of any third person (Article 4, the preceding Act).

## §7. Good Faith and Fair Dealing

### I. The Doctrine of Bona Fides

*43.* Article 2 lays down the doctrine of trust and good faith (bona fides) stating that:

(1) The exercise of rights and performance of duties shall be in accordance with the doctrine of trust and good faith.
(2) No abuse of rights shall be permitted.

This Article may be invoked where an unjust solution will be deduced under the relevant provision(s) of *lex scripta*. In applying this Article, various interests of the parties should be weighed and evaluated against each other, and not merely the purpose and wording of provisions concerned but also the influence of the fundamental rights set forth in the Constitution should be taken into account.

Article 2 as a general provision is applicable throughout the entire private law under various circumstances, i.e., to all the civil affairs. In effect, however, paragraph 1 is usually concerned with the relation between specific persons (including contract), while paragraph 2 is useful mainly where there is no such relation, e.g., in case of the exercise of *rei vindicatio* (*see supra* paragraph 39).

## II. The Functions of the Doctrine of Bona Fides in the Law of Contract

*44.* The doctrine of bona fides carries out some important functions with regard to the law of contract.

First, contents of the contractual obligation shall, as a rule, be determined by way of the interpretation of the contract in question (*see infra* paragraphs 152 ff.). However, since it is in practice impossible to provide for all the eventualities in contract, the doctrine of bona fides may give a guideline to fill the gap (based on the reasonable role-expectation of the parties toward each other). In this sense, this doctrine may create collateral/incidental obligations which are not set forth by way of an agreement (*see infra* paragraph 154). As a result, even in the absence of an explicit agreement and provision in *lex scripta*, the parties may be obliged to provide certain information or to act with due care. In this context, the doctrine of bona fides carries out a "creative/supplementing" function.

*45.* Second, the court occasionally restricts the rights of the parties based on this doctrine (a "restrictive" function). For instance, the lessor may rescind the lease for the future, if the lessee assigns his/her rights without obtaining the consent of the lessor (Article 629). However, the Supreme Court found that the lessor may not rescind the contract, unless the act of the lessee amounts to a destruction of mutual trust (*see infra* paragraph 378). On the other hand, the exercise of one's right may be regarded as abusive if it unreasonably infringes another's rights or interests. In this regard, the Supreme Court requires in principle the intention to harm on the part of the holder of the right (e.g., 2004Da44285. *See* also 2003Da40422), about which most scholars (except me) raise doubts. Abuse of rights is usually concerned with the case where the right in question is one arising from the real property law or torts. However, an abuse of contractual rights may also occur. For instance, a defense that a contractual right has been extinguished by prescription is on occasion rejected by the court based on this doctrine (2002Da32332. the principle of promissory *estoppel*).

*46.* The duty to perform an obligation may undergo change pursuant to this doctrine, if circumstances which became the basis of contract have radically changed after the contract was entered into and if the parties would not have entered into the contract or would have entered into a contract with different contents had foreseen this change (an "adaptive" function). Although there is no explicit provision (such as section 313, BGB), in 2007 (after restraint for a long time) the Supreme Court has approved "in principle" *clausula rebus sic stantibus* (*see infra* paragraphs 175 f.).

Furthermore, the so-called unwritten/judge-made law may be referred to as an outcome of this function.

## §8. Style of Drafting

### I. Introduction

*47.* The style of legislation and the interpretation of legislation are linked in a circular relation, and again the style of drafting of contract and the interpretation of contract are linked in the same way.

As mentioned above (*supra* paragraph 4), Korean law is generally in a simple, systematic and intelligible form; however, owing to its dogmatic, conceptual and systematic characteristics, it is not easy to understand for a layman (in some cases even for expert lawyers).

### II. Style of Drafting of Contracts

*48.* In the Common law system, law is primarily the unwritten/judge-made law found in decisions of the court, and legislation is in principle regarded as an intervention in the (unwritten) Common law. Therefore, the Common law style of drafting of contracts is complex and comprehensive to minimize such intervention. (The lawyer pursues usually completeness, even though he/she knows that not everything that he/she lays down in contract is necessary.)

On the contrary, under the Civil law system, the lawyer may rely on the supplement by application of suppletive/optional provisions (*see* Article 105). In other words, the gap may be filled mainly by way of a complementary application of *lex scripta*. Additionally, customs and the doctrine of bona fides (Articles 106 and 2) may be of use. Therefore, it is not required to provide for all the possible eventualities. On the other hand, a short and brief style of drafting leaves room for negotiation between the parties in cases where a conflict arises. As a result, his/her text is usually short and simple. In short, the Korean style of drafting of contracts is much less detailed and comprehensive than the Anglo-American style. In Korea, everyday transactions are often concluded not in writing or with a few rather short clauses. However, in cases of contracts dealing with important interests, clauses in such contracts may be detailed and elaborate.

§9. SOURCES OF THE LAW OF CONTRACT

## I. Overview

*49.* In Korea, there is no single Act which embraces all the topics surrounding contract, and the law of contract is found in parts of the Civil Code, the Commercial Code, and related statutes.

Provisions on contract are in principle optional in that they apply insofar as the parties do not agree otherwise (Article 105). Furthermore, the parties can develop atypical contracts, some of which have been inserted into the Code (e.g., financial lease in the Commercial Code), and may conclude a named contract with new/modified contents. However, provisions in *lex scripta* play an important role in that they furnish a reasonable standard for the equilibrium and balance between the interests of both parties.

## II. The Civil Code

*50.* The Civil Code is the most general law applicable to almost the whole civil affairs including contract. Chapter 2 of Part Three, following Chapter 1 on General Provisions of Claims, deals with contract. Chapter 2 is divided into two parts: general part and special part. The former contains general provisions on contract, i.e., on the formation, effects and rescission of contract, while the latter enumerated at the beginning fourteen types of so-called named/typical contract (*contractus nominati. See supra* paragraph 30): gift, sale, contract of exchange, loan for consumption, loan for use, lease, contract of employment, contract for work, advertisement offering prizes, mandate, bailment, partnership, life annuity and comprise. In addition thereto, in 2015 (Enforcement date: February 4, 2016), the package tour contract was added.

On the other hand, Chapter 1 of Part Three contains general provisions on obligation. These provisions —which deal with for instance extinction of claims, effects of the failure to perform and assignment of claims— shall apply to all the obligations including of course those arising from contract.

In addition, since a contract is a species of juristic act (*supra* paragraph 17), relevant provisions on juristic act in General Part (Part One) shall apply to contract. For instance, a contract, as an outcome of a declaration of intention, can be void or voidable on various grounds set forth in General Part (e.g., mistake, fraud, duress). The agency is also contained in General Part.

## III. The Commercial Code

*51.* Provisions on contract are also found in the Commercial Code. Part Two of this Code furnishes typical commercial contracts, such as sale, account current, undisclosed association, limited partnership, commercial agents, brokerage, commission agency, forwarding agent business, carriage business, hospitality business, warehousing, financial lease business, franchise business and bonds purchasing business, and Part Four of this Code deals with insurance.

Since, under Article 1 of the Commercial Code, provisions of this Code, as a special law in relations to the Civil Code, have priority over those of the latter insofar as a contract falls within the category of commercial activities (*see* also *supra* paragraph 14), it is necessary to explain commercial activities as a criterion for application. The Commercial Code is applicable to commercial affairs and provides for a list of basic commercial activities, e.g. sale or lease of movables, immovables, securities or any other assets, or undertaking of agency for commercial transactions (Article 46, the preceding Code). In addition, activities of a merchant for the purpose of his/her business shall be deemed to be commercial activities, and activities of a merchant shall be presumed effected for the purpose of his/her business (Article 47, the preceding Code). On the other hand, a merchant is defined as a person who carries out commercial activities in his/her own name (merchant by nature of business. Article 4, the preceding Code) or a person who engages in a business in the same manner as a merchant through a store or similar facility and a company, irrespective of the commercial activities (merchant by legal construction. Article 5, the preceding Code).

## IV. Other Acts

*52.* Besides the Codes just mentioned, there are numerous statutes which deal with specialized matters and modify and/or supplement provisions of the Codes:

(1) Some Acts, e.g., the Deposit Act, supplement the Codes.
(2) The inevitable by-product of modernization is an emergence of socially or economically deprived persons such as workers and house lessees. In order to protect such persons, statutes have been enacted to modify provisions of the Codes (e.g., the Housing Lease Protection Act and the Labor Standard Act). Some developments could be seen in particular with regard to the consumer protection (e.g., the Framework Act on Consumers, the Act on the Regulation of Terms and Conditions, the Installment Transactions Act and the Door-to-Door Sales, etc. Act).
(3) With the rapid advance in the information/communication technology, some new statutes, e.g., the Framework Act on Electronic Documents and Transactions and the Act on the Protection in Electronic Commerce, etc., have been enacted to protect laypersons.
(4) In 2004, Korea has ratified the United Nations Convention on the International Sale of Goods (CISG). CISG was enacted on March 1, 2005.

## V. Substantive Law and Adjective Law

*53.* Similar to other jurisdictions, the distinction between substantive law and adjective law is generally accepted in Korea. With regard to contracts, the former deals with legal relation (i.e., rights and/or duties) between parties as well as legal institution such as formation or rescission of contracts. Adjective law provides, by contrast, for the procedure in which the existence and/or contents of obligations are confirmed/approved officially and such obligations are enforced: procedural law. As to this, *see* also Article 389 and *infra* paragraphs 273 ff.

# Part I. General Principles of the Law of Contract

## Chapter 1. Formation

### §1. Offer and Acceptance

### I. Overview

*54.* In principle, a contract comes into existence when intentions of the parties to produce certain legal effects coincide. A contract consists of declarations of intention of the parties made with respect to one another, and they should coincide in contents. The first of these is denoted as an offer and the second as an acceptance. However, a clear distinction between offer and acceptance may not be drawn especially in cases where lengthy negotiations precede. In these events, the coinciding intentions of the parties themselves is decisive.

Offer and acceptance are declarations of intention, to which not solely Articles 527 ff., but also general provisions on the juristic act in Chapter 5 of Part One shall apply (*supra* paragraph 50). This Chapter deals particularly with matters such as the question about whether an offer or an acceptance is valid, void or voidable. The court may treat conduct(s) (including silence) of the parties as a declaration of intention (i.e., as an offer or acceptance. *See* also *infra* paragraph 105).

### II. Offer

#### A. *Introduction*

*55.* Offer is a declaration of intention which is addressed to and should reach another person before it has legal effects. By means of an offer, one person (offeror) proposes to the other person (offeree) to enter into a contract in such a manner that in principle the only requirement for the conclusion of contract is the assent thereto (acceptance) of the offer.

An offer should be sufficiently clear and detailed (i.e., specify sufficient details so that contents of the prospective contract may be determined) and indicate the definitive willingness to contract, so that the other party may simply accept it to produce certain legal effects. In this regard, it should be distinguished from an invitation to offer/treat (*invitatio ad offerendum*), which is a mere demonstration of intention of one party to invite the other party to make an offer. A tentative proposal such as delivered price list, call for tender or commercial advertisement is usually construed as an invitation to offer. However, on one hand, in some cases it is difficult to distinguish *invitatio ad offerendum* from an offer, and on the other hand, contents of an advertisement may become terms of the prospective contract (of course, depending upon circumstances concerned).

*56.* An offer shall become effective at the time when the notice thereof has reached the person(s) to whom it is addressed (Article 111, paragraph 1). Apart from the revocability of an offer under Article 527, an offer may be withdrawn if the notice of withdrawal reaches the addressed person(s) before or at the same time as the offer reaches. In this event, no offer has been made.

An offer is generally addressed to one or more specific persons, but can also be addressed to the public in general.

### B. *Revocability of Offer*

*57.* In Anglo-American law, an offer, even if set forth explicitly to be irrevocable, may be freely revoked until it has been accepted. The Civil Code has not adopted this model: An offer may not be revoked (Article 527). In cases where the offer was revoked beforehand, revocation itself is without effect, and therefore upon acceptance to the (on the part of the offeror: revoked) offer in good time a contract shall come into existence, although there exists apparently only an acceptance.

However, since this Article is not mandatory, an offeror may make his/her offer revocable, i.e., may reserve the right to revoke the offer at any time even in case of the offer specifying the period for acceptance. The reservation may be indicated by way of a clause to this effect in the offer or drawn from another juristic act or usage. In such cases, an offer may be revoked if a notice of revocation reaches the offeree before the offeree has dispatched an acceptance to the offer. In addition, some Acts furnish the "cooling-off" period in order to protect the interest of consumers. In such case, the consumer may revoke his/her offer. (This revocation deserves in effect a rescission without any burden of damages.) As to the cooling-off, *see infra* paragraphs 352 ff. On the other hand, the Supreme Court ruled that an offer of an employee to terminate contract of employment is revocable until acceptance of the employer reaches the offeror (2003Da1632).

### C. *Termination of Offer*

*58.* An offer may terminate by revocation thereof, lapse of time (Articles 528 and 529), or rejection thereto. Upon termination, the offeree cannot "accept" the offer which no longer exists.

On the other hand, the validity of offer shall in principle not be affected, even if the offeror dies or loses his/her capacity to act after he/she has sent the notice thereof (Article 111, paragraph 2).

## III. Acceptance

### A. Introduction

*59.* An acceptance is also a declaration of intention which should reach the offeror, i.e., the very person who made the offer. By way of acceptance the offeree assents to the proposal made by the offeror.

As mentioned above (*supra* paragraph 54), an acceptance may be in the form of spoken or written words, gestures or conduct. In this respect, it should be mentioned that a silence itself shall in principle not be regarded as a declaration of intention (*infra* paragraph 105). However, in some exceptional cases silence deserves to be a declaration (especially in accordance with the practice established between parties). In such cases, silence means in principle a consent (to certain legal effects), and therefore can constitute an acceptance (e.g., in a case where the offer has been made in the exclusive interests of the addressee). On the other hand, Article 53 of the Commercial Code prescribes that "When a merchant has received an offer to enter into a contract that falls within his/her business types from a person with whom such merchant is in regular business transactions, he/she shall send a notice of acceptance or rejection without delay. If he/she has neglected to send such notice, he/she shall be deemed to have accepted the offer."

### B. Acceptance with Modification

*60.* As a consent to an offer, the acceptance should coincide with the offer precisely (the "mirror image rule"), and if the former does not correspond to the latter (i.e., in case of the lack of consensus), a contract shall not come into existence. In this sense, Article 534 states that in cases where the offeree has accepted an offer but subject to a condition or with any other modification, he/she shall be deemed to have rejected the original offer (which no longer exists) and thereby simultaneously has made a new offer (i.e., a counteroffer). However, this Article does not provide for an exception thereto, such as Article 19, paragraph 2 of CISG, which provides that "However, a reply to an offer which purports to be an acceptance but contains additional or different terms which do not materially alter the terms of the offer constitutes an acceptance, unless the offeror, without undue delay, objects orally to the discrepancy or dispatches a notice to that effect. If he/she does not so object, the terms of the contract are the terms of the offer with the modifications contained in the acceptance." Pursuant to CISG, legal effects of the acceptance with minor modifications may be different from those under Article 534 "in theory" (by virtue of implicit acceptance to the counteroffer the result may not differ in substance).

On the other hand, in cases where both contracting parties refer to their own standard terms (general conditions or standard business/transaction terms), the so-called battle of forms may arise. There is no explicit provision on this topic and, similar to other jurisdictions, scholarly opinion is presumably between the last shot rule and the knockout rule.

*C. Time Limit for Acceptance*

*61.* An offer stands only for a limited time, and the offer not accepted in good time terminates by lapse of time.

An offer specifying a period for acceptance continues to stand before lapse of the period specified and shall lose its effect per se if the offeror does not receive a notice of acceptance within such period (Article 528, paragraph 1). In cases where a notice of acceptance had arrived after lapse of the period specified in the offer, if it was dispatched at such a time that under normal circumstances it would have arrived within that period, the offeror must dispatch, without delay, to the other party a notice of late arrival (*ibid.*, paragraph 2). If the offeror has neglected to give this notice, the notice of acceptance shall be deemed not to have been late (*ibid.*, paragraph 3), and a contract comes into existence from the time when the notice of acceptance was dispatched (Article 531). An offer, which does not specify a period for acceptance, stands for a reasonable period and loses its effect if the offeror does not receive a notice of acceptance within such period (Article 529). In this case, the reasonableness of length of period depends upon circumstances concerned, and the offer remains in principle open for the time the other party needs to decide whether to accept the offer or not and to communicate. By contrast, Article 51 of the Commercial Code states that "An offer to enter into a contract made *inter presentes*, shall lose effect, if the offeree does not immediately accept such an offer."

In case of the delayed acceptance, the offeror may deem such acceptance as to be a new (counter-)offer (Article 530), and upon acceptance thereto the contract shall come into existence.

## IV. Time and Place of Contract

*62.* An acceptance, as a declaration of intention toward the offeror, shall be effective at the time when the notice thereof has reached him/her (Article 111, paragraph 1: the so-called arrival rule). In this context, Articles 528 and 529 require, as a rule, that a notice of acceptance should reach the offeror before the offer terminates by lapse of time. On the other hand, unlike e.g., Article 18, paragraph 2 of CISG, Article 531 of the Civil Code adopts the so-called dispatch rule: "A contract *inter absentes* shall come into existence at the time when a notice of acceptance is dispatched." Therefore, the offeree may not change his/her mind after dispatch of the notice of acceptance. In other words, an acceptance, once dispatched, will prevail over a revocation of that acceptance even if the notice of revocation reached the offeror prior to the notice of acceptance (e.g., by way of telegram). This Article emanates from the "mailbox/postal rule" derived from an English case (*Adams v. Lindsell*, 1 B & Ald 681). (Most scholars are of the opinion that this approach is not desirable, and Article 531 is not mandatory.)

With regard to the discrepancy between the arrival rule (under Articles 528 and 529) and the dispatch rule (under Article 531), it is generally accepted that a contract shall come into existence at the moment when a notice of acceptance is dispatched, unless the notice does not reach the offeror within the time set forth in Article 528 or 529.

In addition, the question about "where" the contract was formed shall also be determined in accordance with Article 531 (in my opinion: the place of dispatch).

*63.* The notice of acceptance should in principle be addressed to and reach the offeror. However, there are some exceptions to this rule.

At first, Article 532 provides for the formation of contract by way of the so-called realization of intention (equivalent to the German term *Willensbestätigung*): In a case where no notice of acceptance is necessary by reason of declaration of intention to that effect by the offeror or usage/practice, the contract shall come into existence upon occurrence of an event which ought to be construed as a declaration of intention to accept. Although there is a controversy surrounding the legal nature of realization of intention, performance of contractual obligation(s) addressed to a third person, for instance, should be regarded as an (implied) acceptance.

In addition, Article 533 lays down the so-called crossed offer: Where offers of the same content are sent to each other, the contract shall come into existence at the time when each of the two offers has reached each other party.

In both cases, the intentions of the parties coincide, and on this basis the Civil Code provides only for the time of contract.

## V. Preengagement and Earnest Money

### A. *Preengagement*

*64.* The prospective parties to a contract may reach a separate agreement that a certain contract will come into existence in the future. This agreement (usually referred to as preengagement, pre-contract or option contract) is a special kind of contract, i.e., a contract to contract (*pactum de contrahendo*).

Since, in such a case, the conclusion of a certain contract depends in principle upon the intention of the obligee of preengagement (i.e., one or each of the parties), contents of the prospective contract should be —at least on the main points (*essentialia negotii*) — sufficiently determined or determinable.

As to the preengagement to secure an obligation, *see infra* paragraph 396.

*65.* A line may be drawn between different types of preengagement:

(a) One or each of the parties to the preengagement shall be obliged himself/herself toward the other party to enter into a certain contract when the latter (obligee) expresses his/her intention to enter into this contract. In this case, such contract shall become effective upon cooperation of the former including, e.g., the transfer of a thing (in case of real contracts) or in writing (in case of formal contracts).

(b) Certain contracts shall become effective per se when the obligee of preengagement declares his/her intention to complete a prospective contract. In other words, whether such contract shall become effective or not depends solely upon the intention of the obligee, i.e., irrespective of the intention or cooperation of the other party. This type of preengagement is only available in consensual contracts.

Article 564, paragraph 1 lays down the second type of preengagement concerning the contract of sale: A unilateral preengagement to sell or purchase shall become effective as a sale from the time when the other party declares his/her intention to complete the sale. (By reason of this provision, a preengagement is presumed to be a second type.) In cases where no period is specified for the declaration of intention to complete the sale (in such a case duration of the right to complete the contract may not exceed ten years from the date of preengagement), the obligor of preengagement may give a peremptory notice to the other party (obligee), specifying a reasonable period, to give a definite answer as to whether he/she will or will not complete the sale within that period, and if the obligee fails to give an answer within that period, the preengagement shall lose its effect (*ibid.*, paragraphs 2 and 3). This Article shall apply *mutatis mutandis* to contracts for value other than sales (Article 567).

In cases where several persons have the right to complete a contract, whether one or each of the parties may exercise the right in respect of his/her portion, should be determined taking the interests of and relation between the parties into account (i.e., depending upon circumstances concerned). Therefore, if several buyers were to be co-owners, each buyer "may" exercise the right and acquire his/her portion of ownership (2010Da82530). (In the past, the Supreme Court ruled that the right "should" be jointly exercised, which was overturned recently.)

*66.* The preengagement should be distinguished from a contract to negotiate. The parties to such contract are obliged to negotiate in good faith, and the precontractual liability may arise therefrom. On the other hand, the preengagement differs also from a conditional contract in that the latter modify or qualify legal effects of contract (*see infra* paragraphs 168 ff.), while the former relates to the formation of contract.

### *B. Earnest Money* (Arrhes)

*67.* In some contracts, especially in a sale of immovable property, it is usual that one of the parties (in general: the buyer) pays a certain amount of money (about 10% of the purchase-price) to the other party. This money deserves to be evidence for the conclusion of contract and may be construed as an advance payment. In addition, the agreement to pay a certain amount of money may be an agreement of penalty if the parties have agreed thereupon. (In this case, such money is presumed to be an amount of liquidated damages under Article 398, paragraph 4.)

However, earnest money is presumed to be the rescission money pursuant to Article 565, paragraph 1, which states that "When one of the parties to a contract of sale has delivered, at the time of entering into the contract, money (or other things) under the name of down payment, assurance deposit, etc., to the other party, unless otherwise agreed upon between the parties, the deliverer by giving up such money, and the receiver by repaying twice its amount, may rescind such contract, until either party has commenced performance of the contract." To exercise the right to rescind a contract, for instance, the seller should tender actually double the amount of the earnest money received before either party commences to perform. In this regard, the Supreme Court found on one hand that the right to rescind a contract at will on the part of the receiver arises upon actual and full payment or tender of double the "agreed" (not received) amount of the money (2014Da231378). This means that a mere agreement to pay the earnest money or partial payment of the agreed money is in principle not enough to confer the right to rescind a contract at will, and that the rescission money contract should be construed as a real contract (although recently some scholars raise doubts thereabout). On the other hand, the Supreme Court ruled that either party may deprive the other party of the right to rescind a contract by way of performance (including successful tender) prior to due date, unless otherwise agreed upon between the parties (2002Da46492).

This Article shall apply *mutatis mutandis* to contracts for value other than sales (Article 567).

## §2. Formal and Evidential Requirements

### I. Overview

*68.* The starting point of the Korean contract law is that a contract is concluded, in principle and in general, by way of mutual consent of the parties without being subject to any requirement regarding its form (the principle of the freedom of contract). In accordance with this rule of consensualism, contracts may be concluded orally, in writing or even by the conduct of the parties from which the intentions of the parties to a contract may be deduced.

In principle, the legal effects of a contract not in writing do not differ from those in writing. However, the form not in writing may weaken effects (especially with regard to the binding force) of a contract. For instance, a contract of gift which is not in writing may be rescinded by either party (Article 555), although the rescission of the contract shall not have any effect in respect of any portion as to which performance has been completed (Article 558).

In Korea, many contracts are not always made in writing. However, it does not mean that contracts are generally made orally. In business transactions, contracts are normally made in writing (usually after a long negotiation process), and people used to make contracts regarding significant impacts (e.g., a sale or lease of immovable properties) in writing. In addition, some contracts are subject to a requirement of writing, and this requirement may be either formal or evidential.

It should be added that the Anglo-American concept of contract "under seal" is unknown in Korean law.

## II. Formal Requirements

*69.* There are some statutory exceptions to the rule of consensualism. In addition, the parties may agree that a contract is to be made in writing, and in this case, the formality is required pursuant to the party autonomy. In these cases, if the formal requirements are not complied with, then the contract is non-existing (not null and void).

The requirement of form has in general two functions. At first, it promotes legal certainty which shall reduce the possibility of conflicts in that it makes clear the existence itself and/or contents of contract and the moment when it takes effects. In addition, it has also a cautionary effect in that it urges the parties to reflect on themselves before they enter into a contract.

*70.* A statutory exception is seldom in the Civil Code. Nevertheless, a suretyship contract is required to be in writing (Article 428-2. *See infra* paragraph 407).

In this regard, Article 4, paragraph 1 of the Framework Act on Electronic Documents and Transaction admits the legal relevance of electronic documents, stating that "No electronic document shall be denied legal effect as a document solely because it is in an electronic form, except as otherwise expressly stipulated in other Acts." In this Act, the term "electronic document" means information, prepared, transmitted, received or stored in an electronic form by an information processing system (Article 2, No. 1).

Moreover, some juristic acts shall be entered into in an authentic deed. A guardianship contract is an example (Article 959-14).

*71.* On the other hand, some Acts (especially the so-called consumer law) require the issue of (written) contract document, in order to protect the socially or economically weaker party (e.g., consumers) who has been unfairly persuaded by the seller to make an unnecessary purchase, and to secure their withdrawal of the offer (*see supra* paragraph 58). For instance, the Door-to-Door Sales, etc. Act provides that in a case where a door-to-door seller (including telemarketer) enters into a contract of sale of goods or services with a consumer, the seller shall (explain and) issue to the consumer a document stating important matters (e.g., the identity information of the seller, the price and specifications of goods or services, conditions and procedures for exchange or return of goods or services, standard terms of transactions) (Article 7, the preceding Act). It should be added that such contract does not belong to formal contracts (i.e., even without the issue of contract document, the contract comes into existence).

It should be added that some Acts require permission from a competent administrative agency. For example, any parties intending to enter into a land transaction contract (including any preengagement) on transfer or establishment of the ownership or superficies over the land located within the permitted area shall jointly obtain the permission from the head of a competent local government (Article 11, paragraph 6, the Act on Report on Real Estate Transactions, etc.).

## III. Evidential Requirements

### *A. Introduction*

*72.* In civil litigations, the party who alleges certain facts should, in principle, prove them, although there is no provision which provides for this rule (on the burden of proof) explicitly. In this regard, the form of contract may affect the evidential issues. For instance, the contract concluded orally or tacitly by the conduct of the parties is, in principle, not null and void, but may cause trouble with regard to the proof of certain matters.

For reference, the Civil Procedure Act enumerates, as forms of evidence, witness (Articles 303 ff.), expert testimony (Articles 333 ff.), documentary evidence (Articles 343 ff.), inspection (Articles 364 ff.) and examination of the parties (Articles 367 ff.).

### *B. Permissibility and Probative Value of the Evidence*

*73.* In contrast to the Criminal Procedure Act, the Civil Procedure Act does not impose any restriction on the permissibility of evidence. Matters related to the examination of evidence which are not documents, but drawings, photographs, recording tapes, videotapes, magnetic discs for computers and other articles created to put the information therein, are permissible without any restraint (Article 374, the preceding Act). In this sense, the parties may use any form of evidence (including even the evidence produced after the filing of a lawsuit), although their probative value would be another matter.

*74.* Article 202 of the preceding Act lays down the principle of the free evaluation of evidence, stating that "A court shall determine, by its free conviction, whether or not an allegation of facts is true, taking into account of the whole purport of pleadings and the results of examination of evidence, on the basis of the ideology of social justice and equity in accordance with the principles of logic and experiences." In this sense, any form of the conceivable evidence may in general be used without any restraint, and the judge is completely free in his/her evaluation of evidence.

*75.* Of course, there are some exceptions to this principle, especially with regard to documentary evidence.

At first, the court found that with regard to the official document, the judge is, in principle, obliged to interpret the contract in accordance with the literal meaning of the words used in the document (2001Da78768). In this context, when a document is admitted to have been prepared by a public official in the course of his/her duties, in view of its preparation method and purport, it shall be presumed to be an authentic official document (Article 356, paragraph 1, the preceding Act). The right recorded in the registration of real estate shall also be presumed to be in existence. In addition, the purpose of an authentication of a deed by a notary public is usually concerned with issues of evidence. The Notary Public Act, revised in 2009, adopted an oath to confirm the authenticity of the contents of a document (When a notary public provides authentication to a deed signed by a private person, and if a client takes an oath to confirm the authenticity of the contents of a deed signed by a private person in the presence of the notary public and sign or seal the deed, or confirms the signature or seal on the deed signed by a private person, the notary public shall write such fact of oath on the deed. Article 57-2, paragraph 1, the preceding Act), and in that case, the authenticity of contents of the document shall be presumed.

On the other hand, there is a special restriction on the probative value of the written document established by the court. In cases where a contract is put down in a "document of disposal," the judge is in principle obliged to deem the contents of the document to be true (97Da1013). In this sense, the form of "in writing" is of great significance. (By contrast, the Supreme Court found, on the basis of the principle of *falsa demonstratio non nocet*, that if the literal meaning of the words used in the (written) contract document is not accordant to the "common" intentions of the parties, the latter shall prevail. 93Da2619,2636) In such a case, contrary to the official document just mentioned, the authenticity of documents should be attested (Article 357, the Civil Procedure Act); however, in some cases, the authenticity shall be presumed (e.g., in cases where the document bears the signature, seal or thumbprint of the principal or of his/her representative. Article 358, the preceding Act).

All aforementioned cases belong to a de facto compulsory evidence, subject to exceptions in case of counter evidence.

*76.* The parol evidence rule of the Common law, pursuant to which the use of evidence as regards contemporaneous oral declarations shall not be accepted in case of a written contract, is unknown to Korean law, although in business transactions a merger/integration clause carries out the same or similar function.

### C. *Function of the Notary Public*

*77.* The position of the notary public is set forth by the Notary Public Act. Article 2 of this Act defines "notary public" as a person appointed by the Minister of Justice to perform duties concerning authentication (appointed notary public), and a person who obtains authorization for authentication from the Minister of Justice pursuant to this Act (authorized notary public). The duties of notaries public shall be to manage (1) the preparation of notarial deeds on juristic acts or facts concerning any other private right, (2) the authentication on deeds signed by a private person or an electronic document, etc. (excluding the same prepared officially by a public official), and (3) affairs to be managed by notaries public as set forth in this Act and other *lex scripta*. With regard to these duties, a notary public shall be deemed to have the status of a public official (Article 2, the Notary Public Act). In addition, a notary public may prepare a notarial deed stating the intention to recognize and accept the compulsory execution attached to a bill or check (Article 56-2, the preceding Act), and may prepare an authentic deed mentioning the tenor of accepting compulsory execution against a request for the transfer or return of buildings or land, or movables prescribed by the Presidential Decree (Article 56-3, the preceding Act).

As mentioned above (*supra* paragraph 76), a notarial instrument is generally used for evidential purposes with regard to contracts.

### *D. Contracts in the Field of Evidence*

*78.* Occasionally, the contracting parties insert into their contract the additional agreement on evidence to prevent uncertainty and/or to take advantage in litigations. The validity of this agreement is in principle not denied in Korea. However, the validity of the agreement in contravention of the rule set forth in mandatory law shall be denied. At first, with regard to the permissibility, agreements on evidence fall into two categories in line with whether the judicial effect is at the free disposal of the parties or not. For instance, an agreement concerning the confession (a contract to finding of a certain fact requiring attestation), is in general valid; however, an agreement on the evaluation of evidence shall be null and void, because this agreement is contrary to the principle of the free evaluation of evidence (Article 202, the Civil Procedure Act). In addition, in the field of ex officio examination of evidence, an agreement to exclude the right of the party to furnish evidence is also null and void.

On the other hand, a clause in standard terms, which imposes the burden of proof on customers without any justifiable reason, shall be null and void under Article 14 of the Act on the Regulation of Terms and Conditions.

## §3. Consideration and Natural Obligations

### I. Consideration

*79.* The Anglo-American concept of consideration is unknown in Korean law, in that a gift (donation) is also provided for as one of named contracts, although the binding force of gift is weakened in some respects (*see infra* paragraph 344).

### II. Natural Obligations

*80.* In Korea, similar to other legal systems those have stemmed from the Roman law, most scholars give assent to a category of non-enforceable obligations (*obligaio naturalis*; natural obligations), although recently, some scholars raise doubts about the usefulness of this category. An obligation arising from an agreement not to bring a lawsuit or an obligation in a case where the obligee has withdrawn a lawsuit after the final and conclusive judgment on the merits of the case (Article 267, paragraph 2, the Civil Procedure Act) is an archetype of a natural obligation, while a moral (i.e., not legal) obligation shall in my opinion not be regarded as a natural obligation. On the other hand, there is a controversy especially concerning an obligation with completed extinctive prescription or one performed for illegal cause (Article 746).

A natural obligation also has legal effects of obligation except for enforceability. Therefore, the obligee may accept performance of a natural obligation, and a claim for restitution is excluded. (However, in case of the performance of a moral obligation, a claim for restitution may also be excluded. Article 744)

## §4. Pre-contractual Liability

### I. Pre-contractual Liability

*81.* Up to the time when a contract is concluded, the contractual relations between the prospective parties do not take place. However, even before the conclusion of a contract, under certain circumstances, it is necessary and desirable that they may invoke the contractual basis for their claims, because, by reason of their willingness to negotiate, they are assumed to enter into the relationship of confidence (e.g., the offeree may, in reliance on the offer, incur considerable expenses in examining it). At this stage, the prospective parties may be found liable for an act or omission in the process toward concluding a contract. The doctrine of bona fides may apply to the pre-contractual negotiations.

The pre-contractual duty is in essence an obligation to protect the reasonable interest (expectation) of the negotiating partner and includes, for instance, a duty of the party in the superior position to provide information regarding (and explain) certain facts and a duty to maintain confidentiality. Concerning the former, Article 436-2 (the former Article 5, the Special Act on the Protection of Guarantors) provides for this duty with regard to the suretyship explicitly (*see infra* paragraph 408). (In addition, for instance, Article 47 of the Financial Investment Services and Capital Markets Act lays down a duty to explain material facts that may produce a significant impact on the investor's reasonable judgment or the value of relevant financial investment instrument, such as risks contingent upon the investment, with such sufficiency as to allow the ordinary investor to understand them.) In case of an inexcusable breach of any of these duties, the breaching party may be liable for damages.

*82.* On the other hand, in accordance with the principle of the freedom of contract, either negotiating party is in principle free to cease the negotiation and is not liable for the failure to reach an agreement. However, even if no contract has been concluded, the negotiating parties may enter into a certain stage in which either party may reasonably expect that a contract will come into existence. At this stage, either party should be under a duty to take care of the reasonable (at the same time worth protecting) reliance of the other party based on the doctrine of bona fides, and a breach of this duty constitutes a civil wrong and results in a claim for damages. For instance, a breakdown of the negotiation (including revocation of the offer), which has continued for a considerable time, may be contrary to bona fides if a reasonable/justifiable expectation of the other party is destroyed. The Supreme

Court ruled that under such circumstances, a person who breaks off the negotiation without any legitimate reason is liable —as a tort-feasor (The legal nature of the liability has been an issue of severe controversy.)— for the loss caused to the other party, who has acted on the basis of a trustworthy expectation and therefore suffered a loss (2001Da53059). In this case, the damages may not cover the expectation loss (equivalent to the German term *"positive Vertragsinteresse"*) including the loss of profits which one party would have made out of the prospective contract, but only the reliance loss (tantamount to the German term *"negative Vertragsinteresse"*), i.e., the loss caused by reason of reliance (e.g., expenses incurred on account of relying that the contract will be concluded). In Korea, neither the court nor the scholars are of the opinion that the court may grant an injunction to continue the negotiation or deal with the contract as coming into existence. It should be added that the prospective parties may agree upon the free withdrawal from the negotiation (e.g., by way of an MOU), and in such a case, the liability just mentioned shall not come into effect.

On the other hand, a person who enters into or continues a negotiation with no real intention of reaching an agreement may be liable for any loss caused to the other party.

## II. Culpa in Contrahendo

*83.* Article 535 states as follows:

(1) In a case where a contract, whose objective is unattainable, is concluded, a party to the contract who was aware of or ought to have been aware of such unattainability, shall be liable for damages suffered by the other party who relied upon the contract as valid. However, the amount of damages to be recovered may not exceed the profit which would have occurred if the contract was valid.
(2) The provisions of the preceding paragraph shall not apply in a case where the other party was aware of or ought to have been aware of such unattainability.

Under this Article emanated from the German concept *culpa in contrahendo*, the contract is deemed to be null and void, if the performance owed is impossible from the very beginning (initial impossibility), and in case of the synallagmatic contract, obligations of both parties do not take effect. On the other hand, a bonafide party may claim damages suffered on account of relying upon the validity of contract, in a case where the other party was aware of or ought to have been aware of such unattainability. In short, the obligor shall be liable to compensate the other party's reliance loss (not expectation loss), regardless of any fault on the former's part.

*84.* Most scholars raise doubts about legal effects of the initial impossibility implied in this Article, as was the same in Germany regarding section 306 of BGB before the revision of the law of obligations which came into force on January 1, 2002. (As a result of the revision, currently, despite the obstacle to the performance of the obligation, which already exists when the contract is entered into, the contract remains effective, even though neither party can claim the performance of the contract. In this case, the obligee may, at his/her choice, demand damages in lieu of performance (i.e., compensatory damages) or reimbursement of his/her expenses incurred. This does not apply if the obligor was not aware of the obstacle to performance when entering into the contract and is also not responsible for his/her lack of awareness. Section 311a, BGB.) In this context, the Supreme Court attempts to limit the sphere of application of this Article. For instance, in case of a partial shortage of quantity in a contract of sale, Article 574 on the seller's liability for the warranty shall prevail over Article 535 (99Da47396).

On the other hand, the legal nature (and necessity) of *culpa in contrahendo* is a highly controversial issue. A majority of scholars are of the opinion that this liability is a contractual liability and contributes to protect the victim, in that he/she may avoid the restriction on or the inconvenience with regard to the tort claim (e.g., the burden of proof or the period of extinctive prescription), while some influential scholars raise doubts about necessity of this concept in Korea (because this concept was originally developed because of the unique deficiencies in BGB regarding tort-liability, and in Korea, the liability based on this concept may and should be characterized as tort-liability) and the court takes this view.

# Chapter 2. Conditions of Substantive Validity

## §1. Capacity to Act of the Parties

### I. Legal Capacity

*85.* The legal capacity, emanated from the German term *Rechtsfähigkeit*, is the capacity to be a subject of rights and duties.

All the physical (natural) persons shall be a subject of rights and duties throughout their lives (Article 3). It is not possible to deprive a person of his/her legal capacity (although up to a certain era, such deprivation was possible).

*86.* A person's legal capacity begins upon completion of birth. However, under certain circumstances, the legal capacity begins before the birth. An unborn child (child in womb, embryo or *fetus*) can inherit if he/she is subsequently born alive (Article 1000, paragraph 3). In addition, an unborn child shall, in respect of the tort-claim for damages, be deemed to have been already born (Article 762). In such situations, the child becomes entitled to claim damages once born.

On the other hand, a person's legal capacity ends on his/her death. In this regard, although the Internal Organs, etc. Transportation Act provides for brain death (Article 4, No. 4: The term "living person" means a person other than a brain-dead person, and the term "brain-dead person" means a person whose brain is diagnosed as having irreversibly and completely ceased to function in accordance with the criteria for determinations for brain death and the procedures for determinations for brain death pursuant to this Act), the concept of brain death should be confined to the transportation of internal organs.

Upon a person's death, an inheritance shall be commenced (Article 997), and the inheritors are determined according to the priority of inheritance (Article 1000), unless there is a will (testament) in conformity with the formality set forth in the Civil Code.

To prevent disputes about the status of inheritor, the Civil Code lays down some provisions regarding the death. At first, in a case where more than two persons died of the same peril, it is presumed that they died at the same time (Article 30. In principle, an inheritance shall not take place between them). Second, if it is uncertain for five years whether an absentee is alive or dead, the court shall, upon application of any person interested or of a public prosecutor, make an adjudication of disappearance (Article 27, paragraph 1. In cases where the absentee was on a battlefield, aboard a sunken vessel or a downed aircraft, or exposed any other danger that could be a cause of death, he/she can be declared missing one year after the incident. *Ibid.*, paragraph 2). A person against whom an adjudication of disappearance has been made is deemed to have died upon elapse of the period just mentioned (Article 28).

*87.* The legal capacity of a person shall be determined by the law of nationality of the very person (Article 11, the Act on Private International Law). On the other hand, since such entitlement is not generally prohibited under Korean law, foreign citizens are also entitled to be a subject of private rights in principle. For example, with regard to foreign investments, except as otherwise prescribed by *lex scripta* of the Republic of Korea, foreign investors and foreign-capital invested companies shall be treated in the same way as nationals of the Republic of Korea or Korean corporations in respect of their business operation (Article 3, paragraph 2, the Foreign Investment Promotion Act). However, there are some exceptions thereto. For instance, with regard to the land acquisitions (Article 3, the Foreigner's Land Acquisition Act), instead of the equal treatment of Korean and foreign citizens, the principle of reciprocity shall apply. Article 7 of the State Compensation Act also states that when the victim is a foreign citizen, this Act applies only in cases where a mutual guarantee with a corresponding nation exists.

## II. Capacity to Act

### *A. Introduction*

*88.* As mentioned above, every person has legal capacity. This means that he/she can, for instance, become an owner of property and/or an obligor. However, not every person can act on his/her own and thereby obtain rights and/or assume duties. In this regard, the legal capacity should be distinguished from the capacity to act (especially capacity to contract. This term is equivalent to the German term "*Geschäftsfähigkeit*"). The latter is the capacity to enter into a "valid" legal transaction, for example, to conclude a contract and incur liabilities by a juristic act.

*89.* Since a person with limited capacity to act cannot act on his/her own, his/her juristic act requires prior consent (in substance: approval) of his/her legal representative to be legally binding.

A juristic act of a person with limited capacity without obtaining the consent of the legal representative is not null and void, but voidable (with some exceptions thereto). Even in a case where a person with limited capacity has not suffered any detriment or where the other party was not aware of and should not have been aware of such limited capacity, a juristic act of the person with limited capacity may be voided. The person listed in Article 140 (including the person with limited capacity himself/herself even before e.g., attaining the age of majority) may invoke limited capacity, and mere ground of the limited capacity is sufficient to void the juristic act (in such a case, the opposite party resisting the voidance may allege and prove the existence of the consent of the legal representative as a cause of plea).

On the other hand, with regard to unjust enrichment, a person with limited capacity shall be liable to make reparation therefor to the extent that he/she is still enriched by reason of such act (Article 141), even though he/she is in bad faith (as to the normal amount of benefits to be returned by a person enriched in bad faith, *see* Article 748, paragraph 2 and *infra* paragraph 452). In addition, a third person (even acting in good faith and without negligence) shall not be protected (as to the effect of voidance against a third person, *see infra* paragraph 142). In this context, it should be emphasized that the main (in my opinion: only) purpose of the capacity to act is to protect the person with limited capacity.

*90.* Although there is no explicit provision such as section 105, paragraph 2 of BGB, an act of a person who cannot dispose of a normal will at time of the juristic act and therefore is incapable of appreciating the implication and effects of his/her act, is deemed to be null and void, even in the absence of judicial recognition of incapacity. For instance, in a case where duress deprives the free exercise of will of the declarant entirely (*vis absoluta*), his/her declaration shall be null and void, while a declaration of intention made under duress (*vis compulsiva*) shall be voidable (Article 110, paragraph 1).

As to the capacity to assume liability. In cases where a minor has caused loss to others, if the minor was not of sufficient intelligence to appreciate the liability for his/her own act, he/she shall not be liable for damages resulting therefrom (Article 753). A person who, while in a state of mental unsoundness, has caused damage to others, shall not be liable for damages resulting therefrom, unless he/she has brought upon himself/herself his/her state of mental unsoundness either intentionally or by negligence (Article 754). In cases where a person without the capacity to assume liability is not liable in accordance with Articles just mentioned, the parents or guardians of such person shall in principle be liable to compensate the loss (Article 755: the vicarious liability). With regard to wrongdoings of a minor with the capacity to assume liability in tort, the Supreme Court ruled that the parents shall be held liable as co-tort-feasors, if there is a causal connection between the negligence of parental supervision and the loss (93Da13605).

### *B. Minor*

*91.* Anyone who has attained the age of majority has the capacity to act in principle. Under the Civil Code, the age of majority is attained upon completion of 19 years of age (Article 4. Before the Revision in 2013: 20 years of age). Anyone below that age is referred to as a minor. In contrast to the general rule regarding the calculation of period, the day on which a person was born shall be included in counting age (Article 158). On the other hand, in a case where a minor enters into a (legal) marriage, he/she shall be deemed to have attained the age of majority (Article 826-2) and be released from the parental authority.

A minor has limited capacity to act. This means that a juristic act of a minor requires the prior consent of his/her legal representative to be legally binding. In principle, those who have the parental authority over a minor become the minor's legal representatives (Article 911). In cases where there is no person with parental authority or a person with parental authority is unable to exercise the power of representation with respect to the juristic act of a minor, a guardian shall be appointed for the minor (Article 928). A guardian of a minor shall become the legal representative of the minor ward (Article 938, paragraph 1) and have the same rights and duties as a person with parental authority with respect to matters set forth in Articles 913–915 (i.e., rights and duties to protect and educate child(ren), right to designate place of residence and right to take disciplinary action) (Article 945). On the other hand, if a parent of a minor is to perform acts of conflicting interests between the parent and his/her child, the parent shall apply to the court for appointment of a special representative on behalf of the child. Where a parent of a minor is to perform acts in which the interest of one child conflicts with that of the other child(ren), the parent shall, on behalf of one party, apply to the court for appointment of a special representative on behalf of the other child(ren) (Article 921). This article shall apply *mutatis mutandis* to a guardian (Article 949-3), and for certain acts, the guardian needs the consent of supervisors of guardianship (Article 950).

*92.* A juristic act of a minor without obtaining the prior consent of the legal representative is voidable. (Article 5, paragraph 2. There is no provision which divides the legal effect in line with the standard of age, such as section 104 of BGB.) Such a juristic act may, however, be ratified subsequently by the person having the right to void a juristic act (including the former minor himself/herself after attaining the age of majority), in which case the act shall not be voided (Articles 143 and 144).

As to exceptions to this rule (The burden of proof lies with the party resisting the voidance): (1) a juristic act performed by a minor is legally binding to the extent that the act concerned is one merely to acquire rights or to be relieved of obligations (Article 5, paragraph 1). For instance, a minor may accept a gift of a book on his/her own. (2) In regard to the property of which a minor has been permitted by his/her legal representative to dispose within the scope specified by the latter (e.g., pocket-money), the minor may dispose of it at his/her will (Article 6. The purpose of disposal is of no significance). A minor can, for instance, independently buy a bicycle with the money which his/her parents have given him/her, and under this Article, the minor may dispose of his/her earnings. (3) A minor who has been permitted to carry on a specific business by his/her legal representative shall have in relation to such business the same capacity to act as a person of full age (Article 8, paragraph 1). In this case, the registration thereof shall be required (Article 6, the Commercial Code), and the minor may conduct the litigation in relation to such a business on his/her own (Article 55, paragraph 1, the Civil Procedure Act). (4) Pursuant to the Labor Standard Act, neither a person with parental authority nor a guardian may enter into a labor contract on behalf of a minor (Article 67, paragraph 1, the preceding Act). Therefore, only a minor can enter into a labor contract with the consent of his/her legal representative. On the other hand, a minor may claim wages in his/her own right (Article 68, the preceding Act). (5) In my opinion, any juristic act necessary for everyday life and the price for which is not excessive should be unavoidable by way of analogy (*see* Article 10, paragraph 4 and *infra* paragraph 94).

### *C. Guardianship for Adults*

*93.* Not every person of full age (adult) can act on his/her own, and acquire rights and/or assume duties by a juristic act. For an adult who cannot dispose of a normal will and therefore is unable to appreciate what he/she does or what his/her actions lead to, i.e., is not mentally capable of taking care of his/her personal affairs or property, a legal assistance program whereby another person assists in decision-making with regard to or in looking after the rights and interests is necessary.

In the beginning, the Civil Code provided for "incompetency" and "quasi-incompetency." However, because of the stigma effect and possibility of an excessive limitation on the capacity to act, the (quasi-)incompetency-based system has not been used properly or generally. To improve this situation, the revision of the Civil Code in 2011 introduces a new adult guardianship system (Enforcement date: March 11, 2013). The fundamental idea of the revision is to reinforce the self-determination on the part of persons to be protected and their normalization. While the previous incompetency-based system focused mainly on property-related affairs, the revision contains additional provisions enabling the guardian to take care of the ward's personal affairs more actively. With the revision, the term "incompetent" was abolished and the concept of the limited capacity replaces it (including minor).

In order to respect the wishes of the ward and to maximize the capacity to act of the ward, four types of guardianship program are furnished: adult, limited, specific and contractual guardianship programs. The former three are judicial in nature, while the last is contractual in nature.

*94.* The Family Court shall adjudicate on the commencement of adult guardianship for an adult who is continuously lacking the capacity to manage personal affairs due to mental restraints caused by a disease, disability, old age or by any other cause, upon application of the relevant person listed (including the person in question (principal), public prosecutor or the head of a local government) (Article 9, paragraph 1). Upon such adjudication, an adult guardian shall be appointed ex officio by the Family Court, and the guardian shall become the legal representative of the adult ward (Articles 929, 936 and 938). Multiple guardians may be appointed and a corporation is also eligible for an adult guardian (Article 930), while the guardian for a minor should be a natural person, and there shall be no more than one person.

Since an adult ward is "continuously" lacking the capacity to manage personal affairs, any juristic act performed by an adult ward is voidable, even in case of the act with the prior consent of the guardian (Article 10, paragraph 1). However, the Family Court may determine the scope of unavoidable juristic acts of adult wards (*ibid.*, paragraph 2). In addition, the guardian may ratify an act performed by an adult ward. On the other hand, an adult ward shall make a decision independently on his/her personal affairs insofar as his/her conditions permit (Article 947-2, paragraph 1).

Despite the resemblance of requirements and effects to an incompetency-based program, the adult guardianship program is a quite different one, in that the latter opens ways to expand the capacity to act of the ward, e.g., any juristic act necessary for everyday life and the price for which is not excessive, such as purchase of daily necessities, shall not be voided by an adult guardian (Article 10, paragraph 4).

*95.* Limited guardianship program confers the guardian with the right to consent and the power of representation to the extent necessary in the interests of the adult ward. For those who lack the capacity to manage personal affairs owing to the mental disturbance, upon application of the relevant person enumerated, the Family Court may adjudicate on the commencement of limited guardianship (Article 12). The Family Court may determine the scope of acts for which a limited ward should obtain the consent from his/her guardian (Article 13, paragraph 1), e.g., business-related act, borrowing money, act which aims at the acquisition, forfeit and alteration of a real right over or title to immovables or important property and so on. Such a juristic act performed without obtaining the prior consent of the limited guardian is voidable (*ibid.*, paragraph 4). (In this respect, there is a controversy concerning whether a limited ward is a person with limited capacity or not.)

Specific guardianship program (Article 14-2), i.e., ad hoc (temporary) guardianship for any specific affairs, does not limit the capacity to act of the ward (although the Family Court may confer the authority of agency on the guardian. Article 959-11, paragraph 1), and therefore may open the door for a more effective one of the judicial guardianship programs.

Contractual guardianship program (Article 959-14) is a voluntary guardianship system whereby the guardian and the ward enter into a guardianship contract which sets out the respective rights and obligations. This contract shall be entered in an authentic deed (Article 959-14, paragraph 1), and take effect at the time when the Family Court appoints a supervisor of voluntary guardianship (*ibid.*, paragraph 3).

*96.* In cases where the principal is an adult ward, limited ward or specific ward, the Family Court shall, if it intends to appoint a supervisor of voluntary guardianship, adjudicate on the termination of the former adult guardianship, limited guardianship or specific guardianship (Article 959-20, paragraph 2). In this respect, contractual guardianship takes priority over the former three guardianships. In other words, the guardianships which are judicial in nature (*supra* paragraph 93) are of the appendant nature.

### *D. Legal Means for the Other Party to an Act Performed by a Person with Limited Capacity*

*97.* The other party to an act performed by a person with limited capacity to act may give a peremptory notice to the latter (only after attaining full capacity) or his/her legal representative requesting a definite answer within a period, which shall not be less than one month, on whether the latter or his/her legal representative ratifies the voidable act or not. If the person with limited capacity or his/her legal representative fails to dispatch a definite answer within such period, the act is deemed to have been ratified (Article 15, with an exception in case where special formalities, such as the consent of supervisor of guardianship under Article 950, are required). In addition, the other party acting in good faith may withdraw his/her declaration of intention until it has been ratified (Article 16, paragraph 1).

On the other hand, in cases where a person with limited capacity has used fraudulent means to induce the belief that he/she is a person of full capacity or has obtained the consent of his/her legal representative, the act performed by the person with limited capacity may not be voided (Article 17).

## III. Juristic Person

### A. Introduction

*98.* As in other jurisdictions, juristic/legal persons have legal capacities, as well. The Civil Code lays down two types of juristic persons: association and foundation. (This two-tiered system emanates from BGB, which distinguishes between *Verein* and *Stiftung*.) A foundation is a set of properties endowed for particular purposes. By contrast, an association is a group of persons to achieve particular purposes, which is of considerable social relevance including various types of corporations. In this context, the Commercial Code defines a company as a corporation incorporated for the purpose of engaging in commercial activities and any other profit-making activities (Article 169), and companies are categorized into five types: partnership companies, limited partnership companies, limited liability companies, stock companies, and limited companies (Article 170).

*99.* The Korean private law divides in principle associations into profit-making and non-profit-making associations, while foundation is non-profit-making in nature. Profit-making associations are regulated by the Commercial Code (Article 39, paragraph 2, the Civil Code).

On the other hand, there are some statutes with regard to the juristic persons for the public interests (e.g., the Private School Act). In particular, the Act on the Establishment and Operation of Public-Service Corporations, the purpose of which are to enable juristic persons to maintain their public interests and to continue their sound activities by supplementing the Civil Code on the establishment, operation, etc., of juristic persons (Article 1, the preceding Act), shall apply to juristic persons, either incorporated foundations or incorporated associations, with the purpose of conducting activities concerning aid or payment of school expenses, scholarships or research expenses, sciences and charities in order to contribute to the general interests of society (Article 2, the preceding Act).

### B. Capacities of Juristic Persons

*100.* No juristic person can come into existence other than in compliance with provisions of *lex scripta* (Article 31).

In order to establish an incorporated association or foundation pursuant to the Civil Code, the founder(s) shall draw up articles of incorporation containing the particulars listed in the Code, and in case of the foundation, endow a certain property (Articles 40 and 42). In addition, the permission of the competent authorities is necessary (Article 32. For reference, with regard to the establishment of a company such permission is not necessary.) and a juristic person shall come into existence by making registration for incorporation at the seat of the principal office of the juristic person (Article 33).

On the other hand, a juristic person shall be dissolved upon expiration of the period of its duration, completion of the undertaking which forms the objective of juristic person or impossibility of such completion, happening of any cause of dissolution specified by the articles of incorporation, bankruptcy or annulment of the permission for incorporation (in a case where a juristic person engages in acts harming public interests, the competent authorities may cancel the permission. Article 38), and an incorporated association shall be dissolved in cases where no member remains, or by resolution of a general meeting (Article 77). In case of dissolution, the juristic person shall have the rights and duties only within the scope of liquidating purpose (Article 81), and the directors shall become the liquidators except in case of bankruptcy, unless otherwise set forth in articles of incorporation, or by the resolution of a general meeting (Article 82).

*101.* A juristic person shall have rights and/or assume duties within the scope of the purpose set forth by the articles of incorporation subject to *lex scripta* concerned (Article 34). Transactions exceeding this scope are null and void (*ultra vires*), and in such a case the other party (even acting in good faith) or a third party shall not be protected (as to tort liability, *see* next paragraph). The court ruled that acts "within the scope of the purpose" under Article 34 cover not merely acts which meet the purposes explicitly set forth, but also acts which are necessary directly or indirectly to achieve these purposes, and the latter shall be determined by the objective nature of the transaction, not by the subjective intention of the relevant party (91Da8821).

On the other hand, the corporate veil can be pierced in cases where a juristic personality is merely a veil or is abused as a means to avoid the legal responsibility (e.g., attachment from the obligee of the member or endower). In this regard, the Supreme Court found, on the basis of the doctrine of bona fides, that the juristic personality (in reality, the separation of the assets of juristic person from that of the member or endower) may be denied, and therefore, for instance, the obligee of a stock company may attach the assets of the only shareholder and vice versa (e.g., 87DaKa1671).

*102.* A juristic person can act solely by its organs. Each director shall represent the juristic person in all of its affairs (Article 59, paragraph 1). However, the limitations on the authority of agency of directors can be set up against a third person (including the other party to a juristic act of a juristic person as well), if the limitation is explicitly provided for by the articles of incorporation and registered (Articles 41 and 60). (In contrast to the Civil Code, other statutes, e.g., Article 389 of the Commercial Code or Article 3, paragraph 2, Number 7 of the Act on the Establishment and Operation of Public-Service Corporations, provides for the representative director.) In such a case, an act of a director with limited authority of agency shall not be effective against the juristic person; however, the latter may ratify the act of the former. In cases where the limitations are not registered, the juristic person may not assert them against third persons (according to the ruling of the Supreme Court: even those acting in bad faith (91Da24564), about which some scholars raise doubts). By contrast, with regard to organizations without juristic personality, since the registration is not possible, the limitations may not be pleaded against third persons acting in good faith (2002Da64780). As to commercial companies, *see* Articles 209 and 393 of the Commercial Code.

As to abuse of the authority of agency: In cases where a transaction is within the authority of agency of directors, the juristic person shall be bound by it. However, in cases where the director carried it out not for the juristic person itself but in the interests of the director or a third person, this consequence is contrary to the doctrine of bona fides and is improper. Therefore, the Supreme Court held that the juristic person may be exonerated in cases where the other party knew (in some decisions: or should have known) the abusive purpose of the director (e.g., 86DaKa1522).

On the other hand, a juristic person shall be liable for any loss caused by its directors or other representatives in the course of performance of their duties; however, the liability of a juristic person shall not relieve directors or other representatives of their own liabilities for damages sustained thereby (Article 35). Thereby, the aggrieved party may claim damages against the director who is directly responsible for damages or the juristic person, or both. In addition, a juristic person may be liable for damage caused to a third person by the former's employees in the course of the execution of the undertaking (Article 756).

### *C. Organizations Without Juristic Personality*

*103.* There are some organizations (associations) without juristic personality, e.g., the family members of the same clan (*chongjung*) peculiar to Korea, and protestant churches. These organizations usually refrain from applying for a juristic personality in order to avoid the burdensome procedure for establishment (including in particular obtaining permission of the competent authorities) and/or the supervision by the competent authorities. Nevertheless, these organizations are treated as juristic persons under certain circumstances by *lex scripta*: the capacity to sue and to be sued (Article 52, the Civil Procedure Act) and the capacity to apply for registration of real estate (Article 26, the Registration of Real Estate Act) are granted to such organizations, and what is more, the Civil Code itself lays down the type of ownership by the members of an organization (association) that is not a juristic person, as the collective ownership (Article 275, paragraph 1). Therefore, administration and disposition of the property of such an organization shall be determined by resolutions from a general meeting of the members, while each member is entitled to use and take profits from the property in accordance with the articles of the organization (Article 276). Therefore, the assets of the organization are also separated from those of the members. On the other hand, the rights and duties of members concerning the property of the organization shall be acquired or lost by acquiring or losing the membership therein (Article 277). In addition, the court applies the relevant provisions on the juristic person by way of analogy.

§2. Defective Declarations of Intention

## I. Introduction

### A. *Declaration of Intention*

*104.* A declaration of intention (*Willenserklärung*), together with a juristic act (*Rechtsgeshäft. supra* paragraphs 17 ff.), is one of the essential and structural characteristics of the German civil law, and the Civil Code accepts this model. Although in recent years, some scholars have raised doubts about the usefulness and desirableness of this model, the declaration of intention and the juristic act are central concepts for a comprehensive understanding of the Civil Code.

On the other hand, a declaration of intention should be distinguished from a juristic act. A declaration of intention is a constructive element of a juristic act; however, it is not the juristic act itself, since a juristic act may require elements other than a mere declaration of intention. For instance, a bilateral juristic act, such as a contract, requires more than two declarations of intention to coincide, although a unilateral juristic act, such as will (testament), consists of a declaration of intention of only one person. In order to transfer the ownership of a movable property, in addition to a juristic act consisting of the agreement that the ownership shall pass, the physical handing over of the thing in question is necessary (Articles 188–190). There is also an act which requires other elements, such as permission of the competent authorities (e.g., concerning incorporation of juristic persons. Article 32. *supra* paragraph 100), to be effective. In short, the juristic act is a broader concept than a mere declaration of intention.

In addition, a declaration of intention is to be distinguished from a statement to which *lex scripta* attaches legal effects without reference to the will (intention) of the person making such a statement. For instance, the other party to an act performed by a person with limited capacity may give a peremptory notice to the part of the latter requesting a definite answer within a certain period (in the German term: *Mahnung*), and the legal effect thereof is created by law (Article 15), not in accordance with the will of the part of the latter (*supra* paragraph 97). However, the provisions on declaration of intention may be applicable (by way of analogy) to such statements, if appropriate.

*105.* A declaration of intention is composed of the external and internal elements. With regard to the external elements, a declaration of intention may be in form of an implicit declaration, i.e., (apart from a conscious and deliberate act, such as speaking or writing) in the form of any conduct from which a reasonable assumption that there is such an intention may be made. In this regard, as a rule, silence does not constitute a declaration of intention. However, in some exceptional cases, *lex scripta* attaches legal effects to silence, and in these cases, the silence is deemed to be a consent (Article 639. *See* also *supra* paragraph 59). (In case of a peremptory notice, the silence is dealt with as an approval or a refusal to ratify depending upon circumstances concerned. Article 15, paragraphs 1 and 3).

On the other hand, regarding internal elements, it is generally accepted that a consciousness of the declaration (in the German term: *Erklärungsbewußtsein*) is not an element of a declaration of intention, despite the diversity of the grounds therefor. Therefore, in spite of the lack of consciousness of the declarant, a declaration of intention may come into existence, although it can be voided on the ground of mistake (Article 109).

*106.* A declaration of intention is an expression of intention (will), which is aimed to produce certain legal effects (i.e., to acquire, abandon or alter rights and/or duties), and these effects take place because the declarant (i.e., person who declares/ expresses his/her intention) wishes them. In this sense, since a declaration of intention is a legal means to realize the party autonomy, emphasis should be put on the subjective intention of the declarant. On the other hand, since a declaration of intention made to another person(s) is at the same time a means of communication, in order to protect the interests of the addressee and to promote the commercial certainty, the objective meaning of the declaration should also be taken into consideration. Therefore, with regard to the declaration of intention (as well as the juristic act), we should aim for a fair balance between the parties' interests.

In this context, the distinction between the declarations of intention made to others and those which do not need to be received is important. The latter, such as will (testament), becomes effective as soon as the intention of the declarant has been declared, and the interest of any other person does not matter. By contrast, a declaration of intention made to another person shall be effective at the time when the notice thereof has reached him/her (Article 111, paragraph 1). The declaration of intention can be withdrawn at any time prior to the arrival thereof, and by reason of the withdrawal in time the declaration becomes without any legal effect (*See* also *supra* paragraph 57). The arrival requires that a declaration of intention has been placed in the sphere of control of the addressee in such a way that the addressee may take cognizance of it (e.g., the letter containing a declaration of intention is deposited in the addressee's mail box), and therefore the interests of the addressee are also of significance.

*107.* It should be added that Article 12 of the Act on the Regulation of Terms and Conditions deals with the deemed declaration of intention. Any of the following clauses in standard terms concerning declaration of intention shall be null and void: (1) a clause which provides that once a certain act of feasance or omission has occurred, customers shall be deemed to have expressed or to not have expressed a certain intention (this shall not apply where customers are separately notified that if they fail to express their intention within a given period, which is a considerable length of time, the customers shall be deemed to have expressed or not have expressed their intention, or where it is impossible to issue such notice due to unavoidable circumstances); (2) a clause which imposes unreasonably strict restrictions on the requirements for or the way in which customers may express their intention; (3) a clause which provides, without any substantial reason, that the intention of a business person, which may materially affect the interests of customers, is deemed to have been communicated to customers; and (4) a clause which provides for an unreasonably long or indefinite term during which a business person may express his/her intention which may materially affect the interests of customers.

*B. Defective Declarations of Intention*

*108.* Legal effects of a contract arise from the intentions of the parties. In this sense, the intention of the declarant and its declaration should coincide in order to give rise to the "intended" legal effects. However, on occasion, the declaration of one (or each) of the parties was not intended by that party. In this case, a party makes a declaration, which does not correspond to his/her wish (intention). For instance, a person may declare his/her intention mistakenly.

On the other hand, a contractual obligation must derive from the "free" intentions of the parties. In this regard, the agreement between the parties should have been made freely. However, a declarant may be under undue influences.

These instances may be denoted as defective declarations of intention. If a declaration of intention suffers from certain defects, then it is void or voidable. For reference, provisions on defective declarations of intention shall not apply to procedural acts, such as a withdrawal of an appeal.

## II. Mistake

*A. Introduction*

*109.* A contract comes into existence when the intentions of the parties to create certain legal effects coincide. However, on occasion, the intention of one (or each) of the parties does not correspond to his/her declaration (except in a case where the declarant himself/herself was aware of the discrepancy), and therefore, despite the "apparent" existence of a mutual consent, the intentions of the parties do not coincide. In this case, the interest of the declarant may conflict with that of the opposite party: the former wishes usually to be exonerated from the binding force of the contract by invoking the absence of an intention in a declaration; however, the latter may be in a position to the contrary. In this respect, the mistake differs from the lack of consensus, in that the former concerns the discrepancy between intention and declaration in one and the same declaration of intention, while the latter is related to the discrepancy between "two" (or more) declarations of intention, and also in that the former causes the voidance of the very declaration of intention, while in the latter case, the contract itself is non-existing. On the other hand, in cases where the pleading of the declarant is justifiable, not merely the opposite party, but also a third party may suffer a detriment. Taking these situations into account, Article 109 seeks a compromise: If a declaration of intention is made mistakenly, the declaration will nevertheless be valid; however, the declaration may be voided. On the other hand, the voidance of a declaration of intention may not be set up against a third person acting in good faith.

The mistake may result in the right of voidance, but not lead to the right of modification (*Reurecht*), and the Supreme Court found that the declarant shall not be liable for damages even if the other party relied upon the validity of the declaration (97Da13023).

*B. Requirements of Voidance Based on a Mistake*

*110.* Since an error is inevitable (*errare humanum est*), it is of particular significance to determine under which circumstances a declaration of intention may be voided on the ground of mistake.

In this regard, Article 109, paragraph 1 provides that "A declaration of intention may be voided if made under a mistake in regard to any essential elements of the juristic act, unless there has been gross negligence on the part of declarant." Under this provision, requirements of the voidance are as follows: (1) the existence of a mistake, (2) the mistake in regard to any essential (material) elements of the juristic act, and (3) the absence of gross negligence on the part of declarant.

It should be noted in advance that these requirements is to limit the right of voidance and thereby to protect the reliance of the other party. Therefore, if the opposite party (recipient) is not worthy of protection, e.g., in cases where a mistake has been induced by the recipient (including the breach of a duty to provide certain information), the declaration may be voided regardless of the fulfillment of any of the requirements.

On the other hand, as to the voidance on the ground of mistake, a restriction on the period, such as "without undue/culpable delay" (section 121, BGB), does not exist, although Article 146 provides for the lapse of the right of voidance, as a whole.

*111.*

(1) As to the existence of a mistake. The court and a majority of scholars draw a line between mistake regarding elements (in substance) and mistake as to motive. The former can arise under various circumstances. For instance, in addition to the archetype, such as slip of a tongue or pen, the declarant made a mistake relating to the subject matter of the transaction because he/she was not familiar with certain measures; the declarant has confused the identity of the opposite party; the declaration of intention is communicated inaccurately (e.g., wrongly delivered by messenger); the declarant signed an instrument which is not in accordance with his/her intention. On the other hand, in case of the mistake as to motive, there is no discrepancy between intention and declaration; however the intention was formed on error. An example of this (besides the archetype such as false/wrong assessment of the financial risk of contract) is a case where a person purchases a piece of land believing that he/she can construct a building thereon; however, due to the inability to obtain the urban planning permission the construction was impossible.

The former may be voidable, while the latter does not in principle constitute a ground to void the declaration. The Supreme Court ruled therefore that mistake as to motive does not affect the validity of the declaration of intention, unless the motive is explicitly made known to the opposite party in such a manner as to incorporate it into the juristic act (2000Da12259). However, some scholars are of the opinion that the division of mistakes into these two categories is rather vague, and that even if the motive is not explicitly made known to the opposite party, there are cases where the declaration may be voided.

*112.*

(2) As to the significance of the mistake. Only mistakes concerning any essential elements of the subject matter to which the agreement relates grant the right to void for the declarant. This requirement shall be determined by two criteria, i.e., a subjective criterion and an objective one. The former relates to the causal connection between mistake and declaration of intention (causation): The assumption that the declarant would not have made the declaration (or not with the same contents) with knowledge of the factual position is sufficient. The latter, by contrast, is concerned with the weight of the mistake, which excludes the right to void in case of trivial/insignificant mistake. The mistake should be significant enough so that a reasonable person (not the declarant himself/herself) would not have made the declaration (or not with the same contents) with such knowledge. In this context, the Supreme Court found that in a case where the declarant does not suffer any detriment despite the mistake, the voidance based on mistake is not permitted (98Da47924).

Whether this requirement is complied with or not, depends upon circumstances concerned. If, for instance, the declarant has confused the actual person with whom he/she is dealing, the confusion of identity of the opposite party may not grant the right to void in cases of sale of daily necessities. In other words, the mistake as to the identity of the other person may be a cause of voidance only in cases where the identification of this person is one of the principal causes of the agreement (e.g., in a gift or suretyship). (In addition, the attribute or quality of the subject matter may constitute an essential element in some cases.) With regard to this requirement, decisions of the court show its elastic attitude in consequence.

*113.*

(3) As to the gross negligence. Since an error is inevitable, the possibility of invalidation (i.e., exoneration from the binding force of a contract) by way of voidance may be justified. However, in case of gross (in substance: inexcusable) negligence on the part of declarant, there is no need to protect the interests of him/her at the cost of the opposite party. In this case, the declarant may not invoke his/her mistake.

## *C. Common Mistake*

*114.* On occasion, both the contracting parties enter into a contract based on the same error, and it is assumed that they would not conclude the very contract with knowledge of the factual position. This case concerns the mistake as to motive, but a solution under Article 109 may lead to an improper consequence, if the motive of only one of the parties is explicitly made known to the other party, or if there has been gross negligence on the part of only one of the parties. On the other hand, the rectification of a contract on the basis of the existing circumstances may correspond with the genuine intentions of the parties. The Supreme Court ruled therefore in such a case that the court may supplement the intentions of the parties which are deduced from the presumed situation with a correct assumption (2005Da13288), although there is another view that the solution in accordance with the German doctrine of "*subjektive Geschäftsgrudlage*" is desirable.

## III. Misrepresentation

*115.* There is no concept that is directly equivalent to the Anglo-American concept of misrepresentation in Korean law. However, some categories of defective declarations of intention are worthy of being mentioned in this regard. (In addition, fraudulent misrepresentations shall be dealt with under Article 110. *See infra* paragraphs 119 ff.).

*116.* The first category is a declaration of an untrue intention (mental reservation: *geheimer Vorbehalt*). A declaration of intention shall be valid, even if the declarant has made it with knowledge that the declaration does not reflect his/her true intention. However, such a declaration shall be null and void if the other party was aware, or ought to have been aware, of the true intention of the declarant (Article 107, paragraph 1). In the latter case, the interest of the opposite party is not worthy of protecting at the cost of the declarant. For instance, a person who has handed in his/her resignation as a joke shall be nevertheless bound to his/her declaration. However, if the opposite party ought to have been aware that it was a joke, the juristic act is null and void. In addition, although there is no explicit provision such as section 118 of BGB (*Mangel der Ernstlichkeit*), in a case where a declaration is not seriously meant and is made in the expectation that its lack of serious intention will not be misunderstood, then the declaration is null and void. In such a case, the declarant will not be liable for damages even if the opposite party relied on the validity of the declaration.

*117.* The second category is a fictitious declaration of intention made in collusion with the opposite party. In this case, while the parties apparently concluded a certain contract, their true intentions are that the very contract will not take effect between them. Such a declaration shall be null and void (Article 108, paragraph 1), because the act does not reflect the parties' true intentions, and there is no need to protect the interests of the parties. With regard to legal effects of such an act (sham/simulated transaction: *Scheingeschäft*), two types are to be differentiated. On the one hand, in cases where the parties intended their relation in existence to remain unaltered (e.g., an obligor assigned his/her real property in order to avoid the attachment from his/her obligees), the sham transaction shall be entirely null and void. On the other hand, if a sham transaction is intended to hide another legal transaction (e.g., in a case where a transaction is actually intended to be a gift, but is disguised as an onerous transaction such as sale in order to avoid any of the restriction on the gift or to evade the tax), such a transaction is null as a sham transaction (i.e., as a sale), but may be valid as a hidden (i.e., secretly intended) transaction (i.e., as a gift) under the provisions on the latter transaction.

*118.* In these two categories, the nullity of a declaration of intention may not be set up against a third person acting in good faith (Article 107, paragraph 2; Article 108, paragraph 2). Thereby, the interests of a third party who relied upon the validity of declaration will be protected (*see infra* paragraphs 141 f.).

On the other hand, an innocent (i.e., non-fraudulent) misrepresentation has no legal effects under Korean law, except insofar as it may produce a mistake.

## IV. Improper Pressure

*119.* A declaration of intention made by fraudulent means (deceit) or under duress (threat) may be voided (Article 110, paragraph 1). In this case, a fraud or duress must be committed intentionally, and the declarant has been induced by it to make the declaration of intention. As a result, the existence of the declaration itself and/or its contents may be against the intention of the declarant, and his/her freedom to determine as to the declaration has been infringed. Therefore, the right to void is granted, irrespective of the detriment, and in this context, in contrast to the case of mistake, the requirements with regard to the motive as well as essential elements (*supra* paragraphs 111 and 112) are not necessary. (e.g., a deceit as to the value of foreign currency may constitute a fraud, while a mistake as to that does in principle not make the declaration of intention voidable.) In addition, in case of fraud or duress, the declarant may claim damages in tort (Article 750).

As to the common requirements of improper pressure: (1) The declaration of intention should be induced by fraud or under duress (causation). This requirement shall be determined by a subjective criterion, i.e., in the position of the very declarant (not a reasonable person). The negligence on the part of declarant is irrelevant, i.e., can only be taken into account in assessing damages. (2) The conduct by fraud or under duress should be unlawful (illegitimacy). This requirement shall be determined by an objective criterion. In this regard, for instance, trivial deceits may be justified in accordance with customs.

In cases where a third person has committed a fraud or duress inducing any person to make a declaration of intention to the other party, such declaration of intention may be voided only if the other party was aware, or ought to have been aware, of the fact (Article 110, paragraph 2). In this regard, the Civil Code does not distinguish between fraud and duress of a person other than the opposite party, in contrast to some legal systems which provide for effects of undue influence of a third party only with regard to fraud, not concerning duress (e.g., section 123, paragraph 2, BGB and Article 96, paragraph 2, the Japanese Civil Code).

*120.*

(1) As to fraud. Not only an active deceit (e.g., a knowingly wrong answer to a certain question from the opposite party) but also a passive one, such as omission, may constitute a deceitful conduct. In this regard, a particularly contentious issue is under which circumstances silence (with regard to a fact which, if the declarant had known it, would have prevented him/her from making the declaration) may constitute a fraud. In most contracts, either party should in principle look after himself/herself because the interests of the parties conflict with each other generally. Therefore, the other party may only exceptionally be under a duty to provide certain information, which depends on circumstances concerned. For instance, the value of the object of a sale is in general not the subject of this duty, but the Supreme Court found, in case of a sale of an apartment house, pursuant to the doctrine of bona fides, that the seller must inform the buyer of the fact that a landfill site will be built nearby, and in case of a breach of this duty, the buyer shall have the right to void (2004Da48515). In addition, *lex scripta* requires the duty to inform with regard mainly, but not exclusively, to consumer-related matters to correct the disparity of the bargaining powers (including the accessibility of information) between the parties, and Article 436-2 lays down the obligee's duty to notify regarding suretyship (*infra* paragraph 408).

On the other hand, a fraud causes mistake as to motive. Since fraud and mistake have different purposes, the declarant may invoke any of them as grounds for voidance. (In this regard, it should be added that in 1999, the Act on Fair Labeling and Advertising was enacted to prevent unfair labels and advertisements for products and services that deceive or mislead consumers in labeling and advertising, and to promote provision of correct and useful information to consumers, thereby establishing fair trade order and protecting consumers.)

*121.*

(2) With regard to duress. Threats not merely to persons (including the person other than declarant) but also to properties may constitute duress. In determining the illegitimacy of the duress, especially in case of the exercise of a right, a reasonable proportion between the right exercised and the advantage obtained should be taken into account. In addition, in a case of enforcing the debt by a threat of legal action, there should be a direct connection between the right which gives rise to the threat and the debt which is performed. (For reference, the Fair Debt Collection Practices Act was enacted in 2009 to contribute to the development of fair practices in debt collection by deterring debt collectors from abusing their rights or using unlawful methods in debt collection and the protection of decent lives and peaceful living of debtors while ensuring due exercise of creditors' rights.)

### V. Gross Disparity

*122.* As a rule, the contracting parties are free to determine the content of the contract, and a mere lack of equivalency in value as such may not constitute a sufficient ground for nullity. Even a contract with an extreme disparity in value (i.e., unilaterally onerous contract) such as gift or suretyship may be valid, if it was concluded out of a motive of generosity or business motives. Therefore, in principle, the Code does not raise an issue of the imbalance of exchange. In this regard, the Supreme Court ruled in obiter dicta that the doctrine of the "just price" (*iustum pretium*) as such is not a part of Korean law (2009Da50308).

However, in cases where the disparity in value is an outcome of one party's exploiting the "state of need" of the opposite party, the principle of the party autonomy or the freedom of contract may not be invoked. In this context, a juristic act which has conspicuously lost fairness (at time of the conclusion of the contract) on account of strained circumstances, rashness or inexperience of the parties shall be null and void (Article 104). This Article aims particularly at transactions that involve undue exploitations of inequality of bargaining power, to which Article 103 may also apply (to which dominant scholars assent). A contract containing clause(s) excessively disadvantageous to one party which is intentionally induced on account of a strong bargaining power of the other party can be null and void under Article 103 or 104. In this context, Article 104 may be comparable with the Anglo-American doctrine of undue influence or economic duress.

*123.* There are some provisions in the Civil Code that share *raison d'être* of Article 104. For instance, Article 607 prescribes that, if the borrower has promised to substitute any other property right in lieu of the object borrowed, the value of the substituted property shall not exceed the aggregate value of the original amount borrowed plus the interest thereon. Any agreement entered into by the parties which is in violation of this Article and is prejudicial to the borrower is not valid (Article 608. *See also* Article 339 concerning the ban on forfeited pledge). In addition, Article 6 of the Act on the Regulation of Terms and Conditions states that "Any clause in standard terms which is contrary to the doctrine of bona fides and is not fair shall be null and void." and lists clauses which are unreasonably unfavorable to the customers as an example thereof (*see infra* paragraphs 155 ff. As to the regulation of interest, *see infra* paragraph 394).

## §3. Other Conditions of Validity

### I. Cause

*124.* The requirement of a *cause*, which was one of the distinguishing characteristics of the French legal family (however, this has been abolished by the Revision of the French Civil Code in 2016), is not introduced into Korean law (as to Article 746 which restricts claim for restitution of performance for illegal causes, *see infra* paragraph 455). Thereby, a contract without any *cause* shall be valid.

## II. Determinability of the Obligations

*125.* Although there is no explicit provision, the rights and duties (generally from a contract, because otherwise they are usually specified in detail by the relevant provisions) should be determined or determinable. However, the contents of a contract need not be determined at the time of the conclusion of a contract. They may also be ascertained afterward. In this respect, besides the preengagement, for instance, the customary practice which the parties to a transaction share (e.g., determining the purchase-price at the market price) may be of importance (Article 106). On the other hand, the parties may agree to leave the power to determine to one of the parties or a third person. The power to determine should be exercised in accordance with the doctrine of bona fides, which may be reviewed by the court.

## III. Initial Impossibility

*126.* In some cases, performance of obligations was impossible already at time of the conclusion of a contract (*ab initio*). For instance, before that time, the object of a sale has been perished or belongs to the person other than the seller. In the latter case, the contract may be valid under Article 569, which states that "In the case where a right, which has been made the object of a sale, belongs to another person, the seller shall acquire such right and transfer it to the buyer." In case of the seller's failure to perform, the buyer may rescind the contract, and a bona fide buyer may additionally claim damages (Article 570. *See infra* paragraph 263).

With regard to the former example, by contrast, the contract is null and void (*impossibilium nulla obligatio*). There is indeed no explicit provision such as section 306 of BGB before the revision in 2002. However, this principle is implicit in particular in Article 535. (In this case, the obligor may be liable for damages if he/she should have been aware of the prior loss of the subject matter. *See supra* paragraphs 83 f.). However, the Supreme Court found that the partial shortage in articles sold by quantity does not lead to the nullity (as well as claim for damages) under this Article, but results in the seller's liability for warranty under Article 574 (99Da47396).

## IV. Illegality and Public Policy

### *A. Introduction*

*127.* As mentioned above (*supra* paragraph 27), a contract, as an expression of free intentions of the parties, is binding in principle. On the other hand, in order to be recognized and enforced by law, the subject of a contract (including the purpose and result thereof) may not infringe the public interests as one of the fundamental purposes of law. In this regard, a contract which is illegal or contrary to public policy shall be null and void.

*B. Illegality*

*128.* Juristic acts are required to comply with law to be enforced through the juridical system. In this regard, the Civil Code states that if the parties to a juristic act have declared an intention which differs from any provision of *lex scripta*, which are not concerned with social order, such intention shall prevail (Article 105). Therefore, the parties may deviate from statutory provisions, unless these provisions concern the social order (i.e., are mandatory). Whether a provision in question is mandatory or optional, is usually not set forth explicitly by *lex scripta*. Roughly speaking, provisions in Part Two (Real Rights) and Part Four (Relatives) are in general mandatory, while provisions in Part Three (Claims), especially concerning contracts, are generally optional, with some exceptions, especially to protect the weaker party.

*129.* On the other hand, mandatory provisions may aim to regulate either the act itself or its validity. In this sense, juristic acts in violation of mandatory provisions are not always null and void.

In determining validity of the act in question, whether the nullification of the act itself is inevitable to achieve the goal set by the mandatory provision or not and whether the nullification leads to unfairness between the parties or not, are of importance. Especially, violations of provisions in the administrative law which prohibit certain acts in the way in which an otherwise legal transaction may be carried out shall not make such acts null and void, even though they may result in administrative penalties. For instance, a person who sells foods without a necessary business license incurs an administrative penalty (Articles 37 and 94, the Food Sanitation Act); nevertheless, the contract itself is valid.

*C. Public Policy*

*130.* The legislator cannot foresee all the eventualities and take into account all the possible interests and relationships. To make a just solution possible in such situation, a general clause which protects the public interests based on the value evaluation is laid down in the Civil Code. Therefore, a juristic act which has for its subject such matters as are contrary to good morals and other social order (usually referred to "social order" in short or public policy. Attempts have been made to distinguish between good morals and social order, without success in my opinion) shall be null and void (Article 103). The court may resort to this provision, together with Article 2 (*see supra* paragraphs 43 ff.), in order to find fair and equitable solutions.

Generally speaking, social order (with the political and moral contents) embraces the protection of proper functioning of public interests, the preservation of integrity of the family and the maintenance of good morals. In this context, especially the fundamental rights provisions in the Constitution should be taken into account as one of the criteria for value evaluation. (In other words, the constitutional goals may be pursued in the private sphere by means of the general clause such as Article 103.) On the other hand, social order with the economic contents which aims to protect the liberty of commerce effectively is also secured by Article 104 (*see supra* paragraphs 122 f.) and recent legislations with regard to the protection of the weaker parties (especially the consumers).

*131.* Social order (*ordre public*) may be defined as "the legal and moral instincts of all just and reasonable citizens." As a changing/floating concept, nevertheless, the exact implication of social order can be understood by an evaluative concretization of the concept. In this sense, social order varies with place and time (i.e., it changes as social and/or economic conditions and ideas change) and is judged by the court in reference to the general idea of the very society. In determining whether a juristic act is contrary to social order or not, the purpose and effects of the act, the interests of the parties and the social permissibility of an act are of significance. In addition, the question about whether a juristic act is contrary to social order or not shall be answered on the basis of situations at the very moment of the conclusion of the contract.

In cases where one of the parties had a motive contrary to social order, the validity of a contract is an issue of controversy. The Supreme Court ruled that the contract may be null and void, if this motive has been expressed, or the other party was aware of the motive (99Da38613). (The motive contrary to social order not in a recognizable form gives rise to at most, a moral question.)

*132.* Article 103 as a "general clause" (together with Article 2) leaves broad discretion to the court. In this context, in order to obtain stability and predictability, the grouping (i.e., a typological review) of decisions of the court is necessary and useful. Some important examples of contracts contrary to social order which are ruled by the Supreme Court: a loan for consumption for gambling money (*infra* paragraph 342), contracts concluded by means of the abuse of a dominant position of one of the parties such as clause stating an immoderate penalty for the breach of contract (92Da46905. *See also* 97Da2221) and a prohibition clause of competitive business which restrict the freedom of employees too excessively (2009Da82244). In addition, the Supreme Court ruled recently that a contingent fee agreement in criminal cases may be evaluated as contrary to social order (2015Da200111).

*133.* In cases where one of the parties to a null or voided contract has performed his/her obligation(s) in whole or in part, he/she may in general demand return of the subject matter performed (*condictio*). However, those who gave something on illegitimate (according to the ruling of the Supreme Court: contrary to social order) grounds, are in principle not entitled to restitution (Article 746. *infra* paragraph 455).

In this context, the effect of double transfer of an immovable property is worthy of being mentioned. For example, the owner O, after a contract of sale with X, made a second contract of sale for his/her immovable with Y. Owing to the principle of relative effect, Y is not obliged to respect the interest of X, and X may not deny the validity of the second contract in principle (*See infra* paragraph 177). At this stage, if the ownership of immovable passes to Y upon its registration, the remedy for X shall, as a rule, be claimed against O (not Y) for damages in lieu of performance (*infra* paragraph 252. As to the exceptional possibility of tort liability of Y, *see infra* paragraph 183). However, if O committed a crime of the breach of trust (Article 355, paragraph 2, the Criminal Code), and if the probability of condemnation of Y is equivalent to that of O, e.g., in case of the inducement of Y to encourage O to frustrate the lawful exercise of a right by X, which the Supreme Court expressed as "positive participation" of Y in the crime of O, the second contract may be null and void (2009Da23283). In this case, X can exercise O's right of restitution against Y (*action subrogatoire*: Article 404, paragraph 1), although O himself/herself shall not be entitled to restitution as mentioned above (83DaKa57). By contrast, double transfer of a "movable," according to the recent ruling of the Supreme Court, does not constitute a crime of the breach of trust (2008Do10479), and therefore, the above solution shall not apply.

## §4. The Consequences of a Lack of Substantive Validity

### I. Overview

*134.* The Civil Code distinguishes between a juristic act (in some exceptional cases: declaration of intention, which hereafter will be left out), which is null and void on the one hand, and one which is merely voidable on the other hand. A null juristic act has no legal effect (i.e., cannot bind the parties to the contract) from the very beginning and without any claim to that effect. On the contrary, a voidable juristic act is for the present (provisionally) valid (i.e., shall bind the parties to the contract); however, it can be voided subsequently. The voidance has the retroactive effect: Upon voidance, the act shall in principle be deemed to have been void from the beginning (*ab initio*. Article 141).

The practical consequences of this distinction are: (1) that a voidable contract may be subsequently validated by ratification (confirmation) by the person protected by the nullity, while a void contract may in principle not be ratified (confirmed); and (2) that the right to void may be extinguished by the lapse of time (Article 146).

Roughly speaking, important grounds for nullity or voidance of contract (to the extent that the Civil Code provides for) are as follow: Juristic act contrary to social order (Article 103), unfair juristic act (Article 104), illegal juristic act, and juristic act which are composed of declaration of untrue intention or fictitious declaration of intention in collusion (Articles 107 and 108), are null and void. In addition, incapability of appreciating the implication and effects of his/her action (*supra* paragraph 90) or initial impossibility (*supra* paragraphs 83, 84 and 126) may lead to the nullity of a contract; On the other hand, juristic acts which consist of declaration of intention by mistake or declaration of intention by fraud or under duress (Articles 109 and 110) are merely voidable. Juristic acts of a person with limited capacity are also voidable.

## II. Nullity

*135.* If a juristic act is null and void, the intended legal effects cannot come into existence. As a result, either party may refuse to perform obligations and/or demand return of benefits resulting from his/her performance (restitution).

Nullity operates automatically (per se), and a judgment of the court which sentences that the act is null and void has merely a declaratory meaning (in other words: is not necessary with regard to the validity of the act itself) in the sphere of the substantive law. With regard to adjective law, however, the situation differs: in a civil litigation, a party who insists on the nullity of a juristic act should in principle allege (and prove) the fact that the act in question is null and void.

If a part of a juristic act is null, the juristic act as a whole shall be made null. However, in a case where it is deemed that the juristic act would have been performed if the null part had not existed, then the rest of the act shall not become null (Article 137). This Article is not mandatory.

*136.* Article 138 lays down the conversion (reinterpretation), i.e., the replacement of a null juristic act by another juristic act: In a case where a null juristic act meets requirements for another juristic act, and it is deemed that if the parties had known the nullity, they would have intended to do the other juristic act, such a null act shall have the effect as the other juristic act.

On the other hand, Article 139 provides for the ratification (confirmation) of a null act: A null juristic act shall not become effective by ratification; however, if the party has ratified it with knowledge of its nullity, he/she shall be deemed to have performed a new juristic act. In contrast to the ratification of voidable act, the ratification of a null act does not have a retroactive effect (i.e., *de novo*).

## III. Voidance

*137.* In contrast to a null juristic act which does not have any legal effect per se (therefore, "anyone," even other than the parties, can invoke its nullity), a voidable juristic act is for the present (i.e., provisionally) valid; however, it can subsequently be voided (invalidated). A voidable juristic act may be voided only by entitled persons listed in Article 140 (i.e., a person with limited capacity, a person who has made a declaration of intention by mistake, fraud or duress, or such person's agent or successor). It depends primarily upon the choice of these persons whether a voidable juristic act will be valid or void. The voidance is a unilateral juristic act, which may be executed implicitly (e.g., implied in a defense against a claim for performance or as a ground for claim for restitution), and shall be effected by declaring (i.e., notifying the exercise of the right to void. In this sense, the court merely confirms that the voidance was valid or not valid) to the other party in a case where the other party to a voidable act is an identified person (Article 142). In this context, it is worthy of adding that Article 15 furnishes the right of peremptory notice of the other party only regarding the act of the person with limited capacity (*see supra* paragraph 97. As a result, the right to void may be excluded).

On the other hand, the Supreme Court held that in cases where a contract was rescinded on the ground of a failure to perform contractual obligations, the mistaken party may void the contract (91Da11308), and thereby he/she may avoid consequences of his/her failure to perform (i.e., liability for damages).

*138.* The voidance has a retroactive effect: Upon voidance, the act shall be deemed to have been void from the beginning (*ab initio*. Article 141. Therefore, with regard to consequences, a voided juristic act does not differ from a null act.) Thereafter, either party may refuse to perform his/her obligations, and may demand return of benefits resulting from his/her performance (*restitutio in integrum*). For example, an article sold should be returned and monies paid should be repaid. Concerning the amount of benefits to be returned, the parties shall in principle be deemed to be enriched in good faith until they became aware of the exercise of the right to void (*see* Article 748 and *infra* paragraph 452).

However, the retroactive effect of voidance may not apply to contracts which have as contents a continuous performance over a period (e.g., contract of employment or of partnership). In these cases, the successful challenge of a declaration only makes the declaration invalid *ex nunc*, i.e., from the moment when it is voided, and therefore the restitution shall not matter. The reason therefor is that in such situations, restitution is impracticable and/or impossible. In a recent ruling, the Supreme Court has explicitly assented to this view asserted by most scholars (2013Da25194,25200).

*139.* A voidable juristic act may be ratified by the persons entitled to voidance, and after the ratification (confirmation), it may not be voided (Article 143). Ratification shall not become effective, unless it is made after causes for voidance have ceased to exist (Article 144 with an exception in case of the voidance of a representative by law).

On the other hand, in contrast to a null juristic act in which anyone can claim its nullity "at any time," a voidable juristic act is subject to the limitation on period of the right to void: the right to void shall be exercised within three years from the time when it becomes possible to ratify the act (e.g., from attaining the age of majority), or within ten years from the time of act (Article 146). According to the ruling of the Supreme Court, these periods are not the prescription period but the period of exclusion (2008Da27301,27318. *See infra* paragraph 234). Once either period lapses, the voidable act becomes valid firmly. (The restriction on exercise of the right to void such as "without culpable/undue delay" in section 121 of BGB is not provided for by the Civil Code.) In addition, in cases where any of the listed events (i.e., performance of a voidable act in whole or in part, demand for performance of such act, novation of such act, furnishing of security, assignment, in whole or in part, of any right acquired as a result of such act and compulsory execution by the voidable act) takes place after it has become possible to ratify, the act shall be deemed (not presumed) to have been ratified, unless any objection is reserved (Article 145).

## IV. Restitution

*140.* Since a void or voided contract is in principle without legal effect, there can be no claim for performance of contractual obligations as well as no claim for damages based on the failure in performance. On the other hand, since in such a case a valid contract which constitutes the legal ground for the retention of performance of the other party does not exist, either party of a void or voided contract may demand the return of benefits resulting from his/her performance (*restitutio in integrum*. Article 741). In cases where recovery is not possible (e.g., carriage of passengers or destruction of the delivered article), the person enriched (i.e., the recipient of performance) shall return the value of performance (Article 747, paragraph 1). In this regard, it should be added that in a case where a person granted property or rendered service for an illegal cause, he/she may not demand return of benefits resulting therefrom (Article 746. *infra* paragraph 447), and the scope of restitution of a person with limited capacity shall be limited to the extent that he/she is still enriched (Article 141. *supra* paragraph 89).

On the other hand, although entering into a null or voidable contract with knowledge thereof may constitute an unlawful act to the other party, the liability for damages of the person declaring voidance (*see* section 122, BGB) shall be denied. The Supreme Court also denied liability of the declarant who voided the declaration of intention on the ground of mistake (97Da13023), although there is a crucial controversy thereover. As a result, the interest of the recipient who relied on the validity of the declaration is less protected than that of the declarant.

## V. Effects of Nullity or Voidance on the Third Party

*141.* If a contract is invalid (i.e., void or voided), the contract shall, in principle, be without effect not merely between the parties thereto but also to a third party. Nevertheless, in certain situations, the interest of a bona fide third party who relied upon the validity of contract shall be protected.

At first, only regarding movables, Article 249 provides for a bona fide acquisition (with an exception in cases of the stolen or lost articles. Articles 250 and 251), stating that "If a person who is in good faith and without negligence commences the possession of a 'movable' peaceably and openly by an act of transaction, he/she shall acquire its ownership immediately even if the assigner is not a legal owner." In this case, the right of a third party may not be prejudiced. (By contrast, in case of immovables, a bona fide acquisition is not permitted, no matter through how many hands it has passed.) In addition, the acquisitive prescription (especially with regard to immovables. Article 245) shall also protect the interest of a third party.

*142.* On the other hand, the nullity or voidance of a declaration of intention may not be set up against a third person acting in good faith in cases of a declaration of an untrue intention (Article 107, paragraph 2), a fictitious declaration of intention in collusion (Article 108, paragraph 2), a declaration of intention by mistake (Article

109, paragraph 2) and a declaration of intention by fraud or under duress (Article 110, paragraph 3). In these cases, the parties may not allege that the act is null or voided against a bona fide third party.

For instance, if X and A collude to pretend to conclude a contract of sale and X registers his/her building under the name of buyer (A), in order to avoid the attachment from X's obligees, the contract shall be null and void between X and A (Article 108). In this situation, X, as the owner, may claim A for cancellation of registration, alleging a claim for removal of the disturbance against the article owned (*rei vindicatio*. Article 213). However, if A has sold the building to a third party Y (subsequent purchaser), who believed that A was the genuine owner, and registered the building under Y's name, X may not exercise his/her *rei vindicatio* against Y under Article 108, paragraph 2. In this case, since X has created the external untrue appearance that A was an owner and Y relied on it, X should bear the result thereof. Some important examples of such a bona fide third party in the decisions of the Supreme Court: a transferee who acquires ownership of immovables from the fictitious transferee (94Da12074), a bankruptcy administrator, where a bankruptcy acquires a sham claim (2004Da10299), and a subsequent purchaser from a third party (2012Da49292).

For reference, the rights of third persons shall not be prejudiced by rescission (Article 548, paragraph 1. *See infra* paragraph 285), in such case, whether the third person is in good faith or not, does not matter.

# Chapter 3. Contents of a Contract

## §1. Introduction

### I. Obligation

*143.* Legal effects of a contract are to create, modify or extinguish obligation(s), and in this sense, the obligation constitutes the primary contents of a contract.

As the main effect of a contract, an obligation is a legal duty to do (e.g., duty of a seller (obligor/debtor) to transfer the ownership sold to a buyer (obligee/creditor), and duty of the latter to pay the purchase-money to the former under the contract of sale) or not to do, and is one of the component elements of the property. Even something the value of which cannot be assessed in money, may be the subject of a claim (Article 373).

On the other hand, a contract may be concluded to terminate a contract in existence. In such a case, an implicit consent to terminate the contract in existence shall be sufficient.

*144.* The content of an obligation may be any act (including, of course, payment of money) or forbearance, i.e., to do or not to do.

With regard to a method of the compulsory execution (Article 389), obligations may be divided into an obligation to give, to do and not to do something. The obligation to give is fulfilled usually by way of delivery of something, irrespective of (but usually including) passing of the ownership or some other real right. (In this context, the obligor is bound to preserve any specified thing with the care of a good manager until it is delivered under Article 374 or to procure the thing in species in case of the fungible claim under Article 375.) The transfer of a real property by a juristic act takes effect upon its registration (in case of immovables: Article 186) or by delivery of the article (in case of movables: Article 188, paragraph 1). On the other hand, in case of an obligation to do something, personal performance will often be required, while in case of an obligation to give or not to do something, the person of obligor will usually be of little importance. In addition, in contrast to most cases, in case of an obligation not to do something or an obligation to give something to a third person, the obligor may perform his/her obligation without any cooperation from the obligee.

### II. Burden of Proof, Obligation of Means and Obligation of Result

#### A. *Burden of Proof*

*145.* The burden of proof lies in principle with the party who alleges certain facts (e.g., a party, in whose interests an exception is inserted, has to prove the existence of such exception). Although there is no provision which lays down the apportionment of the burden of proof in civil litigation explicitly, the apportionment shall, in general, be deduced from substantive law. For instance, on the one hand, Article 390 provides that "If an obligor fails to perform in accordance with the tenor and purport of the obligation, the obligee shall be entitled to claim damages. However, this shall not apply in cases where performance has become impossible and where this is not due to the obligor's intention or negligence." On the other hand, Article 750 states that "Any person who causes losses to another person by an unlawful act, willfully or negligently, shall be bound to make compensation for damages arising therefrom." Both provisions require the obligor's intention or negligence to claim damages. However, the structure of both provisions indicates the apportionment of the burden of proof, i.e., under the former, the obligor should prove the absence of his/her intention and negligence, while according to the latter, the burden of proof lies with the obligee (injured party).

*146.* As to the exception thereto.

First, there are some provisions which lay down explicitly with whom the burden of proof lies. For example, Article 437 prescribes that the burden of proof regarding the defense of demand/peremptory notice and reference/inquiry lies with the surety (*see infra* paragraph 411).

Second, some provisions presume certain facts (presumption provision), by means of which the burden of proof shall be mitigated. For instance, Article 30 states that "In a case more than two persons died of the same peril, it is presumed that they died at the same time." In addition, Article 344 of the Civil Procedure Act provides for the obligation to submit document e.g., of the party who holds the document quoted in a lawsuit, by means of which the burden of proof of the other party may be made easier. On the other hand, especially regarding torts, there are some provisions in the Civil Code as well as in other Acts which shift the burden of proof to the obligor. For example, Article 4 of the Product Liability Act provides for exemptions of the manufacturer from liability.

Third, especially with regard to the so-called a modern type of tort, e.g., medical malpractice, the court presumes the existence of ground for responsibility (i.e., intention or negligence) and/or causation, in order to protect the obligee (injured party), and thereby his/her burden of proof shall be mitigated. In addition, in some cases, especially in a case of liability for environmental damage, the court approves a prima facie proof based on the probability (81Da558), which means the de facto shift of the burden of proof.

### *B. Obligation of Means and Obligation of Result*

*147.* The French distinction between obligation of means (*obligation de moyens*) and obligation of result (*obligation de résultat*) is also introduced into Korea; however, some scholars raise doubts about whether this distinction is useful and desirable in Korea. In an obligation of means, the debtor's obligation is not to achieve a certain result, but to exercise due care. By contrast, in an obligation of result, the obligor is bound to achieve the result he/she has promised.

In general, an obligation to give something belongs to the obligation of result and an obligation for an act (i.e., to do or not to do) to the obligation of means. However, in some cases, this matchup may be incorrect, e.g., a duty of carrier is the obligation of a means as well as of a result. On the other hand, some contracts may generate both types of obligation in the form of an attenuated obligation of result within the general obligation of means (e.g., a lawyer is, in principle, an obligor of an obligation of means, but he/she should file an appeal in time).

*148.* This distinction is concerned primarily with the meaning of the failure in performance. In an obligation of result, the failure to achieve certain result(s), which the obligor has undertaken, constitutes a failure in performance. However, he/she can escape from the liability by showing that his/her failure to produce the result promised is due to a cause beyond his/her control (i.e., the obligor can set up the absence of intention and negligence as a defense). A typical example is an obligation of a seller. By contrast, an obligation of result to the exclusion of the availability of defense (according to the opinion of dominant scholars: except a defense based on "force majeure"), e.g., a monetary debt (An obligor of monetary debt may not raise the defense of the absence of negligence. Article 397, paragraph 2), is generally denoted as an obligation of guarantee.

On the other hand, in an obligation of means, the negligence to take reasonable care to achieve the purpose of a contract leads to a failure in performance, irrespective of the result. A typical example is an obligation of a doctor who is bound to take reasonable steps to cure his/her patient; however, he/she is not liable if, in spite of such steps, no cure is achieved. Therefore, impossibility as such is, in principle, out of question in this case.

*149.* This distinction also plays an important role concerning the burden of proof. (The practical difference lies in cases where the cause of a failure to perform is unknown.) In both cases, the burden of proof of the fact that the obligor has not performed his/her obligation lies with the obligee (Article 390. *See infra* paragraph 237); however, the implication of the failure to perform differs. In an obligation of result, the fact that the result agreed upon is not achieved constitutes a failure in performance per se, and therefore, the obligee has merely to show that the result has not been achieved, and then the obligor should, to be relieved of claim for damages, allege and prove as a defense the fact that the failure to perform shall not be imputed to him/her.

To the contrary, in an obligation of means, not the fact that the result agreed upon is not achieved, but the fact that the obligor does not exercise the reasonable care constitutes a failure in performance, and therefore, the obligee should allege and prove the fact that the obligor did not make the efforts required. (Standard of the efforts required will, in general, depend upon circumstances concerned.) In short, the obligee should show that the obligor was at fault.

## §2. Ascertaining the Contents of a Contract

### I. Introduction

*150.* In accordance with the principle of freedom of a contract (*supra* paragraphs 22 ff.), the parties may decide contents of the contractual relationship. In this sense, the coinciding intentions of the parties are the primary source of contractual obligations. Therefore, what is agreed upon by the parties is the first and foremost important standard to ascertain the contents of a contract.

*151.* However, not all of the contractual obligations are agreed upon explicitly, because it is in practice impossible or unnecessary to provide for all the eventualities in a contract (*see supra* paragraph 48). In such a case, legal effects should be supplemented in diverse ways.

First, legal effects which are not set forth explicitly (such as auxiliary/supplementary duties) may be found through interpretation (more precisely: by way of reading between the lines of the agreement). These effects may be referred to as the implied terms. (The meaning of the implied terms differs from that of the Common lawyers. For instance, under the Common law, the seller's liability for latent defects or the burden of risk shall be expressed as an implied term, which in Korea is set forth in the Civil Code as an optional provision.) In this context, the doctrine of bona fides may contribute to assume the implied intentions of the parties (*see* also *supra* paragraph 44).

Second, if there is a custom (usage or practice) that differs from any provision of *lex scripta* which are not concerned with social order, and if the intention of the parties to a juristic act is not clear, such custom shall prevail (Article 106). In this respect, a custom means a certain line of conduct which used to and may be expected to be taken with regard to a certain kind of contract.

Third, *lex scripta* will apply to fill the gaps left, intentionally or by negligence, by the parties. As mentioned above, the Civil Code lists typical contracts, and thereby the normal incidents of every type of a contract may be dealt with by operation of law. In this regard, a line needs to be drawn between rules which merely fill gaps left by the parties (optional provision) and those which concern the public interests and may not therefore be excluded (mandatory/compulsory provision). The former do not apply if the parties' intention is to exclude them (i.e., the contracting parties may derogate from them), while a contract cannot override a mandatory provision (*see also supra* paragraphs 128 f.).

## II. Interpretation

### A. *Introduction*

*152.* Offer and acceptance must correspond with each other for a contract to come into existence. In this sense, the starting point of the law of contract is common/coinciding intentions of the parties. However, cases in which the intention of one or each of the parties is not clear or in which they have failed to provide for the matter in issue at all, are not seldom.

In such cases, the objective of the interpretation of contract is whether coinciding intentions of the parties exist or not and/or what is agreed upon between the parties (i.e., the meaning attached to and legal effects arising from the contract). On the other hand, in cases where doubt about the parties' intentions cannot be excluded in spite of the interpretation, the contract shall not come into existence.

*B. Goal of Interpretation*

*153.* The purpose of interpretation is to clarify the coinciding intentions of the parties and to determine the contents of a contract. In this context, on the one hand, the internal/genuine intention of the declarant may be regarded as the primary goal of interpretation of a declaration of intention, and therefore, with regard to contract, emphasis should be put on the genuine consent, pursuant to the principle of party autonomy. On the other hand, the objective expression of intention should also be respected, because those who depend upon the objective expression shall be protected (in this sense, Article 111 requires, as a rule, arrival of the declaration of intention), and therefore, concerning a contract, stress may be laid upon the external appearance of the consent, in interests of commercial convenience and security of transactions (*see also supra* paragraph 27). Generally speaking, the former approach can be said to be more generous to the declarant in case of defects of the consent than the latter.

In general, the court seems to place more emphasis on the external/objective expression of intention, as the other party would have understood it, rather than the internal intention. However, in my opinion, stress should be laid upon the genuine intention of the declarant, because the external appearance is, at best, a source to deduce the genuine intention therefrom. On the other hand, in a case where there was, in fact, a true consensus between the parties, there will be a contract with effects in accordance with the true consensus, even if the statements made do not objectively correspond with their common intentions. In this sense, the literal sense of the term stipulated in a document is not decisive, and the Supreme Court also approved this theory which is referred to as *falsa demonstratio non nocet* (93Da2619,2636. *See* also *supra* paragraph 75).

*C. Criteria for Interpretation*

*154.* Since under the Civil Code there is no explicit provision on the interpretation of a juristic act (although some scholars consider Article 106 as a provision on interpretation. *See* also *supra* paragraph 151), it is left to the court to determine (clarify and supplement) the contents of a contract.

In doing so, internal/genuine intentions of the parties should be of great importance as mentioned above. In examining the internal intention, the literal sense of words set forth in contract is not decisive. Since the genuine intention is not always clear, conduct and expressions of the parties in pre-contractual phase may affect the contents of a contract. In addition, the nature of a contract and the doctrine of bona fides may play a role.

On the other hand, in cases where the parties have failed to provide for matter(s) in issue at all, there will in principle be no contract. However, this is the case only with regard to the essential elements of a contract. By contrast, in a case where the lack of consensus relates only to the supplementary elements of a contract, such as time or place of delivery, then there may still be a valid contract, and the gap shall be filled subsequently pursuant to optional provisions, or, prior to this, in a case where there is a custom which differs from optional provision and the intention of the parties to a juristic act is not clear, by the de facto custom (Article 106. *See supra* paragraph 151). In this context, in case of the lack of consensus, it should be determined whether the lack thereof relates to the essential elements of a contract or to the supplementary elements. This will depend on how much importance the parties (including the presumed parties in some instances) attached to the element(s) in question.

## III. Standard Terms

### *A. Introduction*

*155.* In modern society, a person or company who supplies goods or services (e.g., supply of gas or electricity, insurance, banking, transportation) usually offers general conditions, i.e., standard terms of contract which are drafted in advance to use in a large number of contracts and which one party (i.e., a party to a contract, who offers standard terms to the other party as the content of contract: referred to in the Act on the Regulation of Terms and Conditions as "business person") enforces upon the other party (i.e., a party to a contract, who has been offered standard terms from a business person as the content of contract: referred to as "customer") to conclude each individual contract.

*156.* For business persons, this practice is very convenient to deal with plenty of routine transactions. However, as demerits of this practice, customers (in most cases ordinary laypersons) have no right to decide the contents of the contract concerning such goods or services, but have merely the possibility of choice of whether to enter into a contractual relation or not. Especially in cases where these goods or services are indispensable to everyday living, the freedom on the part of consumer is confined to "take it or leave it."

In addition, a business person may abuse his/her prominent position and force the consumer to accept unfair or unjust contract terms. In other words, the prepared standard terms may contain clauses disadvantageous to those in the weaker bargaining position (e.g., concerning limitation of liability). In addition, standard terms are in most cases so complicated (and in fine print) that they are not intelligible to ordinary laypersons.

*157.* Taking these circumstances into consideration, the Act on the Regulation of Terms and Conditions entered into force in 1993. The purpose of this Act is to establish sound order in business transactions, and thereby to protect consumers and promote the balanced improvement of people's lives by preventing business persons from preparing unfair standard terms and using them in business transactions by taking unfair advantage of their bargaining power and regulating unfair standard terms (Article 1).

*B. Statutory Control over Standard Terms*

*158.* In order to restore a balance of interests between the parties (more precisely, in the interests of consumer), the preceding Act lays down judicial control over standard terms step by step. (As to the administrative regulation, Articles 17 ff. of this Act stipulate.)

*159.* At first, a business person should afford any customer a reasonable opportunity to take cognizance of standard terms. Therefore, a business person shall provide standard terms in Korean and use standardized and systemized terms so that customers can easily understand details of standard terms, and explicitly indicate important details thereof with signs, color, bold and large letters, etc., so that customers can easily recognize them (Article 3, paragraph 1, the preceding Act). In addition, a business person shall in principle explain important details set forth in standard terms of a contract so that customers can understand them (*ibid.*, paragraph 3). If a business person fails to do so, he/she may not claim that the relevant clause in standard terms constitutes the content of a contact (*ibid.*, paragraph 4). This implies that standard terms constitute the contents of contract because the customer accepts them (i.e., they are not rules). This step is usually referred to as an incorporation control.

*160.* Second step is a so-called interpretation control. In a case where a business person and a customer agree upon a matter in a manner that is different from the manner set forth in standard terms, such agreement (i.e., individually agreed terms) shall prevail over such standard terms (Article 4, the preceding Act). On the other hand, standard terms shall be construed impartially in accordance with the doctrine of bona fides, and shall not be construed differently depending upon customers (Article 5, paragraph 1, the preceding Act). If the meaning of standard terms is not clear, it shall be construed in favor of customers (*contra proferentem. Ibid.*, paragraph 2).

*161.* Third and most important step is referred to as an unfairness control. This control aims to rule unreasonably onerous stipulations out and is divided into two dimensions. On the one hand, Article 6 of the preceding Act lays down general principles: Any clause in standard terms which is contrary to the doctrine of bona fides and is not fair shall be null and void (*ibid.*, paragraph 1). Whether a clause is unfair or contrary to the doctrine of bona fides shall depend upon relevant circumstances including the further content of contract and the actual and apparent interests of the parties. In this respect, a clause which is unreasonably unfavorable to customers, a clause which customers would have a difficulty anticipating in light of various circumstances including the type of transaction the contract represents (usually referred to as “a surprising clause”), or a clause which is so restrictive of essential rights set forth in a contract that the purpose of contract may not be achieved, shall be presumed to be unfair (*ibid.*, paragraph 2). On the other hand, Articles 7 through 14 of the preceding Act list null and void clauses in standard terms case by case: clause concerning prohibition of exemption clauses (Article 7), predetermination of amount of damages (Article 8), rescission or rescission for the future of contract

(Article 9), performance of obligations (Article 10), protecting rights and interests of consumers (Article 11), deemed declaration of intention (Article 12), additional obligations of agents (Article 13) and prohibition, etc. of filing a lawsuits (Article 14).

*162.* Especially, with regard to contents of a contract, Article 11 of the preceding Act states that:

> The following clause in standard terms concerning the rights and interests of customers shall be null and void: (1) a clause which, without any substantial reason, excludes or limits a customer's rights of defense, offset of damages, etc., which are provided for by Acts; (2) a clause which, without any substantial reason, deprives customers of the right to perform their obligations during a given time; (3) clause which unreasonably limits a customer's right to enter into contracts with a third party; or (4) clause which, without any justifiable reason, allows a business person to divulge confidential information of customers he/she has obtained in the course of his/her business.

*163.* In cases where the whole or any part of standard terms fails to constitute the contents of a contract or is null and void, the contract shall remain effective with only the remaining parts of standard terms (*favor contractus*). However, if it is impossible to achieve the objective of the contract with only the effective parts or such effective parts are unreasonably unfavorable to one party, the relevant contract as a whole shall be null and void (Article 16, the preceding Act. As to Article 137 of the Civil Code with the opposite direction, *see supra* paragraph 125). In case of a partial nullity, provisions of *lex scripta* shall take place of invalid clause(s).

## §3. Supplementary Terms

### I. Exemption Clauses

*164.* The contracting parties may agree to exempt one or each of the parties from liability for the failure to perform obligations arising from contract. A clause which excludes the liability for such failure (exclusion clause) is in principle valid based on the principle of the freedom of contract. For instance, the parties to a contract may agree that certain facts shall be regarded as force majeure in their relationship (i.e., the obligor shall not to be liable for the failure to perform due to those facts). They may also agree to limit the extent of damages payable or alter the burden of risks pursuant to *lex scripta*. In addition, the warranty liability may be excluded, limited or tightened. Especially, a clause on an upper limit of damages (limitation clause) is also in principle valid as a species of exemption clause as well as liquidated damages.

*165.* However, since exemption of damages in cases based on the intention or gross negligence shall be contrary to social order (Article 103), it is generally accepted that clauses excluding liability in cases where one or each of the parties fails to perform willfully or with gross negligence are invalid. This approach is based on the fear that such an exemption clause may encourage recklessness. (In addition, if the exemption clause has been incorporated into contract under undue influence, that clause may be voidable under Article 110. *See supra* paragraphs 119 ff.).

On the other hand, Article 7 of the Act on the Regulation of Terms and Conditions denies the validity of following exemption clauses in standard terms: (1) a clause which exempts a business person from liability for intention or gross negligence on the part of the business person, his/her agents or his/her employees; (2) a clause which limits, without any substantial reason, the extent of indemnification payable by a business person, or which passes a risk to be borne by a business person to a customer; (3) a clause which, without any substantial reason, excludes or limits the warranty liability of a business person, or tightens requirements of customers to exercise the rights under the warranty thereof; or (4) a clause which excludes or limits the warranty for the subject of contract for which a business person has provided a sample, or has indicated the quality, performance, etc., without considerable reasons.

It should be added that a contractual exemption clause will be no bar to a tort-claim.

## II. Penalty Clauses

*166.* The parties to a contract may determine in advance the amount of damages payable in the event of a failure to perform an obligation (Article 398, paragraph 1).

This agreement has in general two purposes: to liquidate damages in advance and to compel the obligor to perform. In this context, although this agreement is presumed to determine in advance the amount of damages (i.e., to constitute liquidated damages. *Ibid.*, paragraph 4), pursuant to Korean law, in contrast to the Common law, a penalty clause is also valid. In cases of liquidated damages, the agreement is primarily to rule the burden of proof of occurrence as well as bothersome and difficult calculations of damage out (although with the indirect purpose to compel the obligor to perform). Therefore, the aggrieved party does not need to prove the occurrence and/or the amount of loss, and may not be awarded larger or smaller sum (i.e., irrespective of the actual amount of loss) unless otherwise agreed upon by the parties (about which some scholars raise doubts). By contrast, in case of a penalty, the only purpose is to put pressure on the obligor, and therefore, compensation for damages is another matter.

*167.* Where the amount of damages determined in advance is unduly excessive, the court may reduce the amount to a more reasonable and appropriate sum (Article 398, paragraph 2). To do so, an application/request of the obligor is not required. The Supreme Court ruled on the one hand that this paragraph is applicable only to the liquidated damages (i.e., not to the penalty in its original sense. 68Da491), and on the other hand, that in cases where the amount of penalty is unduly excessive, the penalty clause may be contrary to social order (Article 103) and therefore null and void totally or partially (2000Da56976). In addition, Article 8 of the Act on the

Regulation of Terms and Conditions lays down that “Any clause in standard terms which obligates customers to pay unreasonably heavy loss, including but not limited to, excessive liquidated loss for delay, shall be null and void.”

On the other hand, the determination in advance of the amount of damages shall not affect the obligee’s claim for performance or rescission of contract (Article 398, paragraph 3). The obligee may claim to perform and to pay the amount of money determined under penalty clause; however, the obligor may not choose to pay the latter in lieu of the former of course.

## §4. Conditional Contracts

### I. Introduction

*168.* There may be clauses in a contract which qualify or modify the effect, i.e., enforceability of obligation (i.e., not the existence itself, in that a conditional obligation or an obligation subject to a time limit is also in existence from the moment of the conclusion of contract), as a result of which it may be uncertain whether it will have effects or whether it will keep its effects. Such a provision is either a condition or a specification of time. Conditions and time limits may be set forth implicitly. It is worthy of mentioning that no condition may be attached, nor a time limit may be assigned, to a unilateral juristic act in principle (*see* Article 493, paragraph 1).

### II. Conditions

*169.* An obligation is conditional when it depends upon a future and objectively uncertain (at time of the stipulation of condition) event, either by suspending its enforcement until such event occurs or by extinguishing it if such event occurs. In other words, a condition is a provision which makes effects of a juristic act and the enforcement of obligation(s) arising therefrom dependent upon a future and uncertain event.

In cases where a condition is contrary to social order, the juristic act subject to the condition shall be null and void (Article 151, paragraph 1).

*170.* The conditions may be either suspensive, in that the obligation will not be effective unless and until the indicated event occurs, or resolutive, in that the obligation will cease to be effective if the indicated event occurs.

A juristic act subject to a suspensive condition (condition precedent) shall become effective upon fulfillment of the condition (Article 147, paragraph 1). In this case, the obligation is without effect until the fulfillment of the condition, and therefore, the obligation may not be enforced until then. If this condition has already been fulfilled at time of the applicable juristic act (more precisely: at the time of stipulation of the condition), such act shall be unconditional, and if nonfulfillment of this condition was already certain at time of the juristic act, such act shall be null and void (Article 151, paragraphs 2 and 3). In addition, most scholars are of the opinion that in cases where fulfillment of a suspensive condition depends solely upon the will of the obligor, the obligation shall be null and void.

By contrast, a juristic act subject to a resolutive condition (condition subsequent) shall cease to be effective upon fulfillment of the condition (Article 147, paragraph 2). In this case, the obligation is, for the moment at least, fully effective and enforceable, but will cease to be effective if the indicated event occurs. If this condition has already been fulfilled at time of the applicable juristic act, such juristic act shall be null and void, and in cases where nonfulfillment of this condition was already certain at the time of the juristic act, such act shall be unconditional (Article 151, paragraphs 2 and 3).

*171.* Whether and when a condition is fulfilled is a question of fact. In this regard, the Civil Code furnishes some suppletive provisions. If a party who is to be disadvantaged upon fulfillment of a condition has intentionally obstructed fulfillment of such condition in violation of the doctrine of bona fides, the other party may treat the condition as having been fulfilled (Article 150, paragraph 1), and if a party who is to be advantaged upon fulfillment of a condition has intentionally fulfilled such condition contrary to the principles of bona fides, the other party may treat the condition as not having been fulfilled (*ibid.*, paragraph 2).

*172.* Effects of fulfillment of a condition shall in principle not be affected retroactively. Therefore, for instance, in a case where a person has discharged an obligation subject to a resolutive condition, he/she may not demand return of the subject matter. However, in cases where the parties declare an intention contrary to that effect prior to the time of fulfillment, such intention shall prevail (Article 147, paragraph 3).

Neither party to a juristic act subject to a condition shall, during pendency of a condition (i.e., while it is uncertain whether a condition has been fulfilled or not), do anything to impair the benefit which the other party might derive from such an act upon fulfillment of the condition (Article 148). In addition, the rights and duties of the party concerned during pendency of a condition may be disposed of, inherited, preserved or secured in accordance with the general provisions of *lex scripta* (Article 149).

## III. Time Limits

*173.* An obligation may depend upon the occurrence of a future and certain event. A time limit differs from a condition in that the indicated event is certain to take place (even though the moment at which it will occur may not be certain). In this context, the only question is about "when."

The time limits may also be either suspensive (time of commencement) or resolutive (time of termination/expiration). A juristic act subject to a suspensive time limit shall be effective when the time specified arrives, and a juristic act subject to a resolutive time limit shall cease to be effective when the time specified arrives (Article 152). There is no retroactive effect.

A time limit (in effect: time for performance) is presumed to be stipulated for the benefit of the obligor, and the benefit of the time limit may be waived, but the interests of the other party shall not be prejudiced thereby (Article 153). On the other hand, the obligor may not claim the benefit of the time limit, in cases where the obligor has damaged, diminished or extinguished the security, or has failed to perform the obligation to furnish security (Article 388). In addition, the parties may agree upon forfeiture of benefit of time limit (acceleration clause). In this regard, e.g., in banking transactions, upon the occurrence of events specified, the time for performance shall be due per se or upon demand of the obligee (*see infra* paragraph 246).

## §5. Modifications of Contracts

### I. Modification by the Parties

*174.* Pursuant to party autonomy, the parties may modify the contract. The modification of the existing contract by the parties is based on their mutual consent on new terms of the contract. In other words, this type of modification is brought about in the manner of a new contract (contract of alteration). Therefore, to the agreement to modify the existing contract, the general rule of the contract law shall apply.

In this regard, Article 10 of the Act on the Regulation of Terms and Conditions states that:

The following clause in standard terms concerning the performance of obligations shall be null and void: (1) a clause which, without any substantial reason, gives a business person the power to unilaterally determine or change the details of performance; or (2) a clause which, without any substantial reason, allows a business person to unilaterally suspend the performance of his/her obligations or imputes performance of his/her obligation to a third party.

### II. Modification by the Court

*175.* There is a controversy over whether a contract in whole or in part may be modified or set aside by the court upon application/request of one of the parties (without obtaining the consent of the other party) on the basis of unforeseen circumstances (*clausula rebus sic stantibus*). This issue takes place normally when the circumstances under which a contract is concluded have been changed radically after the conclusion of the contract, and therefore, it is no longer fair to require the party who may suffer therefrom to perform his/her obligations. For instance, in a case where the contract becomes impossible to execute at the price which has been agreed upon due to steep inflation, it may be unreasonable — taking into consideration the doctrine of bona fides — to bind the parties to the contract.

If the change in circumstances is foreseeable at the time of the conclusion of contract, the parties shall take the risk of change in circumstances into account, and according to the allocation of risks agreed upon (even implicitly) by the parties the contract should be maintained in an unmodified form. However, in a case where the change is unforeseeable at the time of conclusion of the contract and is radical, the situation differs completely. A classic example is a German case in which the court ruled increase of the nominal value of pecuniary claim because of severe inflation after World War I (by requiring the revision of agreements in light of inflation and revaluation of the currency after the World War. *See RGZ* 103, 328 in 1922). Under such circumstances, if both of the parties agree to modify or set aside the existing contract, there is no problem. However, in cases where they do not agree to do so (which is usual, because the interests of the parties conflict with each other), one of the parties may suffer a great loss, i.e., significantly changed circumstances may distort the intended equilibrium of the parties or defeat the purposes of the parties.

*176.* In this case, many other Civil law countries furnish the competence of the court to modify or set aside the contract. In Korea, since there is no explicit provision under the Civil Code, most scholars attempt to accept it as *de lege lata.* (However, there are some provisions which are based on the same grounds. For instance, in a case where the rent previously agreed upon by the parties has become unreasonable due to the increase or decrease of the public impost imposed upon the object leased or any other change in the economic situation, either party may demand of the other party to raise or reduce the rent for the future. Article 628).

In this respect, the court previously denied the competence of the court to modify or set aside the contract on the basis of unforeseen circumstances. Recently, however, the Supreme Court acknowledged as a rule that a seller may rescind his/her contract on the ground of severe change in circumstances, stating that the circumstances should not be subjective or personal, but be objective, and form the basis of the contract (2004Da31302), although application of this doctrine was denied in the very case (*See* also *infra* paragraph 281). In addition, unforeseen circumstances should concern the basic assumption on which the contract was made.

# Chapter 4. Privity of Contract

## §1. THE RULE OF PRIVITY OF CONTRACT

### I. The Principle of Relative Effect

*177.* The starting point regarding the effects of contract is that the contracting parties can create obligations only toward each other (i.e., a contract has effects only between the parties thereto, and a third party may not acquire rights or be subject to liabilities therefrom), although a contract may indirectly affect third parties (e.g., a failure to perform contractual obligation(s) on the part of obligor due to a third party's fault may result in his/her tort-liability. *infra* paragraph 183). This principle of relative effect does, in essence, not differ from the Anglo-American concept of "privity of contract."

In this context, it should be mentioned that the general/universal successor, e.g., an heir (inheritor) of the deceased (inheritee), is not a third party. The inheritor stands in the place of the inheritee and succeeds, from the time of commencement of the inheritance, to the blanket rights and duties pertaining to the property of the inheritee, unless they are entirely personal to the inheritee either because the parties so agreed upon or because of the nature of the performance involved (Article 1005). By contrast, in case of a specific/singular succession, an assignee acquires the claim and rights which are accessory thereto (*infra* paragraphs 185 ff.), a third person takes over his/her predecessor's duties or liabilities, or a successor of real property may take benefits or burdens of a "real" character.

### II. Contracts in Favor of Third Persons

*178.* The main exception to the principle of relative effect is a contract in favor of third persons (contract for the benefit of third parties).

In cases where one of the parties to a contract has promised to make a certain performance in favor of a third person (beneficiary), the beneficiary may demand such an act of performance directly from the obligor, and in this case the right of the beneficiary shall come into existence from the time when he/she declares his/her intention to enjoy the benefit of contract to the obligor. (Article 539. In this regard, claim for the performance of the obligation which arises from the contract deserves to be an implicit declaration of intention to enjoy.) The Supreme Court ruled recently that this Article shall apply to a contract which releases a third person from the obligation (2002Da37405). However, on account of a contract any obligation may not in principle be imposed on a third party.

In addition, in a contract of life insurance, a policyholder may designate or change a beneficiary (Article 733, paragraph 1, the Commercial Code), and a benefit may be conferred directly on persons who are even either not yet in existence or not yet identified.

*179.* In a contract in favor of third persons, the right is conferred directly on the beneficiary from the moment of his/her declaration of intention to accept/enjoy the benefit, and after then the parties may not modify or extinguish this right (Article 541). (However, the exercise of the right of the parties to rescind or void the contract itself is another matter.) In the meantime, the obligor may, by specifying a reasonable period, demand of the beneficiary to answer whether or not he/she will receive and enjoy the benefit set forth by the contract. If the obligor has not received a definite answer within such period from the beneficiary, it shall be deemed that he/she has refused to enjoy the benefit (Article 540).

As mentioned above, the beneficiary can claim performance directly from the obligor, and therefore, in case of a failure to perform, the beneficiary shall be entitled to claim for performance and/or damages. However, the beneficiary may not rescind the contract by himself/herself, because he/she is not a party to the contract.

On the other hand, the obligor may raise defenses incidental to the contract in favor of third persons against the beneficiary who is to enjoy the benefit of contract (Article 542).

*180.* There is a controversy surrounding the German concept of a contract with protective effect for third persons (*Vertrag mit Schutzwirkung für Dritte*) which gives rise to certain additional/accessory obligations in favor of persons who are not parties to the contract. Although some scholars are of the opinion that this concept may also be useful in Korea, it is generally accepted that the adoption of such concept is in part superfluous and in part not desirable, because this concept came from the unique deficiencies in BGB concerning (tort-)liability, and in Korea such persons may claim damages based on tort, of course, depending upon circumstances concerned.

## III. Other Exceptions

*181.* First, the French term of "*action directe*" as such is unknown to Korean law; however, the implication of this term has been introduced into *lex scripta*. In some cases, the statutory provisions grant a third party a direct claim against one of the contracting parties. For instance, in case of a legitimate sublease (*see infra* paragraph 378), although lease and sublease are separate contracts and therefore contractual relations between the lessor and the sub-lessee cannot be deduced therefrom, Article 630 allows for the lessor a direct claim against the sub-lessee, saying that "If a lessee has subleased the object with the consent of the lessor, the sub-lessee assumes the obligations directly to the lessor. In this case, the sub-lessee may not raise a defense against the lessor by a payment of the rent to the sub-lessor." And with regard to the liability insurance, Article 724, paragraph 2 of the Commercial Code lays down that "A third party may directly request an insurer to compensate for losses caused by an accident attributable to the insured, within the limit of the insured amount. However, an insurer may assert against the third party with a defense which the insured has in connection with the accident." In addition, Article 14 of the Fair Transactions in Sub-contracting Act also prescribes, in order to establish fair order in subcontract transactions, that in some events (e.g., when the subcontractor has requested direct payment of the subcontract consideration where payment has been suspended, the principal contractor is bankrupt, or other similar reasons exist, or where the principal contractor has become unable to pay the subcontract consideration as permission, authorization, license, registration, etc., relating to the business have been revoked) the person ordering work shall pay the subcontract consideration corresponding to the completed portion of manufacturing, repair, construction, or service.

*182.* Second, on occasion, a third party may raise defenses from a contract to which he/she is not a party against a contracting party, or conversely a contracting party may be allowed to raise defenses from the contract against a third party. For instance, a surety himself/herself may raise any defense which the principal obligor has against the obligee, against the obligee (Article 433, paragraph 1. *See infra* paragraph 410) and *exceptio non adimpleti contractus* based upon a synallagmatic contract may be exercised against the assignee of the claim (i.e., a third party to the contract. *See infra* paragraph 185).

In addition, where an agent by law for the obligor effects performance in lieu of the latter or the obligor effects performance by other person as an employee, the intention or negligence of the agent by law or the other person shall be deemed to be that of the obligor (Article 391). In this context, the intention or negligence of the third party (usually referred to as "assistant to perform" for short), including a subcontractor, may affect the liability of the obligor (*see infra* paragraph 238).

*183.* On the other hand, a contract may affect third parties in that an act of a third party which infringes a contractual obligation may constitute an unlawful act (tort) to one of the contracting parties (e.g., threat against one of the contracting parties not to perform contractual obligations). Whether an act of a third party results in tort-liability or not, depends upon the illegality of the act in question. In this context, the Supreme Court takes into account the contents of the infringed obligation, situation of infringement and (malicious) intent of the third party (2000Da32437).

## §2. Transfer of Contractual Rights and Duties

### I. Overview

*184.* Contractual rights may be transferred in various ways. At first, a transfer of claim (including contractual rights) on the basis of contract is denoted as an assignment (cession), which will be dealt with soon. In addition, replacement of the obligee by a third person (of course including the transfer of claim) by operation of law is referred to as subrogation (*infra* paragraphs 216 ff. As to inheritance *see* also *supra* paragraph 177). Claims may also be transferred by an order of the court (i.e., when there exists an assignment order as a method of encashment of monetary claim, the seized claim shall be transferred to the execution creditor in lieu of the payment. Article 229, paragraph 3, the Civil Execution Act).

On the other hand, a transfer of a claim shall be differentiated from an assumption of obligation, in which not claims, but obligations shall be transferred, and takeover of contract, in which a third person shall succeed to the status of contracting party itself including all rights and duties.

## II. Assignment of Claims

*185.* A claim may be assigned to a third person, except where its nature does not permit the assignment (Article 449, paragraph 1. e.g., a claim from a contract of employment). In cases where the parties have declared their intention to the contrary, a claim shall not be assigned; however, such declaration of intention may not be set up against a third party acting in good faith (*ibid.*, paragraph 2). In this regard, the Supreme Court found on the one hand that a bona fide third party with gross negligence shall not be protected under this proviso (96Da18281), and on the other hand that a bona fide subsequent assignee or a *mala fide* subsequent assignee from a bona fide assignee shall be protected under this proviso (2012Da118020). In addition, some claims, e.g., pension claim or claim for support, may not be assigned owing to the statutory restriction (*see*, e.g., Article 979).

As a result of the assignment of the claim, the assignee acquires claim and rights which are accessory thereto, such as rights arising from hypothec and suretyship (in order to acquire hypothetically, a registration of additional entry of transfer is necessary under Article 186). The accessory rights include right of the assigner to interest and/or penalty agreed upon. On the other hand, assignment of claims does not affect the obligor's defenses.

*186.* Assignment of a nominative claim (in which the obligee is specified unlike securities) can be effected from the very beginning between the assigner and the assignee. However, it may not be set up against the obligor or any other third person, unless the assigner has given notice thereof to the obligor or the obligor has acknowledged/consented thereto (Article 450, paragraph 1). A notice of assignment of a claim shall be given by the assigner as a rule, but the assignee may give such notice as an agent or messenger.

The effects of notice of or acknowledgment (consent) to assignment of a claim except just mentioned (i.e., the primary effect for setting up assignment of a nominative claim) is worthy of being mentioned. On the one hand, in cases where an assigner has given such notice to the obligor, even if assignment has not been made or is null and void, an obligor acting in good faith raise a defense which can set up against the assignee (e.g., the fact that the obligor has effected performance to the assignee), against the assigner (Article 452, paragraph 1), and the notice of assignment may not be withdrawn without obtaining the consent of the assignee (*ibid.*, paragraph 2). In addition, where an assigner has given notice of assignment, the obligor may set up against the assignee any defense, which has arisen against the assigner prior to the receipt of the notice (Article 451, paragraph 2).

On the other hand, if the obligor has given his/her acknowledgment to assignment of a claim without objection (reservation), he/she may not set up against the assignee any defense that he/she could have set up against the assigner. However, in cases where the obligor has paid anything to the assigner for the discharge of the obligation, the obligor may recover it, and if he/she had incurred a new obligation to the assigner, the obligor may treat it as if it had not been incurred (*ibid.*, paragraph 1). In this regard, the Supreme Court ruled that the defense shall be confined to one predictable at time of the acknowledgment. For instance, in cases of the assignment of claims for insurance money, the insurer may set up effects of the exemption clause (except exemption on account of delay of the premium) against the assignee (2000Da13887).

*187.* In addition, the notice of or acknowledgment to assignment of a claim may not be set up against a third person other than the obligor, unless it is put in writing with a certified fixed date, such as a notarized document or registered and certified mail (Article 450, paragraph 2). In case of multiple assignments (e.g., several assignees of one and the same claim; an assignee and a pledgee), the Supreme Court ruled that the priority of the competing assignees shall be determined at first by the existence itself of a certified fixed date and, in case of multiple assignments with certified fixed date, in order of the arrival of the notice or acknowledgement (i.e., the order of a fixed date itself is not decisive. 93Da24223).

*188.* The method of publicizing of assignment of claims pursuant to the Civil Code is inconvenient and, what is more, unsuitable, especially if there are a number of obligors such as consumers who use goods provided based on an installment contract in relation to which the claim has to be assigned. In this context, the Act on Security over Movable Property, Claims, etc. (enacted in 2011) provides for requirements to set up an assignment of a nominative claim in a different way. Any acquisition, loss, or alteration of a security interest in a claim by an agreement shall be a valid defense against a third party other than the obligor of a nominative obligation ("third-party obligor"), when the acquisition, loss, or alteration is registered in the collateral security register, and a secured party or a person who has created a security interest (assigner or assignee if a security interest in a claim is assigned) shall not have a valid defense against a third-party obligor, unless the former notifies the third-party obligor of the registration by delivering the certificate of registration or the third-party obligor acknowledges it. In cases where with regard to the same obligation registration in the collateral security register is completed and a third-party obligor is notified of the assignment or acknowledges the assignment pursuant to the Civil Code, the secured person or the assignee of an obligation provided as security may assert his/her rights against a third party other than the third-party obligor, in order of such registration and the (arrival of) notice of or acknowledgement to assignment of a claim, except as otherwise provided for in any other Act (Article 35, the Act on Security over Movable Property, Claims, etc). It should be added, in this context, that the reversed structure of the requirements to set up assignment of a nominative claim under the preceding Act shall apply only to the assignment with the security agreement (*see* also *infra* paragraphs 428 f.).

*189.* On the other hand, a debt payable to order, such as promissory notes, bills of exchange, and checks, may be assigned by means of endorsement on and delivery of the instrument (Article 508), and a debt payable to bearer may be assigned by means of delivery of the instrument (Article 523).

## III. Assumption of Obligation

*190.* A third person may assume an obligation by way of a contract entered into with the obligee and thereby discharge the obligation for the obligor, except in cases where its nature does not permit such assumption. However, a third person who has no interest in the obligation may not assume an obligation against the will/intention of the obligor (Article 453).

An assumption of obligation requires the person who assumes the obligation to be a party thereto, and needs, in addition, the consent of the obligee, because the creditworthiness of the original obligor shall be changed. If the obligor, the obligee and the third person all agree, the debt shall be transferred to the third person. In a case where a third person has taken over a debt through a contract entered into with the obligor, it shall be effective from the time when the obligee has given the consent thereto (Article 454, paragraph 1). The consent of the obligee may be implicit. For instance, in cases where the obligee demands performance toward the third person, the latter should perform obligation. In this context, the third person or the obligor may request the obligee specifying a reasonable period to answer whether he/she will consent or not, and without a definite answer within such period specifying whether to consent or not, it shall be deemed to be a refusal to consent thereto (Article 455). On the other hand, in the absence of the consent of the obligee, the original obligor is still obliged to perform the obligation against the obligee, but an assumption of fulfillment instead thereof may take place.

*191.* As a result of the assumption of obligation, the third person, as a new obligor, should perform the obligation in lieu of the original obligor, and the latter is totally exempted from performance. Without any declaration of intention to the contrary, the consent to the assumption of obligation shall be effective retroactively from the time of such assumption. However, the retroactive effect may not harm rights of a third person (Article 457).

On the other hand, there are other types of the assumption of an obligation: (1) an overlapped/additional assumption of obligation, in which a third person assumes the obligation additionally, and thereby both the original obligor and the third person shall jointly and severally be liable to perform the original obligation; and (2) an assumption of fulfillment, where a third person is obliged to perform merely against the original obligor, not against the obligee. In cases where a person purchases an immovable property, which is already hypothecated, paying the difference between the purchase-price and the claim secured, the Supreme Court regarded the agreement between the buyer and seller as to the amounts deducted concerning the claim secured in principle as an assumption of fulfillment (2000Da18578).

## IV. Takeover of Contracts

*192.* There is no general provision on the takeover of contracts. However, for instance, if the lease shall be effective against a third person, the transferee (including any person who has succeeded to the right to lease) of a leased house shall be deemed to have succeeded to the status of the lessor (Article 3, paragraph 4, the

Housing Lease Protection Act. *infra* paragraph 386). In addition, as an effect of inheritance, the inheritor succeeds the status of contracting party of the inheritee (Article 1005).

To the takeover of contracts by way of a contract, provisions on assumption of obligation may apply by way of analogy. In order to take over the status of contracting party itself, therefore, there should be an agreement upon the take over of a contract in existence between one of the parties to the very contract and a third person, and the cooperation of another party to the very contract. Apart from the case of tripartite contract to take over, the cooperation means consent to the contract to take over. The form of the cooperation depends upon circumstances concerned.

*193.* As a result of the take over of a contract, the third person shall be the new party in lieu of the original party, and the latter is totally excluded from the contract.

On the other hand, there is another type of takeover of a contract, i.e., an overlapped/additional takeover of contract, where the original contracting party is still a party with the third party (*see supra* paragraph 191).

## §3. The Right of Subrogation and the Right of Revocation of the Obligee

### I. Overview

*194.* In a case where the obligor fails to perform obligations and there is no security right, his/her assets is the only object of compulsory execution. (In this sense, the value of claims depends, at first, upon the assets of the obligor.) As a result, it is in the interests of the obligee to ensure that the assets of the obligor shall be maintained and do not fall below the amount owed. In this context, the Civil Code furnishes two means in the obligee's interests: the right of subrogation (*action subrogatoire*) and the right of revocation (*action revocatoire*).

### II. The Right of Subrogation

#### A. Introduction

*195.* An obligee may, in order to preserve his/her own claim, exercise the rights belonging to the obligor; however, this shall not apply to rights which are exclusive and personal to the obligor (Article 404, paragraph 1). Unless and until the claim of the obligee becomes due, he/she may exercise such rights only with the court's permission or as acts of preservation (*ibid.*, paragraph 2). For instance, A lends three thousand dollars to a used-car dealer B and the repayment is due. B had sold a used-car for two thousand dollars to C 33 months ago (in this case, the prescription period of B's claim is three years. Article 163, No. 6. *See infra* paragraph 230), but does not at all demand to pay the purchase-money against C. B does not have any other assets. In such a case, A may exercise B's right against C, and thereby interrupt prescription (*infra* paragraph 231).

In accordance with the nature of subrogation, the obligee may not exercise rights which the obligor himself/herself cannot exercise. However, the obligee may exercise rights even if it is against the will/intention of the obligor. On the other hand, in cases where the obligor has already exercised his/her rights, the obligee may not subrogate, even if such exercise is improper (in this case, the obligee may exercise the right of revocation).

If the obligee has exercised the right of subrogation against a third person, except any act of preservation, the obligee is bound to give notice thereof to the obligor. After receipt of such notice, the disposition of the rights of the obligor may not be so set up against the obligee (Article 405). On the other hand, the Supreme Court held, with regard to res judicata, that in cases where the obligor was aware of the fact of the pendency of action exercising the right of subrogation, the obligor shall be bound by the judgment of that action (74Da1664).

### *B. The Sphere of Application of the Right of Subrogation*

*196.* The right of subrogation was primarily designed to ensure the performance of monetary debts and was supposed to be a stage prior to compulsory execution of obligations, but thereby the same effect as civil execution may be achieved more easily in some cases. In the example above mentioned, obligee (A) has two options. At first, pursuant to the Civil Execution Act, A may, with an executive title against B, request the issuance of a collection order against B's right toward C, and then demand payment from C (Article 229, paragraph 2, the preceding Act). On the other hand, A may, without such procedures, substitute B and claim payment directly against C. In the latter case, C should in principle pay the purchase-money to B, not A, because the purchase-money constitutes to the assets of the obligor. However, the Supreme Court has allowed that A, in lieu of B, may receive performance directly from C (2004Da70024). In such event, A should return the money received to B; however, A can set off his/her obligation to return against the obligation of B, and thereby the obligee has the de facto priority.

*197.* In order to justify such subrogation, it is, as a rule, necessary that the obligor does not have sufficient assets to satisfy the claim of the obligee (i.e., shall be in a state of insolvency). However, the courts have mitigated this requirement and broadened the sphere of application of this institution.

First, this right may be used to secure the transfer of a specific immovable property. For instance, A purchases an immovable property (X) from B, who had purchased X from C. To be an owner of the property by a contract of sale, the registration is necessary (Article 186), and registration shall in principle be applied jointly by a person entitled to file for a registration and a person obliged to file therefor (Article 23, paragraph 1, the Registration of Real Estate Act). As a result, in a case where B has failed to register X under his/her name, A is also unable to register X in his/her name. However, since A is not a contracting party to the first sale (between B and C), A may in principle not demand C directly to cooperate in registering X in A's name (*see supra* paragraph 177). In this context, the courts have approved that A may exercise B's right against C to demand that C should cooperate in registering X (84DaKa1131,1132). In this case, A's subrogation reaches only to registering X in B's name, and A should, in turn, demand B to cooperate in registering X in A's name.

*198.* Second, as is usual in other jurisdictions, a claim has in principle effect only to the obligor, i.e., a claim is not a right in rem, but a right in personam (*supra* paragraph 177). Therefore, for instance, the lessee of a house may not be fully protected in case of the disturbance of a person other than the lessor. The lessee may on the one hand demand cessation of the disturbance as a possessor of the leased object (Article 205), and on the other hand, ask the lessor, who is bound to maintain conditions necessary for using of and taking profits from the leased object while the lease is in force (Article 623), for necessary measures to terminate this situation (disturbance), such as exercise of the claim of removal of disturbance on the basis of his/her ownership (Article 214. *rei vindicatio*). However, in a case where the lessee does not possess the leased object and the lessor does not take necessary measures, a lessee is not entitled to take action directly against the disturbing person. In this context, the courts have approved that lessees are entitled to exercise those rights belonging to the lessor-owner to the disturbance (93Da59502).

It is irrelevant in such cases whether the obligor has sufficient assets to satisfy the claim of the obligee or not. In these cases, the obligee has priority, because these cases are *in rerum natura* unconnected with preservation of the obligor's assets.

It should also be added that the Supreme Court opens the availability of this right to the cases other than those mentioned above, if the obligee's claim is closely connected to the right subrogated, and the subrogation is necessary to ensure satisfaction of the obligee's claim and may not result in unjust intervention in the sphere of the obligor (99Da38699).

## III. The Right of Revocation

### A. *Introduction*

*199.* Though the value of claim depends in substance upon assets of the obligor, the assets are at his/her free disposal. However, Article 406 provides for the right to revoke an act of the obligor which may harm the interests of the obligee, and to restitute the previous status (*actio pauliana*): If the obligor has committed any juristic act which has a property right for its subject, with knowledge that it would prejudice the obligee, the obligee may apply to the court for its revocation and restitution of its original status (*ibid.*, paragraph 1). For example, X lends ten thousand dollars to Y. Because he/she is unwilling to repay the debt, Y gives away the only immovable property to Z. X may file an action to revoke the transaction between Y and Z, and to demand the return of the transferred assets from Z.

This right of revocation is a legal means to protect the interests of the obligee by preventing an act which leads to a decrease in the obligor's assets, and thereby may render a full satisfaction of the obligee's claim impossible or worsen the situation. A typical example of such act is a sale of property at an unreasonably low price or giving away certain properties. On the other hand, the Supreme Court found that a sale of real property at a "reasonable" price may be harmful under certain circumstances (66Da1535), although the nominal amount of the assets has not changed, presumably because cash is more easily disposed of than real property itself, and in this sense, a sale of real property itself deserves to be estimated as "a decrease in quality." In addition, in cases where the obligor has furnished his/her property as security for one or a few of the obligees in existence, it may constitute a harmful act to another obligee(s), because it gives preference to the obligee(s) secured over the others (86DaKa83). However, a disposition in compliance with the court's order does not constitute a harmful act.

*200.* The right of revocation differs from the right of subrogation in several ways. First, the former should be exercised through the court, and the action shall be brought within one year from the time when the obligee became aware of the ground for revocation, or within five years from the time when the juristic act which led to a decrease in the obligor's assets was performed (Article 406, paragraph 2). Second, the obligation does not have to be due when the obligee exercises his/her right of subrogation. However, the obligee who exercises the right of revocation should in principle acquire the claim before the act concerned of the obligor.

On the other hand, after the commencement of bankruptcy proceedings, obligees are entitled to deny the validity of acts of the obligor committed after his/her property status has become crucial. This right of denial (avoiding power) is provided for by the so-called insolvency legislation. For instance, any custodian may set aside acts for the obligor's assets after rehabilitation procedures commence (Article 100, the Debtor Rehabilitation and Bankruptcy Act).

### *B. Some Requirements of the Right of Revocation*

*201.* The right of revocation may not be exercised in cases where the claim of the obligee concerned is secured or where the remaining assets of the obligor is sufficient to satisfy the claim of the obligee.

The obligor's intent to prejudice the obligee should exist and be proven, but such an intent may be inferred from the relevant circumstances including the nature of transactions. In addition, in nearly all acts of the obligor which harms the interests of the obligee, a third person shall be involved. The revocation of such an act without limitation may affect the interests of those who entered into a transaction with the obligor. Therefore, the obligee may not exercise the right of revocation in a case where a person who has derived a benefit from such act (beneficiary) or a person who has succeeded to such benefit (successor) was, at the time of such act or succession, unaware of the fact that it would prejudice the obligee (Article 406, paragraph 1). In the aforementioned example, if Y (obligor) sold the only immovable property to Z at an unreasonably low price, X (obligee) may not revoke the sale contract between Y and Z, insofar as Z had not known that the sale was harmful to the interests of X. The burden of proof lies with the beneficiary Z (i.e., the beneficiary is presumed to have known the prejudicial nature of the transaction: rebuttable presumption). The same applies where there is a successor from Z.

On the other hand, according to the ruling of the Supreme Court, the obligee should file a lawsuit against the beneficiary or successor (i.e., a lawsuit against the obligor shall be dismissed on account of the lack of standing. 87DaKa1586), because the final goal of such lawsuit is the restitution of the previous status of assets of the obligor.

*C. Effects of the Exercise of the Right of Revocation*

*202.* In the previous example, even if Z is also an obligee against Y and receives repayment by any means from Y, X will try to nullify the transaction by exercising the right of revocation and have the money or assets returned to Y. The revocation and restitution of its original status shall take effect for the benefit of all obligees (Article 407). In this regard, either of the obligees (including Z) may demand distribution of the restituted assets, if he/she has an executive title.

On the other hand, the revocation is required only to restitute the previous status of assets of the obligor, and the restitution is for the compulsory execution of the very obligee in general. In this sense, the revocation has a "relative" effect. The Supreme Court found also that upon revocation the act of the obligor shall be treated as invalid only between the parties to the action for revocation and restitution, i.e., the obligee and a person who is obliged to restitute (91Da13717). Therefore, the act of the obligor remains valid with regard to all the other persons.

# Chapter 5. The End of Contracts

## §1. Performance

### I. Extinction of Claims: Overview

*203.* Claims may be extinguished on various grounds: e.g., performance including accord (substitute performance), deposit, setoff, novation, release, merger and prescription.

### II. Performance of Obligations

#### A. Introduction

*204.* The parties to a contract are obliged to perform obligations they have undertaken, and an obligation terminates usually by fulfillment, i.e., by carrying out the performance owed. In this sense, performance (or payment, which in this context is not confined to paying a sum of money) means a fulfillment of obligation, as a result of which the obligation reaches its goal and shall be extinguished. On the other hand, the obligee may refuse to accept a partial payment of obligation.

In the absence of any agreement to the contrary, the expenses of performance shall in principle be borne by the obligor (Article 473).

#### B. Parties of Performance

*205.* Performance of obligation may also be effected by third persons, unless the nature of such obligation does not permit such performance (e.g., in cases of an obligation to do in personal) or the parties have declared their intention to the contrary (Article 469, paragraph 1). However, a third person who has no interest in an obligation may not effect performance against the will/intention of the obligor (*ibid.*, paragraph 2).

In cases of performance by a third person, this person should have the intention to discharge an obligation of the obligor. (Whether the person effects performance with or without his/her own interests does not matter.) On the other hand, in cases where a person other than the obligor has discharged an obligation by mistake, the obligation shall in principle not be extinguished, and the person may claim restitution (*see* Article 745 and *infra* paragraph 454).

*206.* A person who has performed an obligation on behalf of the obligor may demand reimbursement against the obligor and be subrogated to the rights of the obligee (by acquiring the acknowledgment of the obligee or by operation of law. *See* Articles 480 and 481). A person who is subrogated to the rights of the obligee may exercise all the rights possessed by such obligee as effect of and as security for such right to the extent to which the former may seek reimbursement under his/her own right (Article 482, paragraph 1). In this context, a performance by a third person differs from a performance-in-chain, in that from the legal point of view, in the latter case there is a series of performances, although there is apparently only one performance. The meaning of differentiation relates to the parties of restitution. In case of a performance-in-chain, if a contract to which a person who performs is a party is void or voided, he/she can claim for restitution against only the opposite party of the very contract (i.e., not against the person who has received performance).

*207.* The performance should be effected to a person who is entitled to receive payment, and generally the (genuine) obligee has the right to receive payment.

However, on the one hand, the right of the obligee may be restricted. For instance, in effecting a seizure of a monetary claim, the court shall prohibit the garnishee from making any payment to the debtor and the debtor from disposing of the claims and from receiving the payment (Article 227, paragraph 1, the Civil Execution Act). The obligor may be discharged even in this case; however, the discharge may not be set up against the execution creditor. On the other hand, persons other than the (genuine) obligee, e.g., his/her agent, pledgee (in cases where the claim is offered as a pledge) or possessor of a negotiable instrument, may have the power to receive payment:

*208.* In some exceptional cases performance made to a person who has no power to receive it may be valid, and thereby release the obligor from obligation. First, a performance made to a holder of quasi-possession of the claim shall be effective if it was made in good faith and without any negligence (Article 470). This Article (together with the following Article) aims to protect those who rely on the appearance of a genuine obligee (e.g., the appearance of an invalid assignment order). For instance, if a bank allows someone who comes with a bankbook and a signet to withdraw money from an account, the bank is usually exempted from liability, unless it has not exercised the required standard of care. As an extension of this Article, a performance, made in good faith and without any negligence, to the bearer of receipt may also be valid (Article 471). Second, a performance made to a person who is not authorized to accept it shall be effective to the extent that the relevant obligee has been enriched as a result thereof (Article 472).

In cases of performance to anyone other than a person who is entitled to receive payment, the restitution between the recipient and the obligee may arise.

### C. *Object of Performance*

*209.* With regard to subject of obligations to deliver a thing, the Civil Code distinguishes between obligations to deliver a specified (i.e., certain and determinate) thing and obligations to deliver thing(s) determined as to kind. Concerning the former, Article 374 provides on the one hand for the duty to care for the thing specified, stating that "the obligor is bound to preserve such a thing with the care of a good manager until it is delivered," and Article 462 stipulates, on the other hand, the manner of the duty to deliver, saying that in such case "the obligor must deliver the thing specified in the condition in which it exists at the time when the delivery thereof is due." As to the claim in species (fungible claim), Article 375 states that "Where the quality of such things cannot be identified in accordance with the nature of the juristic act or the intention of the relevant parties, the obligor is bound to deliver things with intermediate quality." and "If the obligor has completed the acts necessary for performance or has identified the thing to be delivered with the consent of the obligee, such thing shall thenceforth constitute the subject of the claim." Upon specification (concretizing), a duty to procure things in species will be changed to a duty to take custody of the thing specified with the care of a good manager, and the impossibility of obligation shall be at issue. (Before specification, the impossibility of the obligor's obligation shall in principle not come into question, in contrast to the obligation to deliver any specified thing.) There is a controversy surrounding whether after specification the obligor may deliver things other than the specified which nevertheless correspond to the obligation.

In addition, Articles 463–465 provide for delivery of thing(s) belonging to another person and delivery of a thing by its owner without the capacity to dispose of it, and their consequential relations.

*210.* On the other hand, a monetary debt (obligation to pay a sum of money) belongs in principle to the claim in species; however, due to special characteristics of monetary debt, Article 375 in the proper sense shall not apply to it. Payment may be made in money or at the time when the obligor credited the account of the obligee with the amount owed. (If the amount of a claim is designated in foreign currency, the debtor may effect payment in the Korean currency at the current rate of exchange at the place of performance when delivery is made. Article 378) This obligation must be performed in principle at its nominal value (Article 376: Where the subject of a claim is to be delivered in one kind of currency, and the currency has ceased to be legal tender at the time the claim becomes due, the obligor is bound to effect payment in another currency of legal tender,) and therefore, the concretizing is meaningless. (As a result, with regard to this obligation, the impossibility does not matter.) To its nonperformance Article 397 shall apply (*see infra* paragraphs 308 and 311).

### *D. Place and Time of Performance*

*211.* The obligor should perform his/her obligations at the right place, otherwise he/she will not be discharged from his/her obligations. In addition, the method of tender of performance (Article 460, as a premise for *mora creditoris*. *See infra* paragraphs 258 ff.), the time when the obligations are discharged, and the burden of risks are related to the place of performance. In this regard, the place is of some importance.

The right place is determined in accordance with the nature of the obligation or the declaration of intention of the parties. Article 467 lays down that if the place of performance has not been identified through the just mentioned standards, (1) delivery of a specified thing should be made at the place where the thing owed existed when the relevant obligation arose, and (2) performance of any other obligation should be effected at the present domicile or business place of the obligee.

*212.* Performance should be made in good time. Time for and delay of performance will be discussed with regard to the failure to perform (*infra* paragraphs 243 f.). Here, it is worth mentioning that in the absence of any declaration of intention to the contrary by the parties, the obligor may make performance even prior to the time when it becomes due; however, he/she should compensate for the damage of the other party (Article 468).

### E. *Tender of Performance*

*213.* To be a valid tender, exact compliance with the tenor of obligation is required. Therefore, the tender of partial performance does not in principle constitute a valid one.

A tender of performance shall relieve the obligor from responsibility for the failure to perform (more precisely: delay) from the time of such tender (Article 461). On the other hand, a tender of performance shall give rise to *mora creditoris* (Articles 400 ff., *infra* paragraphs 258 ff.) and exclude *exceptio non adimpleti contractus* (Article 536. *infra* paragraphs 288 ff.).

*214.* As to the method of tender of performance, Article 460 states: "Performance must be effected by way of actual tender in strict accordance with the tenor of obligation. In a case where the obligee refused its acceptance in advance or where an act on the part of the obligee is required for performance of the obligation, it shall be sufficient to demand the acceptance thereof by giving a notice that all preparations have been made for performance."

With regard to the method of tender of performance, there are three types of obligation: obligation to be collected at the obligor's domicile, obligation to be handed over at the obligee's domicile and obligation to send the thing owed on its way to the obligee. In the first type, the obligor's duty is to make all preparations for performance, and the obligee is required to collect the thing owed from the obligor. In this case, the latter method of tender of performance above mentioned (usually referred to as the "oral tender") shall be sufficient. In the second type, by contrast, the obligor should bring the thing owed to the obligee. In this case, in principle the former method, i.e., the "actual tender," is required (Article 460). In the last case, the obligor should send the thing owed to the obligee.

### F. *Effects of Performance*

*215.* The primary effect of performance is the extinction of a claim. In addition, a person effecting performance may request to issue a receipt and/or demand the return of a document evidencing the obligation (Articles 474 and 475).

On the other hand, Articles 476 ff. provides for the order of allocation (appropriation) of performance in cases where an obligor owes to a single obligee several obligations whose subject is of the same kind, and the tender of performance is insufficient to discharge all the obligations. Allocation takes place in the following order: (1) allocation agreed upon by the parties (although there is no explicit provision thereto), (2) allocation designated in principle by the person effecting performance (Article 476) and (3) statutory allocation in the order of the advantage to the obligor (Article 477, which shall apply *mutatis mutandis* to expenses, interests and principal obligations. Article 479).

## *G. Subrogation*

*216.* The subrogation is a replacement of the obligee of an obligation by a third person as a result of the performance made by him/her to the obligee. The third person can therefore exercise, in addition to his/her own claim for reimbursement to the obligor, the claim of the original obligee and the accessory rights thereto. In this sense, subrogation makes the position of the third person stronger, especially with regard to the availability of security rights connected to the claim of the original obligee. This replacement takes place by operation of law. Some examples: subrogation of a mortgagee next in priority in case of the joint mortgages (Article 368, paragraph 2), subrogation of an obligor to the obligee owing to compensation for damages (Article 399. *See infra* paragraph 313) and subrogation by insurer against third parties (Article 682, the Commercial Code).

*217.* The most important example is subrogation set forth in Articles 480 ff.

A person who has a legitimate interest in effecting performance shall be subrogated *ipso iure* to the rights of the obligee by effecting performance (Article 481. On the other hand, a person without any legitimate interest may be subrogated by acquiring the consent (in substance: approval) of the obligee thereupon (Article 480), in which case replacement of the obligee takes place by operation of law, not by a juristic act).

In a case where a third person has performed a part of the obligation on behalf of the obligor, the former may exercise his/her right together with the obligee in proportion to the value of the performance effected by the subrogee (Article 483, paragraph 1). By contrast, the rescission or rescission for the future of contract by reason of a failure to perform may be done only by the obligee, and he/she should reimburse the subrogee for the value of the performance effected together with the interest thereon (*ibid.*, paragraph, 2).

*218.* A person (subrogee) who has been subrogated to the rights of the obligee may exercise the claim and the right in respect to its security to the extent to which the subrogee may be reimbursed by virtue of his/her own right (Article 482, paragraph 1).

In cases where there are several subrogees, the exercise of the just mentioned right shall among them be restricted in accordance with Article 482, paragraph 2. (By contrast, this restriction, i.e., partial subrogation, shall not apply to the relation between subrogee(s) and the original obligor.) For instance, between surety and a person who has furnished his/her own property as security for the obligation of another (third-party security furnisher), they shall be subrogated to the rights of the obligee in proportion to their numbers, and in a case where there are several third-party security furnishers, they shall be subrogated to the rights of the obligee in respect of the balance excluding the part incumbent upon the surety, and in proportion to the value of each property. In this respect, it should be mentioned that in a case where a surety has furnished his/her own property as security for the obligation of the principal obligor, in assessing the scope of subrogation he/she shall in principle be treated to have only one status (presumably as a surety), according to the recent ruling of the Supreme Court (2007Da61113,61120).

*219.* On the other hand, in cases where there exists a person entitled to the right of subrogation under Article 481 (i.e., who has a legitimate interest to effect performance), if the obligee lost or diminished his/her security due to his/her intention or negligence, the former shall be relieved of his/her liability to the extent it has become impossible for him/her to be reimbursed by reason of such loss or diminution (Article 485).

It should be mentioned that the Supreme Court is of the opinion that the subrogation by the person who has performed obligation (Articles 480 ff.) shall have precedence over the subrogation of a mortgagee next in priority in a case of joint mortgages (Article 368, paragraph 2. 93Da25417).

## III. Set-Off

### *A. Introduction*

*220.* In cases where two persons mutually owe to the other party any obligations with same kind of purpose, if both obligations have become due, each obligor may be relieved of his/her own obligation by setting off each value thereof against the corresponding amount of the obligation of the other obligor (Article 492, paragraph 1).

The setoff set forth by the Civil Code is a unilateral act, i.e., effected by way of a declaration of intention of one party to the other party (Article 493, paragraph 1). The declaration of intention for a setoff shall be deemed to extinguish the obligation to the extent of the corresponding amount when each obligation is suitable for setoff (*ibid.*, paragraph 2. The declaration takes effect retroactively as of the time when the obligations of both parties became due,) which is not mandatory.

*221.* Setoff is laid down as a ground for extinction of claims, which is the basic effect of setoff. However, particularly in banking transactions, setoff may function as a means of security. A bank and a customer, who borrows money from the bank and opens a bank account (especially a fixed-period deposit), usually agree in advance that in cases where the borrower's property status becomes insecure (e.g., the customer's obligee attaches this account), the bank will set off its obligation against the customer's obligation. (Generally, a forfeiture of benefit of time limit is agreed upon at the same time. *See supra* paragraph 173) In doing so, the bank manages to secure at least the amount of the deposit in priority to other obligees. In this case, setoff generally takes effect for the future, and not retrospectively.

### *B. Requirements for Set-Off*

*222.* In order to effect the setoff, both obligations have to be of the same nature (in general: monetary debt), and each party should be the obligee as well as the obligor to the other party.

Under certain circumstances, a setoff is prohibited, for instance, in cases of the intention to the contrary of the parties (Article 492, paragraph 2, although with no effect against a bona fide third person), a setoff against an obligation arising from an intentional unlawful act (Article 496), a setoff against an obligation of which attachment is prohibited (Article 497), and a setoff against any obligation subject to injunction (Article 498).

On the other hand, the legitimate expectation of the party for the setoff should be protected. Therefore, a claim with the completed extinctive prescription may be used for a setoff, if the claim had been suitable for the setoff prior to the completion of prescription (Article 495). Nevertheless, in a case where one party bought a promissory note from a third person who was on the point of bankruptcy at 40% of face amount, in order to effect a setoff against his/her obligee, the Supreme Court held the abuse of setoff (2002Da59481).

## IV. Additional Grounds for the Extinction of Obligations

*223.* First, the obligee may refuse to accept performance other than the one which the obligor has undertaken. However, in a case where an obligor has, with the consent/acknowledgment of the obligee, accomplished an act of performance of obligation different from and in lieu of the one originally owed, such an act (accord. referred to also as substitute performance) shall be deemed to be a valid performance (Article 466). The accord is a means to satisfy the claim of the obligee. Since it is generally accepted that accord is a real contract, before the actual performance, the (original) obligation shall remain in existence. The claim of the obligee is satisfied by the fulfillment of performance other than originally owed (regardless of its value), e.g., by acquisition of a real property in lieu of repayment, and thereby the obligor shall be discharged from his/her obligation. In this sense, it is different from novation, in which the parties agree to alter essential elements (i.e., obligor, obligee or subject matter) of the obligation, and thereby the original obligation (including any rights of security) shall be extinguished and a new obligation arises (Article 500), i.e., except in case of the substitution of obligor, the obligor is still bound to perform an (new/substitute) obligation. In this context, according to the ruling of the Supreme Court, a delivery of promissory notes, bills of exchange or checks with regard to the obligation in existence is deemed to be an act for payment (in the interests of the obligee. 95Da25060), although such an act may extinguish the obligation as an accord. It should be added that in Korea a promise to return substitutes, combined with the provisional registration, was commonly used as a means of security (although some agreements may be prohibited under Articles 607 and 608), which is regulated by the Provisional Registration Security Act (*see* also *infra* paragraph 396).

*224.* Second, in cases where the obligee refuses or is unable to accept the performance tendered, the person who will and can make performance may relieve himself/herself of his/her obligation by depositing the subject of performance with the competent official depository for the obligee. The same shall apply where the obligee cannot be ascertained without any negligence on the part of the person who will make performance (Article 487).

On the other hand, in fact only certain objects, such as money or negotiable instruments are capable of deposit, and in a case where the subject of performance is not suitable for deposit, or there is any danger of its perishing or being damaged, or excessive expense is required for deposit, the person who will perform may, with the permission of the court, sell such property at official auction or for value at the market price and deposit the proceeds (Article 490).

The effect of deposit is to release the obligor from the duty to perform, unless the depositor recovers the deposited article (*see* Article 489).

In addition, the Civil Code furnishes novation (Article 500), release (Article 506. *See supra* paragraphs 227) and merger (Article 507) as grounds for extinction of obligation(s).

## §2. Frustration

*225.* Under the Common law, contractual liability is, in principle, absolute. In other words, the parties are bound to perform what they have promised. The rigidity of this approach may be mitigated by the implied term of the doctrine of frustration. The impossibility of performance may be absorbed into the category of frustration if the impediment has been unforeseeable and irresistible, and thereby the impossibility may result in the termination of contract, i.e., the obligor may be released from his/her obligation.

Under Korean law, by contrast, the unexpected/irregular situation in performance is evaluated to a certain extent from a moral standpoint, and therefore such rigidity may usually not be in question. In other words, the obligor is, in principle, responsible only for damage arising from the failure to perform attributable to himself/herself.

*226.* On the other hand, in spite of term of "act of god" (force majeure) stipulated e.g., in Articles 308, 314 and 336, the Civil Code does not, as a rule, adopt the doctrine of change in circumstances or economic impossibility, the doctrine of disappearance of the foundation of contract (*Störung der Geschäftsgrundlage*. Section 313, BGB), or the doctrine of frustration of the adventure, though the legislator, presumably based on this doctrine, sought to modify the consequence of the drastic change in circumstances (e.g., claim for increase or decrease in the rent. Articles

286 and 628), and the court approves this doctrine exceptionally concerning the rescission of contract (*see supra* paragraphs 175 f.).

## §3. Discharge by Agreement

*227.* If the obligee declares his/her intention to release the obligation to the obligor, such obligation shall be extinguished. However, a release may not be set up against a third person who has a reasonable interest (Article 506). The release under this Article is a unilateral juristic act.

On the other hand, the same effect may be obtained by agreement. If the parties agree to discharge one or both of them, one or both of the parties may be released from obligation(s). As a rule, the parties to a contract may agree to modify their contract pursuant to the principle of the freedom of contract, and modification of course includes discharge. To discharge, general rules of the contract law shall apply.

## §4. Limitation of Actions (Prescription)

### I. Prescription

*228.* Part One (General Part) of the Civil Code provides for the extinctive prescription. (Provisions on the acquisitive prescription are laid down in Part Two as a ground for acquisition of the ownership. Articles 245 ff.) The *raison d'étre* of extinctive prescription is at first that a certain situation which lasts for a long period deserves to be protected, because it is used to form a basis of everyday life irrespective of the legal state, and second, that after a long period, it becomes difficult for the obligor to prove the fact that he/she had performed his/her obligation, and such obligor may need protection. In short, the extinctive prescription contributes to promote legal certainty and to avoid unnecessary disputes, and thereby everyone may rely on the existing factual situation which lasts for a long period as representing a true legal situation.

### II. Requirements

*229.* Although property rights other than an ownership are also a subject of the extinctive prescription, the main subject is a claim, i.e., right to demand another person to perform an obligation, except for those rights arising from family law, as a rule.

The extinctive prescription shall run from the time it becomes possible to exercise a certain right (Article 166, paragraph 1). For instance, a prescription of an obligation to give or to do runs at the day on which the obligation arises, unless either condition or time limit is pended. On the other hand, in cases where it is impossible to exercise a claim for the reason other than legal, the prescription shall run irrespective of knowledge of the claimant; however, recently, the Supreme Court found that in a case where a beneficiary did not know of the existence of an insurance claim due to any cause not attributable to him/her, the prescription shall run from the time of knowledge of the beneficiary (2000Da31168).

*230.* The extinctive prescription of a claim shall become complete, if it is not exercised for ten years. The extinctive prescription of property rights, other than a claim and an ownership, shall become complete if they are not exercised for twenty years (Article 162, paragraphs 1 and 2). (With regard to the tort claim, Article 766 lays down that right to claim for damages resulting from an unlawful act shall lapse by prescription: (1) if it is not exercised within three years commencing from the date on which the injured party or his/her agent by law becomes aware of such damage and of the identity of the person who caused it, or (2) if ten years have elapsed from the time when the unlawful act was committed.) On the other hand, Article 64 of the Commercial Code states that "Except as otherwise prescribed in this Code, the extinctive prescription of a claim arising out of a commercial activity shall become complete if it is not exercised within five years. However, if a shorter period for prescription is stipulated by other Acts or subordinate statutes, such provision shall apply."

The Civil Code provides also for short extinctive prescriptions of three years and one year for some categories of claims (Articles 163 and 164). Especially, the period of extinctive prescription of a claim regarding items received in exchange for products and merchandise sold by producers and merchants shall be three years (Article 163, Nr. 6). On the other hand, the period of extinctive prescription of any right established in a final and conclusive judgment or tantamount thereto (e.g., bankruptcy proceedings, settlement in the court) shall be ten years, even if the period for the original claim is shorter pursuant to *lex scripta* (Article 165).

The extinctive prescription shall, by a juristic act, not be excluded, extended or aggravated; however, it may be shortened or lessened (Article 184, paragraph 2).

## III. Interruption and Suspension

*231.* The extinctive prescription may be interrupted or suspended under certain circumstances. Article 168 lists grounds for the interruption of extinctive prescription: (1) any demand; (2) any attachment, provisional attachment or provisional disposition; and (3) any acknowledgment. A judicial claim (i.e., demand by way of judicial proceedings) shall have no effect of interruption of the prescription, if the action is dismissed, rejected or withdrawn. In such a case, however, if a judicial claim, participation in bankruptcy procedures, attachment, provisional attachment or provisional disposition is made within six months, the prescription shall be deemed to have been interrupted by the first judicial claim (Article 170). According to a recent ruling of the Supreme Court, in order to interrupt the extinctive prescription, the obligee may bring an action several times; however, with regard to res judicata, the court may not render a judgment of the prior action (2018Da22008). A simple demand (i.e., demand not through the court) shall have no effect of interruption of the prescription, unless a judicial claim or equivalent thereto (e.g., participation in bankruptcy procedures or attachment) is taken within six months (Article 174). A simple demand need not be in writing. On the other hand, in order to make an acknowledgment having the effect of interruption of the prescription, no capacity to act or authority for disposition in respect of rights of the other party is required (Article 177).

In cases where the prescription is interrupted, the period of prescription passed until the interruption shall not be computed (i.e., shall be nullified), and the prescription which was interrupted begins to run anew from the time when the ground for such interruption has ceased to exist (Article 178, paragraph 1). The interruption of prescription shall be effective solely between the parties with respect to whom the ground for interruption arose and their respective successors in title (Article 169).

*232.* On the other hand, the suspension is connected with, for instance, limited capacity, inheritance or natural calamity (Articles 179 ff.). In contrast to the interruption, from the time of disappearance of the ground for suspension the prescription period continues to run for six months (one month in case of natural calamity or its equivalent. Article 182).

## IV. Effects of Prescription

*233.* There is a crucial controversy over the effect of completion of the period of extinctive prescription. Some scholars are of the opinion that completion of the prescription does not extinguish the obligation per se, but give the obligor the right to invoke it. However, the Supreme Court ruled that upon completion of the prescription, even without invoking of the prescription, a claim extinguishes per se (in the sphere of the substantive law); however (from the standpoint of the procedural law), the court may not make a judgment based on the prescription unless the party invokes it (i.e., the court may not ex officio apply the prescription. 78Da2157). On the other hand, the Supreme Court grants the right to invoke only to those who have direct interests, such as surety or third-party purchaser of the mortgaged property (95Da12446). According to this approach, once the period of prescription has completed, the claim eventually loses its force and the person originally under an obligation can refuse to perform. However, in cases where the obligor effects performance, he/she may not claim for restitution (Articles 742 or 744. *See infra* paragraph 454).

The effect of extinctive prescription shall be retroactive to the day on which it began to run (Article 167). In addition, in a case where the extinctive prescription of a principal right has become complete, it shall affect its accessory right (Article 183). On the other hand, the benefit of extinctive prescription may not be waived in advance (Article 184, paragraph 2).

In some cases (especially in cases where public authority was abused and thereby the legal benefit of citizens was infringed), invoking of the prescription may be regarded as abuse of right (i.e., contrary to the doctrine of bona fides) by the courts (2002Da32332).

## V. Period of Exclusion

*234.* The period of exclusion is a statutory period of existence with regard to the formative right (equivalent to the German term "*Gestaltungsrecht*"). As a result of the lapse of this period the right perishes *ipso iure*.

This period differs from the extinctive prescription, at first, in that the court should ex officio consider this period in contrast to the prescription. Second, since upon exercise of the formative right, legal relation itself (including claims and/or obligations therefrom) shall be altered, the period of exclusion shall not be interrupted.

# Chapter 6. Remedies

## §1. INTRODUCTION

### I. Overview

*235.* Legal effects of contract are to create, modify or extinguish an obligation, and one of the goals (in my opinion: the primary goal) of the law of contract is to constrain the obligor to perform what he/she has undertaken and to give to the obligee the means of making such constraint effective.

In this regard, in cases where the obligor does not perform his/her obligation voluntarily or the performance does not comply with the tenor of obligation, remedies for the failure to perform obligation(s) (breach of contract, referred to also as "default" or "nonperformance") consist of claim for performance, claim for damages and claim for rescission (usually with retroactive effect). Remedies granted to the aggrieved party (obligee) vary depending upon type of the failure to perform. For instance, in case of *mora creditoris*, the obligee may: (1) claim (specific) performance as well as damages for delay (Articles 389 and 390), (2) claim damages in lieu of performance (Article 395) or (3) exercise the right to rescind the contract and claim damages (Articles 544 and 551).

Restitution as a remedy will be discussed later.

*236.* In this context, types of the failure to perform are of importance. For example, the failure to perform attributable to the obligor and that not attributable should be distinguished, in that only the former gives the obligee a claim for damages (Article 390). In addition, in cases where performance is already permanently impossible, a claim for damages arises immediately; otherwise, the obligor shall be responsible for delay from the time when the demand for performance has been made upon him/her, except in cases where a definite time for performance of a claim is specified (Article 387). Taking these circumstances into consideration, types of the failure to perform will be discussed later.

### II. Imputability of the Failure to Perform

#### *A. Introduction*

*237.* The Common law has thought of contractual obligations as in principle absolute, and therefore, apparently finds no place for fault in contractual liability. By contrast, the Civil law including the Korean Civil Code requires fault, i.e., intention or negligence, for contractual liability. However, the places where the two systems arrive are not substantially different, because under the Common law, contractual liability may be mitigated by the implied term of the doctrine of frustration (*see supra* paragraph 225).

If the obligor fails to perform an obligation, except in cases of nonperformance of monetary debt (Article 397, paragraph 2. *See infra* paragraph 308), fault on the part of the obligor is necessary in order to claim damages. As a result, even in cases where the obligor fails to perform his/her obligation, if this is not due to the obligor's intention or negligence, the obligee may not claim damages (Article 390). Whether an obligor is at fault or not is, as a rule, determined by an objective standard (i.e., how a prudent obligor would have acted in the same position).

However, there are some exceptions. At first, the obligor shall, in principle, be responsible for damages during *mora debitoris* even if he/she is not at negligence (Article 392. *See infra* paragraph 247). In addition, the parties may agree that the obligor shall be liable for events not attributable to him/her including force majeur.

*B. Imputability of a Person Other than the Obligor*

*238.* Where an agent by law for the obligor effects performance in lieu of the latter or the obligor effects performance by other person e.g., as an employee, intention or negligence of the agent by law or the other person (i.e., assistant to perform) shall be deemed that of the obligor (Article 391). For instance, where the obligor performs his/her obligation by a third person, the obligor is liable for the acts of this person to the same extent as the obligor would be liable for his/her own acts. Especially, in a case where an employee of the obligor wrongfully causes damage in the course of the execution of the undertaking, the injured obligee may claim damages against the obligor based on contractual liability (Articles 390 and 391). (In this case, the obligee may at the same time claim damages against the employee under Article 750). With regard to Article 391, the relationship between the obligor and the third person need not be one of social dependency, i.e., for instance, another merchant acting as a subcontractor shall be sufficient. (In cases where the obligor owed a duty to perform obligations "himself/herself," nevertheless employed the other person to perform it, the performance by a third person itself constitutes a failure to perform, and the obligor is liable for any loss therefrom.)

*239.* The contractual liability of the obligor under Article 391 differs in some respects from the tort-liability of employer for damages set forth in Article 756. For instance, in contrast to the former, the latter does not need the contractual relationship between the employer and the injured party, but requires the relationship of social dependency between the employer and the person who has caused loss. In addition, the defense that "the employer has exercised due care in the appointment of the employee and the supervision of the undertaking, or if the damage would have resulted even if due care had been exercised" (proviso to Article 756, paragraph 1) is available only with regard to the latter, although this defense is generally denied by the court.

*C.* Force Majeure

*240.* Pursuant to the Korean private law, the failure to perform a contractual obligation imposes the obligor to compensate the loss which the obligee suffers, unless such failure shall not be imputed to the obligor. The imputability in this context means any fault, i.e., intention or negligence, of the obligor or his/her assistant to perform, and the fault is concerned with the duty to exercise due care which the obligor is bound to. In other words, the obligor shall not be liable for damages, if there is no fault on the part of himself/herself or his/her assistant to perform. In this context, force majeure (act of God) as a defense for the exemption from liability need not be discussed.

On the other hand, there are several statutory provisions in which the term force majeure is laid down (e.g., Article 336 regarding loss of the pledged article). In addition, the dominant view is of the opinion that force majeure may be necessary as well as useful. In cases where the liability without fault (equivalent in substance to the strict liability) shall be imposed (e.g., with regard to damages for nonperformance of monetary debt, the obligor may not set up the absence of negligence as a defense. Article 397, paragraph 2. *infra* paragraph 308), the doctrine of force majeure may mitigate the harsh consequences, although some writers raise doubts thereabout.

*241.* Regarding the concept of force majeure, the objective approach requires absolute impossibility of performance which may apply to everyone. By contrast, according to the subjective approach, it is sufficient that performance had become too harsh for the obligor concerned, unless this was imputable to him/her. In Korea, it is generally supported that the concept of force majeure should be defined objectively. Therefore, force majeure is considered as a cause from outside of the obligor which impedes the performance of an obligation, such as earthquake, riot or blockade of trade, and which the obligor cannot prevent from occurring (i.e., not attributable to him/her). Of course, the cause should be unforeseeable at time of the conclusion of contract even from the point of view of a prudent obligor. The obligor shall not be held liable for such a cause. On the other hand, such a situation as illness of the obligor, even in cases where the obligation should be performed by the obligor in person, does not constitute force majeure.

## §2. Types of the Failure in Performance

### I. Overview

*242.* The content of a contractual obligation aims, in essence, at performance of what has been undertaken. In some cases, however, the contract is not performed in compliance with its terms. For instance, an obligor does not perform his/her obligation in good time or he/she does not perform his/her obligation at all (breach of contract).

In Korea, the predominant view "was" of the opinion that the failure to perform is composed of three (closed) types, i.e., delayed performance (*mora debitoris*), impossibility of performance and imperfect/defective performance, which was the case in Germany before the revision of law of obligations in 2002. Actually, there are some provisions which concern special type (e.g., Article 395 furnishes compensatory damages in case of *mora debitoris. See infra* paragraph 247), and in this sense, the types above mentioned are still meaningful. However, Article 390 lays down that in cases where an obligor fails to effect performance in accordance with the tenor and purport of obligation, the obligee may claim damages. This Article shall apply in all the cases in which the obligee somehow fails to obtain what the obligor has undertaken.

In this context, in my opinion, the failure to perform itself is of great importance and the "type" of such failure is not so important. However, since the remedies granted to the obligee vary depending upon types of the failure to perform, such failure will be discussed based on (not closed, but open/flexible) typology.

## II. Delayed Performance (*Mora Debitoris*)

### A. *Time of Performance*

*243.* The obligor should perform his/her obligations in good time. If no time has been agreed upon by the parties, an obligation may be claimed as well as effected to perform immediately (with exception of the loan for consumption. *See* Article 603 and *infra* paragraph 395).

On the other hand, an obligation may be subject to a time limit of commencement (*see supra* paragraph 173). A time limit is presumed to be stipulated for the benefit of the obligor (Article 153, paragraph 1). As a result, the obligee may not, in principle, claim performance before the due date; however, the obligor may perform earlier (in cases where a time limit is set at the same time for the benefit of the obligee, with compensation for loss of the obligee. proviso to Article 468). In contrast to this, due to the juristic act, the nature of contract or other circumstances, a time limit may be set only for the benefit of the obligee (e.g., obligation of a bailee), and in this case, the obligor may not perform the obligation before the due date, but the obligee may claim performance earlier.

### B. *Delay of Performance*

*244.* In cases where performance is still possible, but the obligor, at his/her fault, does not perform at all or has performed defectively in quantity or in quality (which can be cured), he/she shall be responsible for delay from the time when performance becomes due.

In this regard, Article 387 provides for the time when performance becomes due: "Where a definite/specified time for performance of an obligation is assigned, the obligor shall be responsible for delay from the time of arrival of such time. If an indefinite/unspecified time for performance of an obligation is assigned, the obligor shall be responsible for delay from the time when he/she has become aware of the arrival of such time. In a case where a time for performance of an obligation is not assigned, the obligor shall be responsible for delay from the time when demand for performance has been made upon him/her." (On the other hand, according to the ruling of the Supreme Court and the predominant view, a tort claim shall become due immediately when an unlawful act takes place. 92Da48413).

*245.* The obligee should serve on the obligor a preemptory notice requiring performance, unless a definite time for performance is assigned. As a result, with respect to damages for delay, the obligor is liable for after that moment. The purpose of such a notice is to let the obligor know that the obligee demands performance, and thereby allow a chance to perform once more. Therefore, in cases where the obligor has expressly and firmly/irreversibly refused to perform or where performance has become impossible, such notice is not required. A preemptory notice is also required to rescind the contract (Article 544. *infra* paragraph 280).

*246.* Article 388 provides for the forfeiture of benefit of the time limit. The obligor may not claim the benefit of time limit in cases (1) where the obligor has damaged, diminished or extinguished the security and (2) where the obligor has failed to perform the obligation to furnish security. (A time limit is presumed to be stipulated for the benefit of the obligor. Article 153, paragraph 1. *supra* paragraph 173).

In addition, the parties may agree upon an acceleration clause (i.e., the forfeiture of benefit of the time limit by a contract). In this case, the acceleration arises either upon occurrence of the ground agreed upon per se or upon demand of the obligor. For instance, in a banking transaction, in order to avoid restriction on the setoff under Article 498 ("A third-party obligor who has been ordered not to make payment may not assert the setoff against any after-acquired claim against the relevant attaching obligee." As to requirement for setoff of the third-party obligor, the Supreme Court ruled that his/her claim shall become due before or at the same time as the counterclaim becomes due. 82DaKa200. *See* also 2011Da45521), with regard to some grounds, e.g., application for attachment, acceleration per se shall be set forth.

## *C. Effects of Delay*

*247.* In case of a delay, the obligation remains in existence, and the obligee may apply to the court for enforcement (Article 389. *See infra* paragraphs 273 ff.) or execute real security rights, if the obligation is secured, and at the same time claim damages (Article 390). In this case, the damages covers, as a rule, the loss incurred by delay, but the obligee may claim compensatory damages (i.e., damages in lieu of performance) under Article 395, which lays down that "In cases where the obligor has delayed the performance of an obligation, if he/she fails to perform within a reasonably specified time in spite of the obligee's demand specifying such period or if performance after delay is no longer profitable for the obligee, the obligee may refuse to accept performance and claim damages in lieu of performance."

On the other hand, the obligor shall be responsible for damages during *mora debitoris*. In such cases, the obligor is liable for all the losses, even if he/she was not at fault for the impossibility of performance itself (i.e., regardless of fault). However, this shall not apply to cases where the damage is inevitable/unavoidable even if he/she performed at the time when the time of performance became due (Article 392). In addition, with regard to damages for nonperformance of monetary debt, the obligee is not bound to prove the actual damages nor can the obligor set up the absence of negligence as a defense (Article 397, paragraph 2. *See infra* paragraph 308).

*248.* In case of a failure to perform the obligation pursuant to a contract (not limited to a synallagmatic contract), the obligee is entitled to rescind the contract (Article 544). A rescission of contract shall not affect any claim for damages (Article 551).

### *D. Supplements*

*249.* In a case where the obligor refuses expressly and firmly/irreversibly to perform the obligation owed, the Supreme Court ruled that the obligee is entitled to rescind the contract and claim (compensatory) damages (2004Da53173). As to the legal character of the refusal to perform, some scholars are of the opinion that it is an independent type of the failure in performance, but in my opinion, it is a species of the genus delay, i.e., an anticipated delay of performance.

On the other hand, in cases where there is a justifiable reason for the delay, the obligor is not legally in default. For instance, a tender of performance shall relieve the obligor from responsibility for delay from the time of such tender (Article 461), and *exceptio non adimpleti contractus* (Article 536) also constitutes a justifiable reason.

## III. Impossibility of Performance

### *A. Introduction*

*250.* In cases where the obligor cannot perform his/her obligations, legal consequences of the impossibility vary depending upon circumstances concerned. In this context, the impossibility may be divided into several categories. For instance, in case of a permanent impossibility, the obligor may invoke a defense of impossibility, and the obligee may claim damages in lieu of performance immediately, while in case of a temporary impossibility the obligor is, in principle, still bound to perform. (The German traditional distinction between an objective impossibility (*Unmöglichkeit*) in which it is not possible for anyone at all to perform and a subjective impossibility (*Unvermögen*) in which the very obligor is not in a position to perform, is generally not accepted in Korea.)

The answer to the question about whether an obligation is impossible to perform or not depends on the criteria, which are socially acceptable, including of course, physical or legal point of view (e.g., impediment on account of government measures). Even in a case where performance is not impossible physically, the obligation may be treated as impossible to perform, which depends on circumstances concerned. On the other hand, in cases where the line between impossibility of and delay in performance is not sharp, the key to distinction is the possibility of subsequent performance in view of the obligee. For instance, a case in which the performance should be effected within a certain time in the interests of the obligee, and this time has passed without performance, may be dealt with as an impossibility especially concerning the rescission of the contract (*see* Article 545). And a case in which an obligation not to do was violated also constitutes impossibility.

### *B. Supervening Impossibility*

*251.* Performance of an obligation owed may be impossible from the beginning (initial impossibility) or become impossible subsequently (supervening/subsequent impossibility). In a broad sense, impossibility includes initial impossibility, but the failure to perform is mainly related to the supervening impossibility, because the former constitutes under Korean law, a condition for the validity of a contract (As to the former, *see supra* paragraphs 83, 84 and 126). A typical example of supervening impossibility is a case where a building sold was destroyed after the conclusion of a contract or where after the conclusion of a contract of sale, a third person acquired the ownership of the article sold.

Even in case of the supervening impossibility, a contract and obligation(s) therefrom shall not cease to exist. However, the impossibility will bar a claim for performance to the extent that the impossibility reaches, and thereby the obligor shall be discharged from the original obligation (i.e., duty to perform owed), regardless of whether an obligation has become impossible due to a cause attributable to the obligor or not. (In case of a temporary impossibility due to any cause not attributable to the obligor, the obligor shall be exempted from liability for any damage caused by the delay in performance, but the contract remains in principle and can be enforced when the cause of impossibility ceases to exist.) On the other hand, in case of a claim in specifice, the obligor is liable to procure the thing of the same kind.

*252.* In a case where an obligation has become impossible due to a cause attributable to the obligor, the obligee may claim damages in lieu of performance (Article 390). As mentioned above, however, in a case where the obligor was already in delay at the time when an obligation became impossible to perform, the obligor may not set up the absence of negligence as a defense (Article 392). In addition, in case of the impossibility of a contractual obligation, the obligee is entitled to rescind the contract only if the obligor is responsible for the cause of impossibility (Article 546. *See infra* paragraph 280). A rescission of the contract shall not affect any claim for damages (Article 551).

On the other hand, in a case where the obligor, as a result of the impossibility, obtains reimbursement or a claim to obtain reimbursement for the object owed, the obligee may demand return of what has been received in reimbursement or an assignment of the right to demand reimbursement. Although there is no explicit provision, such as section 285 of BGB, the Supreme Court, assenting to the view asserted by most scholars of those days, approved this right of obligee

(92Da4581,4598). In this case, the damages in lieu of performance are reduced by the value of reimbursement or the right to demand reimbursement the obligee has obtained.

### *C. Burden to Bear Risks*

*253.* In a case where a specified thing, as the subject of the contract, is lost or damaged due to any cause not attributable to the obligor, the obligee may neither demand performance nor claim damages. In this context, if the contract is synallagmatic, the question of the risk of counter-performance, i.e., whether the obligor is still entitled to claim counter-performance in case of an accidental destruction or deterioration, arises. (In case of a unilateral contract, the obligee will anyway suffer the loss arising from the impossibility not attributable to the obligor. However, if the obligor has received any benefit by being relieved of his/her own obligation, he/she shall return such benefit to the obligee: Offset of profits and losses. *See infra* paragraph 313). On the other hand, the risk of counter-performance passes usually to the obligee upon delivery of the thing owed.

*254.* Concerning the burden to bear the risk of counter-performance, the Civil Code accepts obligor's burden in principle: In a case where performance of an obligation of one of the parties to a synallagmatic contract becomes impossible by any cause for which neither of the parties is responsible, the obligor may not be entitled to counter-performance (Article 537). It is generally accepted that this approach is proper and desirable, because this Article is based on the principle of interdependence in a synallagmatic contract (in other words, each obligation is the cause of the other, and therefore the extinction of one obligation requires, as a rule, the extinction of the other. *See supra* paragraph 32). In cases where the counter-performance has already been made, the obligor will be bound to make restitution. However, this does not apply where the obligee has demanded the return of what has been received in reimbursement or an assignment of the claim for reimbursement in place of the performance which was originally owed.

*255.* On the other hand, exceptionally, the obligee may bear the risk of counter-performance. If the performance of an obligation of one of the parties to a synallagmatic contract becomes impossible by any cause for which the obligee is responsible, the obligor may demand counter-performance. The same applies to cases where performance becomes impossible during *mora creditoris* by any cause for which neither of the parties is responsible (Article 538, paragraph 1). In these cases, if the obligor has received any benefit by being relieved of his/her own obligation, he/she shall return such benefit to the obligee (*ibid.*, paragraph 2).

With regard to the case of *mora creditoris*, there is something to be mentioned. In a case where an obligee refuses to accept performance firmly and irreversibly, the obligor shall be relieved of responsibility for the failure to perform (Article 461. In substance, this Article covers merely delay) even without a peremptory notice of acceptance of performance (*cf.* Article 460). The Supreme Court found, nevertheless, that "the" obligee in *mora creditoris* bears risks only in the case where there was at least a tender of the obligation somehow (2001Da79013).

## IV. Other Types

### A. *Imperfect Performance*

*256.* The obligor should perform an obligation in accordance with the tenor and purport of obligation (Article 390) and the doctrine of bona fides (Article 2, paragraph 1). Therefore, in a case where he/she does not perform an obligation consistent with its purported meaning, the obligee may refuse to accept imperfect performance, which does not lead to *mora creditoris*. The third type of the failure to perform is referred to as an imperfect (defective or incomplete) performance or a positive mal-performance, in that the obligation has been performed, but not in a proper manner. (In this regard, cases where an imperfect performance has been made should be differentiated from cases of delay and impossibility.)

An example is a delivery of defective goods in a contract of sale. Another and more important example is a case of additional damage (e.g., where the obligor delivered pullet infected with disease, which later spread to the obligee's chicken farm).

In case of an imperfect performance, the obligee may demand proper performance in lieu thereof within a reasonable period, if possible. In addition, the obligee is entitled to claim damages (Article 390), if in a case where the proper performance is possible the obligor fails to make such performance till the obligation becomes due or if such performance is impossible or impractical. In order to claim damages, there should be fault on the part of the obligor.

*257.* On the other hand, in cases where the obligor culpably breaches duties such as to exercise due care or to report dangers, and thereby causes any harm to the obligee, the obligor is liable for damages. In other words, a person may, on the basis of the doctrine of bona fides, owe a duty to take necessary steps to protect the life, body and property of another person. For instance, the Supreme Court ruled that a hospitality business operator may not be exonerated from liability for personal damage of guests, unless the former proves the fact that he/she has not neglected to exercise due care (96Da47302). (For reference, a carrier shall not be exonerated from liability for damage received in the carriage of passengers unless he/she proves the fact that he/she or his/her employees have not neglected to exercise due care in connection with the carriage (Article 148, paragraph 1, the Commercial Code), but there is no provision equivalent to this in the chapter on hospitality business.) In addition, a travel agent with respect to a package tour contract or an employer may be liable, if he/she had failed to take sufficient measures to protect the traveler or employee (98Da25601). This type stems from the German concept of "*positive Vertragsverletzung.*"

The "duty to care for safety" itself is generally accepted. However, the legal nature of this duty is an issue of severe controversy. This duty may be useful to deal with cases where a remedy in tort is not available or inappropriate, which seems to be the case in Germany. In spite of influential counterviews, most scholars are of the opinion that this duty is contractual. On the other hand, the court regarded this duty principally as tortious, but as contractual occasionally (e.g., 98Da25601).

### *B. Mora Creditoris*

*258.* Although there are cases in which performance of obligations does not need any cooperation from the obligee (e.g., in case of an obligation not to do), in most cases the obligor cannot perform his/her obligation without inevitable cooperation of the obligee (e.g., acceptance of performance an obligation or collecting the thing owed from the obligor), because the fulfillment of an obligation means generally a certain result, i.e., realization of the purpose of obligation on the part of the obligee. Therefore, even in cases where the obligee refuses to accept performance without a justifiable ground (e.g., tender of partial performance) or it becomes impossible for him/her to do so, the obligor shall not be released from the obligation. On the other hand, under Korean law, there is no explicit provision under which the obligee shall be under a duty to accept performance, such as section 433, paragraph 2 of BGB (which says that: "The buyer is obliged to pay the seller the agreed purchase-price and to accept delivery of the thing purchased.").

*259.* In this context, if an obligee is unable to accept performance of an obligation or refuses to accept it, such obligee shall be responsible for delay commencing from the time when the performance has been tendered (Article 400). (In this case, the obligor may deposit the subject of obligation under Article 487. *See supra* paragraph 224).

The delay of acceptance (*mora creditoris*) takes place when performance of obligation(s) is prevented owing to any impediment on the part of the obligee, and the obligor is capable and ready to perform.

*260.* In such case, the obligor is still bound to perform, but his/her responsibility shall be mitigated, in contrast to the case of delay in performance (*mora debitoris*) in which the responsibility of the obligor is strengthened (Article 392. *See supra* paragraph 247). At first, the obligor shall be relieved of responsibility for *mora debitoris* (Article 461). What is more, if the obligor has no intention or gross negligence in respect of the failure to perform (in substance: only impossibility), such obligor shall, during *mora creditoris*, be free of all the responsibility arising from the failure to perform (Article 401). In addition, during *mora creditoris*, the obligor is not bound to pay the interest (Article 402), and the amount of the increased expense owing to this delay shall be deducted from the account of the obligee (Article 403). Furthermore, the obligee shall bear the risk of counter-performance, as mentioned above (Article 538, paragraph 1. *See supra* paragraph 255).

*261.* With regard to the effects of a refusal to accept performance of a contractual obligation, the question about whether or not the obligor is entitled to rescind the contract and/or claim damages, has been an issue of controversy. Until recently, the prevailing view was of the opinion that the obligee owes a duty to accept performance based on the doctrine of bona fides, and his/her failure to do so will give rise to the same effect as the obligor's failure to perform. However, in recent years, there is an influential view that *mora creditoris* is judicial in nature, and therefore, the effects not set forth by the Code, such as a claim for recession as well as damages, may not be granted.

## V. Obligor's Liability for Warranty

### *A. Introduction*

*262.* The Section on the contract of sale includes provisions on the liability for warranty (Articles 570–584). This liability is strict liability, i.e., irrespective of fault on the part of the obligor.

These provisions shall apply *mutatis mutandis* to contracts for value other than sales, unless the nature of such contracts does not so permit (Article 567). Indeed, the Section on contract for work provides for the contractor's liability separately, which will be dealt with later with regard to contracts for work (*infra* paragraphs 364 f.).

Provisions on the seller's liability for warranty are not mandatory. However, even in cases where the seller has made a special agreement to the effect that the seller is not liable in respect of the warranties, he/she may not be relieved of liability with respect to any fact of which he/she was aware and nevertheless failed to disclose, or in respect of any right which he/she himself/herself created in favor of, or assigned to, a third person (Article 584. *See* also Article 7, the Act on the Regulation of Terms and Conditions).

### *B. Seller's Liability for Warranty*

*263.* The seller's liability for warranty arises in cases where he/she does not have full legal rights over the property or where the thing sold is defective.

First, even in cases where a right, which has been made the object of a sale, belongs to the person other than seller, the contract itself is valid, and the seller shall assume an obligation to acquire such right and transfer it to the buyer (Article 569). If the seller cannot acquire and transfer the right he/she has sold to the buyer, or the thing sold is subsequently evicted from the buyer, the buyer may rescind the contract and claim damages (Article 570). Upon rescission, the buyer should return the thing sold and the benefit therefrom to the seller (however, the buyer in good faith shall not be required to return the benefit to the genuine owner under Article 201, paragraph 1), and the seller must return the purchase-price and interest thereon, and pay damages in lieu of performance. On the other hand, proviso to Article 570 restricts claim for damages: if the buyer was aware, at the time when the contract was made, that the right did not belong to the seller, the buyer may not claim damages. However, even the buyer in bad faith may claim damages under Article 390 (not under Article 570), if it is due to the seller's fault (i.e., fault-based liability). In this regard, even in cases where the buyer should have known that the right belongs to a third person, the buyer's negligence shall be taken into account in assessing damages.

There is no time limit with regard to exercising of such rights.

On the other hand, Article 571 lays down that a bona fide seller may, compensating any damages caused to the buyer, rescind the contract (in a case where the buyer is *mala fide*: without damages) (Article 571).

*264.* Second, in cases where any part of the right which forms the object of a sale belongs to another (e.g., a joint owner sells property without obtaining the consent of the other owner(s). *See* Article 264), if the seller is unable to acquire and transfer such part of the right to the buyer, the buyer may demand reduction of the purchase-price in proportion to the value of the part in shortage (Article 572, paragraph 1). If the buyer would not have bought the remaining part, had such alone been the object of sale (i.e., in cases where the purpose of contract may not be achieved due to the partial failure to transfer the right), the buyer acting in good faith may rescind the whole of the contract (*ibid.*, paragraph 2). Furthermore, the bona fide buyer may claim damages in addition to demanding a reduction of the purchase-price or the rescission of contract (*ibid.*, paragraph 2).

This right should be exercised within one year from the time when the buyer became subsequently aware of the fact if the buyer was acting in good faith, and from the time when the contract was entered if the buyer was acting in bad faith (Article 573).

In cases where several properties were sold in one and the same transaction and some of them belong to third person(s), the same rule shall apply. On the other hand, the price-reduction means in substance a partial rescission, and in this regard the buyer may refuse to pay the whole purchase-price until the amount of reduction is specified. In addition, Article 571 shall not apply (i.e., even a bona fide seller may not rescind the contract).

*265.* Third, Articles 572 and 573 (*see* preceding paragraph) shall apply *mutatis mutandis* where there is any shortage in the object of a sale made for a designated quantity or where part of the object of a sale had already been lost at the time when the contract was entered (Article 574). This Article shall not apply to the shortage or destruction occurred after the conclusion of contract.

With regard to the former case, the shortage in quantity should be important enough so that the buyer would not conclude a contract, had known such shortage. Therefore, this Article shall not apply where the quantity is merely to identify the property sold or to calculate the purchase-price as a whole. On the other hand, regarding the latter case, the Supreme Court ruled that this Article prevails over Article 535 (*see supra* paragraph 84).

The bona fide buyer's remedies consist of a reduction of price and a rescission. On the other hand, the Supreme Court ruled that the *mala fide* buyer may demand a reduction of price (99Da58136), about which some scholars raise doubts.

*266.* Fourth, in cases where the object of a sale is subject to a superficies, a servitude, a *chonsegwon* (*see infra* paragraph 419), a right of retention or a pledge (i.e., cannot use and take the profits from the object sold), and the buyer was unaware thereof, he/she may rescind the contract. However, the rescission is possible only if the purpose of contract is unattainable on account thereof. Otherwise, the buyer may only claim damages. This rule shall apply *mutatis mutandis* in cases where a servitude which has been represented as being in existence in favor of immovable property, which is the subject of a sale does not exist, or where a registered lease exists on the immovable property.

These rights shall be exercised within one year from the time when the buyer became aware of the fact (Article 575).

In this case, the impossibility of enjoying (i.e., using of and taking profit from) the object sold constitutes a defect. On the other hand, if the buyer was aware thereof, it shall be reflected in determining the purchase-price, but in my opinion the buyer should be entitled to demand a reduction of price in proportion to impossibility of enjoying (probably in the form of damage), if such defect has not taken into account therein.

*267.* Fifth, in case where the buyer has been unable to acquire or has lost ownership of the immovable which forms the object of a sale by reason of the exercise of a mortgage or *chonsegwon* existing over such an immovable, the buyer may rescind the contract (Article 576, paragraph 1). In case of the existence of such a right, if the buyer has preserved his/her ownership by incurring expenditure for costs, he/she may claim reimbursement of such costs from the seller (*ibid.*, paragraph 2). The buyer may claim damages he/she has sustained from the seller (*ibid.*, paragraph 3). The Article shall apply *mutatis mutandis* to the sale of superficies or *chonsegwon* which have been the subject of the mortgage (Article 577).

There is no time limit.

In this case, the risk of loss of the ownership constitutes a defect. This Article shall not apply in cases where the buyer assumes fulfillment of the obligation secured (*see supra* paragraph 191). On the other hand, the Supreme Court found that in a case where the buyer has lost the ownership of immovables on account of the principal registration after provisional registration, this Article shall apply (92Da21784).

*268.* Finally, the expectation of the buyer that the thing sold possesses the qualities which are necessary for a normal use thereof, as well as those which are necessary for special use set forth by the contract, should be protected. In this regard, the seller is liable for the objects with latent/hidden defects which make the thing sold unfit for such (normal and/or special) use or restrict such use (i.e., not of merchantable quality) that the buyer, if he/she had known the existence of defects, would not have bought the thing or would have done so only for a lower price. (In contrast, delivery of a thing other than the one agreed upon or a thing of a different character (i.e., so-called *aliud*) does not constitute the performance consistent with the purpose of the obligation.)

In this liability, the defect should be latent, i.e., a defect which an ordinary buyer would not be able to find with the care normally required. If the seller can prove the fact that the buyer knew or should have known the existence of defect, the seller can avoid liability. On the other hand, a latent defect means a lack of conformity to the contract. In determining whether the thing delivered conforms to the purpose of contract or not, normal use thereof, intent of the buyer, circumstances surrounding the sale (including the nature of the thing, e.g., new or used, and job of the seller), sample shown or description given to the buyer (i.e., guarantee concerning the nature, quality or suitability of the thing sold), etc., should be taken into account. In addition, a defect does not have to be physical. In a case where a buyer purchased a piece of land in order to construct a building, but on account of unattainability of the urban planning permission the construction was impossible, the Supreme Court regarded such a defect as a latent defect, nevertheless denied the liability under Article 580, because "at the time of the conclusion of contract" the buyer was able to obtain the permission (i.e., change in the plan of the buyer caused the inability) (98Da18506).

When any latent defect exists in the object of a sale, the buyer may rescind the contract, only in cases where he/she is unable to achieve the purpose of contract on account of such defect; however, claim damages at any event (Articles 580 and 575). The buyer may demand not merely a reduction of price to the extent that the defect in the thing sold diminishes its value but also the expenses occasioned by the sale (the so-called reliance damages). On the other hand, in cases where the object of a sale has been specified in kind, if any defect exists in the object specified, the buyer may rescind the contract and claim damages. However, in this case, the buyer may demand the non-defective item without rescinding a contract or claiming for damages (Article 581). (With this regard, in 2017 (Enforcement date: January 1, 2019), the Motor Vehicle Management has adopted the so-called Lemon Law. According to Articles 47-2 ff. of this Act, the buyer of a vehicle may demand a refund of the purchase-money or to replace the vehicle under certain circumstances.)

The buyer has to exercise these rights within six months from the time when he/she was first aware of the defect (Article 582). On the other hand, contributory negligence of the buyer shall be reflected in assessing the damages (94Da23920).

*269.* On the other hand, Article 578 provides for the seller's liability for warranty in cases of a sale by "official" auction (i.e., compulsory execution based the executive title (Article 24, the Civil Execution Act) as well as auction for exercise of security right (Article 264, the preceding Act)). In such a sale, the successful bidder may, in accordance with the above mentioned (except *supra* paragraph 268, as the seller's liability on account of defect shall not apply in a sale by official auction. Article 580, paragraph 2), rescind the contract or demand reduction of the purchase-price against the obligor (as a seller) (Article 578, paragraph 1). In cases where the obligor is insolvent, since the auction is in reality for the satisfaction of the obligee's claim, the successful bidder may demand a total or partial reimbursement of the proceeds against the obligee who has received the distribution of the proceeds (*ibid.*, paragraph 2). In addition, if the obligor was aware of any deficiency in the object or right sold and nevertheless failed to disclose it or if the obligee was aware of such deficiency and applied a sale by official auction, the successful bidder may claim damages either from the obligor or the obligee (*ibid.*, paragraph 3).

However, since the buyer may not resort to the seller's liability for warranty if the sale is invalid, Article 578 shall not apply in cases where the official auction itself is null and void (e.g., in a case of a compulsory execution based the forged executive title or an auction for exercise of security right commenced after the extinction of obligation secured. In such a case, the buyer may demand the obligee to return the proceeds distributed from the auction as unjust enrichment. As to the exceptional revocation of auction, *see* Articles 268 and 96, the Civil Execution Act). On the other hand, a successful bidder's acquisition of immovables shall not be affected by an extinguishment of the security right after application for auction for exercise thereof (Article 267, the preceding Act), and therefore, Article 578 may apply in this case.

On the other hand, if, for instance, the claim sold or the security therefor does not exist, the seller shall be liable to the buyer under provisions on the seller's liability for warranty. In this regard, Article 579 lays down that, if the seller of a claim warrants the solvency of the obligor, the seller is presumed to have warranted solvency at the time when the contract was entered or the claim becomes due (in case of a claim not due yet).

*270.* It should be added that the Commercial Code contains special provisions on sales between merchants. The buyer shall, upon receipt of the subject matter, inspect it without delay, and, if any defect or deficiency in numbers is found therein, immediately give notice thereof to the seller. In cases where he/she fails to do so, he/she has no right to rescind the contract, to demand price cuts (a reduction of the purchase-price) or to claim damages thereby. Even when a defect is not immediately discoverable, the buyer has only six months after receiving the object in which to discover such defect (Article 69, paragraph 1, the preceding Code). However, this paragraph shall not apply to a seller acting in bad faith (*ibid.*, paragraph 2).

### C. *Relation to the Failure in Performance*

*271.* There is a long-pending controversy over the legal nature of the seller's liability for warranty, which concerns relation between provisions on the seller's liability (Articles 570 ff.) and those on the failure to perform an obligations (Article 390). For instance, the question about whether a buyer of a defective thing can avoid restriction arising especially from the limitation of period by seeking a claim based on the failure to perform is of great importance.

In the past, most scholars were of the opinion that the liability for warranty is created by law, because in a sale of a specified thing, the seller should and can deliver the thing sold in the condition in which it exists at the time when delivery is due (Article 462. i.e., regardless of the quality), and that will be enough. However, recently, there is an influential view that this liability is a special form of the failure in performance. In my opinion, even in a sale of a specified thing, the buyer will pay the purchase-price in exchange for the "defect free" thing, and the seller should take it into account. (Since the defect leads to an improper performance in cases of a sale of a right or a thing in species, this dispute is meaningful only with regard to the sale of a specified thing.)

*272.* In a case where a defective article is sold, the seller's liability under Article 580 can be pursued, but it also constitutes an improper performance on the part of the seller, and Article 390 may additionally apply (especially with regard to additional damage).

The liability for warranty and liability based on the fault have different goals in that the former makes up a difference between the prices of the object with and without defects, while the latter aims to ensure compliance with the tenor and purport of obligation. As a result, only by way of the latter, the additional/subsequential damage may be compensated. On the other hand, practical differences between claims under Article 390 and under Article 580 are that, at first, Article 390 requires fault on the part of the seller, while Article 580 imposes strict liability. Second, the latter should be made within six months (Article 582), while the former can be made for ten years (Article 162, paragraph 1). In spite of different views of some scholars, the courts are of the opinion that the buyer may freely choose between them. The Supreme Court found that in case of a sale of right belonging to another person, a *mala fide* buyer may claim damages not under Article 570, but under Article 390, i.e., with proof of fault on the part of the seller (93Da37328). In other cases where a buyer purchased a piece of land, which was buried with waste during the embankment, the Supreme Court ruled that such a defect of the object owed may lead to the liability for warranty as well as the imperfect performance (especially concerning the additional/subsequential damages) (2002Da51586).

## §3. Compulsory Execution

### I. Introduction

*273.* For the case where the obligor does not perform his/her obligation voluntarily, the law furnishes the means of compelling him/her to do so. The obligee may apply to the court for compulsory execution thereof, unless the nature of the obligation does not permit such execution (Article 389, paragraph 1). Although detailed provisions on the compulsory execution procedure are set forth by the Civil Execution Act, a related provision is also laid down in the Civil Code. This implies that the compulsory execution of obligation is the primary remedy for the failure to perform an obligation, and is permitted generally, unlike the Common law system in which the primary remedy is damages (although specific performance is admitted exceptionally). Of course, in case of impossibility, the compulsory execution is not available.

It should be mentioned that compulsory execution shall not affect a claim for damages (Article 389, paragraph 4).

### II. Methods of Compulsory Execution

*274.* The method of compulsory execution depends upon the nature of the obligation.

First, the obligee may apply to the court for "direct execution" (enforcement of specific performance), unless the nature of an obligation does not permit such execution. This method is suitable for the obligation to give something (*supra* paragraph 144). In cases where the obligation owed is monetary, the assets of the obligor (immovables, vessels and movables including cars as well as claims and other property rights) shall be seized/attached and auctioned by the court. The obligee receives distribution from the proceeds of the sale by compulsory auction. In a case where an obligor is liable for delivering specified movables or a specific quantity of fungibles, an execution officer (previously referred to as "bailiff") shall take them away from the obligor and deliver the same to the obligee (Article 257, the Civil Execution Act). In cases where an obligor is liable for delivering any immovables or ship, an execution officer shall deprive the obligor of his/her possession thereof, and deliver the same to the obligee (Article 258, paragraph 1, the preceding Act).

*275.* Second, the method of compulsory execution of an obligation for an act differs from that of an obligation to give something. It is not permitted directly to compel the obligor to do something. The Civil Code lays down instead that in such a case, the obligee may apply to the court for "substitutional/substitutive execution." If the obligation has an act which is not entirely personal to the obligor for its subject, an application may be made to the court to compel performance by a third person at the expenses of the obligor. The obligee himself/herself may perform at the expense of the obligor, which is not a form of self-help. In case of the obligation for a juristic act, application may be made to the court for a decision which shall substitute a declaration of intention of the obligor (Article 389, paragraph 2). On the other hand, in cases where the obligation for nonfeasance (inaction) has been violated by the obligor, an application may be made to the court for removal of the outcome of action performed by the obligor at the obligor's expense and the reasonable precautionary steps against any future action (*ibid.*, paragraph 3).

*276.* Finally, since pressure on the obligor to perform personally is not allowed, the substitutional execution is not applicable to obligations in which performance by the obligor in person is of the essence. In this case, "indirect compulsory execution" may be available: In cases where the nature of debts permits an indirect compulsory execution, the court of first instance shall, upon application of the obligee, render a ruling on ordering such an execution. Such ruling shall clarify an obligation to perform the debts and an appropriate period for performance, and when the obligor defaults on the performance within such period, the court may order him/her to make a reimbursement of a specific amount in proportion to the defaulted period (usually on daily basis), or order him/her to make an immediate compensation for damages (Article 261, paragraph 1, the Civil Execution Act). This institution, an *astreinte*, is a means of putting economic pressure on the obligor to perform and is independent of the remedy of damages. (*Asteintes* should be paid to the obligee, not to the state, and damages shall be assessed irrespective of the *asteinte*.) Even this method shall not be available to cases where it may infringe free will of the obligor (e.g., obligation of a singer or a painter. In this case, only claims for damages shall be allowed). On the other hand, the *astreinte* may be used not only for the enforcement of contractual obligations, but also to secure the abatement of a nuisance or to enforce duties arising out of the family law.

## §4. Rescission

### I. Introduction

*277.* In case of a failure in performance, if one of the parties to a synallagmatic contract does not perform his/her obligation yet, the other party may refuse to perform his/her own obligation, exercising *exceptio non adimpleti contractus* (Article 536. *See infra* paragraphs 288 ff.). However, if he/she has already performed, he/she may claim performance and/or damages. In addition, regardless of his/her performance, in cases where he/she wishes to be relieved of his/her obligation, he/she may claim rescission, and thereby he/she may claim restitution and enter into another (especially more advantageous) contract. In this sense, the rescission (cancellation) is the last remedy.

In contrast to some jurisdictions in which the right to rescind a contract is entitled only to the parties to synallagmatic contracts, under Korean law such a restriction does not exist, i.e., a unilateral contract may also be rescinded based on the failure in performance.

### II. The Right to Rescind a Contract

*278.* Apart from cases in which the parties to a contract may agree to terminate the very contract, in order to rescind a contract, the right to do so is necessary.

The right to rescind a contract may arise by an agreement between the parties to the contract which aims generally to cope flexibly with the change in circumstances. The requirements and/or method of rescission are usually set forth in such agreement. The parties may, in principle, agree to rescind the contract in existence even on the ground of an immaterial failure of performance.

The right to rescind a contract may also arise by operation of law especially as a remedy for the failure to perform contractual obligations. In this regard, despite the absence of explicit provision (such as Article 64, paragraph 1, CISG), the Supreme Court requires that the failure to perform shall in principle be sufficiently serious to justify the rescission of contract (97Ma575). In other words, in order to rescind a contract, the failure to perform ought to be material (i.e., about an essential element of contractual obligations). Whether the failure to perform is material, should be determined in light of the parties' intention which may be inferred from objective circumstances. The answer thereto depends upon circumstances concerned. In this context, contents of the contract and consequences of the failure to perform shall be taken into account.

*279.* On the other hand, Article 9 of the Act on the Regulation of Terms and Conditions lays down that some clauses in standard terms concerning rescission or rescission for the future of a contract shall be null and void: (1) a clause which excludes the right of customers to rescind or rescind for the future the contract pursuant to *lex scripta*, or limits the exercise of such right; (2) a clause which grants a business person the right to rescind or rescind for the future a contract which is not provided for by *lex scripta*, therefore might put customers at an unreasonable disadvantage; (3) a clause which mitigates a business person's requirements to exercise the right to rescind or rescind for the future a contract pursuant to *lex scripta*, therefore might put customers at an unreasonable disadvantage; (4) a clause which, without any substantial reason, obligates customers to pay excessive restitution due to rescission or rescission for the future of a contract, or which unreasonably provides for customers to waive their claim for restitution; (5) a clause which unreasonably reduces the obligation to restore of a business person or his/her duty to pay indemnity in the event of rescinding or rescinding a contract for the future; and (6) a clause in a contract providing for a continuous obligee-obligor relationship which might put customers at an unreasonable disadvantage by providing for a duration that is unreasonably short or long or by allowing implied extensions or renewals of contract.

*280.* The Civil Code distinguishes regarding the requirements between delay and impossibility of performance.

Concerning delay of performance, Article 544 states that "If one of the parties does not perform his/her obligation, the other party may, specifying a reasonable period, give peremptory notice demanding its performance, and may rescind the contract, if no performance is effected within such period. However, if the obligor declares in advance his/her intention that he/she will not perform, no peremptory notice shall be required." In this regard, at first, if, due to the nature of contract or by a declaration of intention of the parties, the purpose of the contract is unattainable unless the performance is made at a designated time and date, or within a designated period, and one of the parties has failed to perform his/her obligation in good time, the other party may, without giving the preemptory notice, rescind the contract (Article 545). Second, the Supreme Court held that even in a case where a reasonable period was not set forth explicitly in the notice, the obligee may rescind the contract successfully after the lapse of a reasonable period (94Da35930). Third, there is a controversy over whether the delay should be imputable to the obligor or not, and the dominant view answers in the affirmative.

On the other hand, with regard to impossibility, Article 546 lays down that "If performance has become impossible for any cause for which the obligor is responsible, the obligee may rescind the contract."

*281.* Concerning the right to rescind a contract, the followings are worthy of mentioning.

At first, in 2007 (after restraint for a long time) the Supreme Court found "in principle" that in an exceptional case of a significant and radical change in circumstances, a contract can be set aside if its enforcement would be unacceptable pursuant to the doctrine of bona fides, and that a test of such a change should be an objective one, i.e., in accordance with the observance of reasonable standards of bona fides (2004Da31302. *See supra* paragraphs 175 f.).

On the other hand, if a holder of the right to rescind a contract has at his/her fault (i.e., intentionally or by negligence) materially damaged the subject of the contract, has become unable to return it, or has caused it to be converted into a different kind of object by processing or altering it, the right to rescind the contract shall be extinguished (Article 553).

## III. Exercise of the Right to Rescind a Contract

*282.* The right to rescind a contract shall be effected by a declaration of intention (unilateral juristic act) to the other party, and this declaration may not be revoked (Article 543). (In exercising this right, an order of the court or a recourse to the court is not necessary, although the court may review afterwards whether the requirement of rescission is complied with.) No condition may be attached to such a declaration (*see* Article 493, paragraph 1).

In cases where one or each of the parties to a contract is composed of more than two persons, a right to rescind a contract shall only be exercised by or against all of them, and in such cases, if the right to rescind a contract has been extinguished with respect to one of the persons who compose a party, it shall be extinguished with respect to the other person(s) (Article 547: Indivisible nature of right to rescind a contract. This Article is not mandatory).

On the other hand, if no period is specified for exercise of the right to rescind a contract, the other party may demand of the holder of the right to rescind a contract, to make a definite answer by specifying a reasonable period on whether he/she rescinds the contract or not, and if no notice of rescission has been received within that period, the right to rescind a contract shall be extinguished (Article 552).

## IV. Effect of Rescission

*283.* There is a crucial controversy over the effect of rescission. Although some scholars are of the opinion that the original obligation is transformed into an obligation to undo the transaction by making restitution (which stems from the German theory of *Rückgewährschuldverhältnis*), the Supreme Court found that the effect of rescission is to make the contract retrospectively null (75Da1394, 81DaKa1110), which was the formerly dominant view and is still supported by influential scholars.

*284.* According to the stance of the Supreme Court, upon rescission of a contract, obligations arising from that contract shall be extinguished and obligations which have not yet been fulfilled need no longer be fulfilled. On the other hand, in cases where one or each of the parties has already performed his/her obligations, the party who has received the performance shall be liable to restore the opposite party to his/her original position (*restitutio in integrum*. Article 548, paragraph 1. In this regard, whether the possessor was in good faith or in bad faith, is irrelevant, and Article 748 shall not apply. As to the normal amount of benefits to be returned, *see infra* paragraph 452). And interest shall be paid on any money to be repaid as from the day on which such money has been received (*ibid.*, paragraph 2). It is the return of unjust enrichment, not in the nature of damage. Benefit gained from having use of the thing or exercise of the right also ought to be disgorged on the same basis. In addition, provisions on *exceptio non adimpleti contractus* shall apply *mutatis mutandis* to *restitutio in integrum* (Article 549).

*285.* On the other hand, in cases where the ownership of the immovable sold has already passed to the buyer, since the validity of transfer of ownership is dependent upon the validity of contract creating the obligation to transfer ownership (*see supra* paragraph 21), the ownership returns to the seller *ipso iure*. In this regard, since a bona fide acquisition is confined to the movable, the retrospective nullity may affect not merely the parties themselves but also a third person, who has acquired real rights over the immovables by way of a contract. In order to protect such a third person, Article 548, paragraph 1 lays down that the rights of the third person shall not be prejudiced by rescission. As a result, in spite of rescission, the interim owner shall be protected. To be protected under this provision, for instance, the purchaser should register the real estate under his/her name. Therefore, in a case where the real estate was leased by the purchaser without registration but with the seller's approval, the lessee will not be protected, even if he/she has met the requirement to obtain opposing power (95Da32037. As to the opposing power, *see infra* paragraphs 379 and 386). It should be mentioned that even after rescission, a bona fide third person shall be protected (2000Da584).

In addition, rescission of a contract shall not affect any claim for damages (Article 551). According to the ruling of the Supreme Court, reimbursement of expenses which one party has made in reliance on receiving performance may be covered by damages (2015Da59115. *See infra* paragraph 297).

## V. Rescission for the Future

*286.* In some cases, a contract shall be valid for a long time on account of characteristics of the contract (e.g., lease of an immovable, contract of insurance or employment) or because of the intention of the parties to develop a long-term business relationship (e.g., contract between a manufacturer and a distributor). In such contracts for successive/continuous performances, facts accomplished already cannot be reversed, and therefore the retrospective effect is inadequate or not necessary. In this context, the Civil Code distinguishes "rescission for the future" (termination) from rescission (with retrospective effect), saying in Article 550 that "If one of the parties rescinds a contract for the future, the contract shall lose its effect for the future."

*287.* In this regard, refusal to renew is worthy of mentioning.

It is not seldom that merchants (usually companies) conclude a contract which shall be valid for a specified period, however shall be automatically renewable, unless either party gives an advance notice of refusal to renew a contract. In such cases, a relationship between the parties is generally based on the mutual trust, and there is a need to protect each party's interests, unless the failure to perform is so significant, so as to break the trust and thereby to make continuance of the contractual relationship improper. In this sense, refusal to renew a contract without any justifiable ground may be contrary to the doctrine of bona fides, and therefore, a refusal to renew may not be permissible, unless there is a reasonable period notice which enables the loss to be recovered, or reasonable compensation therefor, although pursuant to the principle of the freedom of contract, the parties are in principle free to refuse its renewal. For instance, in case of a sole distributorship contract, particularly because of the legitimate expectation for the continuation of relationship upon which investments had been made, the distributor should be given an opportunity to make up for his/her investment, if he/she had acted in good faith. The limit of refusal should be determined by taking into account various circumstances (e.g., the status of both parties, the length of the relationship, the amount of damages presumed to be suffered by the refusing renewal, etc.)

## §5. Exceptio Non Adimpleti Contractus

### I. Introduction

*288.* Since in a synallagmatic contract, the obligations of the parties are concurrent (*supra* paragraph 32), nonperformance of one party justifies that of the other party, and therefore, each party may refuse to perform his/her obligation until the other party performs (or at least tenders) his/her. In this regard, Article 536, paragraph 1 provides for *exceptio non adimpleti contractus* (defense of simultaneous performance): "One of the parties to a synallagmatic contract may refuse to perform his/her own obligation until the other party tenders performance of his/her obligation. However, this shall not apply if the obligation of the other party is not due." For instance, in a contract of sale, the seller can withhold delivery if the buyer does not pay the purchase-price (In this case, the buyer should perform his/her obligation or at least tender the performance in order to claim performance against the seller), or the buyer may withhold payment until the attachment on the thing sold is canceled. In this sense, this *exceptio*, on the one hand constitutes a ground for refusal to perform, and on the other hand, a means of compelling the opposing party to perform his/her obligation.

*289. Exceptio non adimpleti contractus* and a right of retention (Article 320. *See infra* paragraph 420) serve the same purpose in that the holder of a right is entitled to suspend performance of his/her own obligations. However, the *exceptio* is on the one hand much wider, in that a performance which may be withheld is not confined to one to hand over a thing to which the other party is entitled (e.g., obligation for an act may be withheld). On the other hand, a right of retention is not confined to a synallagmatic contract (the obligor to a unilateral contract may retain a thing belonging to another person if the claim secured arises in respect of such a thing). In addition, pursuant to the Civil Code, the right of retention is a real right and therefore constitutes a defense to anyone (including even the owner who is not an obligor of the claim secured).

## II. Requirements

*290.* In principle, the obligation of which the obligor may refuse to perform should be correlative to the obligee's obligation in that both arise from one and the same synallagmatic contract. However, obligations arising from a synallagmatic contract are not always correlative obligations. For instance, the obligation of the lessee to pay rent and the obligation of the lessor to reimburse the useful expenses are not correlative; nevertheless, between both obligations, *exceptio non adimpleti contractus* shall be available.

In case of partial performance, the *exceptio* shall, in principle, be granted to the extent of the failure in performance. In addition, in order to avoid abuse of this *exceptio*, the obligation of the other party should be of comparable importance (i.e., not trivial such as accessory obligation).

*291.* With regard to this requirement, the Supreme Court expands the sphere of application of this *exceptio* to the concurrent obligations which arise out of the same legal relationship (i.e., not from one and the same synallagmatic contract). For instance, this *exceptio* may be available concerning the restitution of the performed in the event that a synallagmatic contract is void or voided. (92Da45025, 2001Da3764. Regarding *restitutio in integrum* resulting from rescission, Article 549 explicitly provides for the availability of this *exceptio*. *See supra* paragraph 284).

*292.* On the other hand, an obligor may exercise his/her right to refuse performance in cases where the claim against his/her obligee becomes due and the obligee does not tender his/her obligation(s). In this sense, as to the obligation which is expected to be performed before that of the other party, there is, in principle, no room for this *exceptio*.

However, there are two exceptions. At first, even in cases where one of the parties to a contract is bound to perform his/her own obligation prior to the other party, if there is any significant cause on account of which the other party's performance becomes difficult, this *exceptio* shall be available (*ibid.*, paragraph 2). For instance, a significant change in the obligee's property status after the conclusion of contract constitutes the grounds for this exception. Similarly, Article 588 provides for buyer's right to refuse payment of the purchase-money where a third person claims certain right: "If a third person claims a right over the subject matter of the sale, and consequently, there is a danger of the buyer's losing what he/she has bought in whole or in part, he/she may refuse payment of the purchase-money to the extent of such danger. However, this shall not apply when the seller furnishes reasonable security." Second, after the obligation of the other party has become due, this *exceptio* shall be available. In this case, according to the ruling of the Supreme Court, the obligor shall be liable for damages for the delay for the period between the due date of the obligor and that of the obligee (90Da19930).

### III. Effects of *Exceptio Nn Adimpleti Contractus*

*293.* After requirements of *exceptio non adimpleti contractus* are complied with, the obligor shall not be in default (i.e., not liable for late performance), irrespective of the exercise of this *exceptio*, because this *exceptio*, as a right to withhold, constitutes a legitimate ground for refusal to perform obligation. (97Da54604,54611. However, the obligor may not use and take the profits from the thing to be returned). As a result, the other party, without performance or its tender, neither claims performance and/or damages, nor rescinds the contract. In this respect, this *exceptio* is closely related to delay. (In my opinion, this *exceptio* should be dealt with in that context.) On the other hand, where the defendant does not plead this *exceptio* against the claim for performance, the court will order performance of the defendant irrespective of the counter-performance in accordance with the oral proceeding system.

## §6. Damages

### I. Introduction

*294.* In cases of failure to perform attributable to the obligor, the obligee shall be entitled to claim damages (Article 390).

The purpose of the award of damages is to compensate the obligee for loss, which he/she has suffered from the failure to perform. In this regard, there are some issues to be dealt with: what constitutes a loss for which the compensation is to be made; is the loss a result of a failure in performance; to what extent damages will be given; how is the amount to be well assessed and so on.

*295.* As a rule, in order to claim damages, an obligee should allege and prove the fact that the obligor has failed to perform obligation(s) and the obligee has suffered loss therefrom, and the obligor may invoke the absence of fault as a defense (Article 390). However, with regard to an obligation of means and monetary debt, the situation shall differ (*supra* paragraphs 147 ff. and *infra* paragraph 308).

In addition, the parties may, in advance, agree that one or each of the parties shall not be liable for the failure to perform his/her obligation, and in such case, the aggrieved party shall not be awarded damages. In addition, the parties may agree upon an upper limit of damages, and in such case, damages should be subject to that limit. As to exemption clauses and penalty clauses, *see supra* paragraphs 164 ff.

On the other hand, in a case where more than two persons are each obliged to compensate the same loss, the relation of their obligations belongs to "untrue" joint and several obligations (*see infra* paragraph 404). In this case, an obligor who has paid for the damage may take recourse against the other obligor(s).

## II. Definition and Types of Damage

### A. *Definition*

*296.* According to the established ruling of the Supreme Court and the general academic opinion, damage means the difference between the actual position in which the aggrieved party (obligee) finds himself/herself as a result of an infringement (failure to perform an obligation) and the presumed position in which he/she would have been if the obligation had been performed (91Da33070), which is usually referred to as a balance theory.

However, in some exceptional cases where there is no difference in spite of a failure to perform (for instance, in a case where the obligee is insured against the loss arising from a failure in performance, he/she has in fact suffered no loss), the concept of normative damage should be approved (in the aforementioned case, the right of the obligee to claim damages will pass to the insurer: subrogation. Article 682, the Commercial Code).

On the other hand, damage should be real, but, a reasonable degree of certainty suffices for compensation.

### B. *Types of Damage*

*297.* Damage arising from a failure to perform obligation(s) (as well as in tort) is divided into the material (pecuniary/property) damage and the immaterial (intangible/moral) damage.

The Supreme Court divides again, the material damage into positive damage (*damnum emergens*) and negative damage (*lucrum cessans*), which is, including the immaterial damage, referred to theory of trisection on loss (*see* 2002Da34581 with regard to tort-claim). The obligee is entitled to damages in respect of the loss which he/she has suffered and the profit of which he/she has been deprived. For instance, in a case where the seller of goods fails to deliver, the difference between the contract-price and the cost to obtain substitutive/replacement goods is the positive damage, and the lost profit which the buyer may earn by an advantageous resale is the negative damage. In addition, the Supreme Court approves in recent years the reliance loss which is to be contrasted to the expectation loss under the Common law, i.e., the loss incurred by the obligee in reliance on the obligor's promise to perform, with regard to damages as effect of rescission (2015Da59115. *supra* paragraph 285). (In my opinion, this loss, as futile expenses (*see* section 284, BGB), belongs to *damnum emergens*, and shall be treated as an issue regarding assessment of damages (in that it guarantees a minimum amount of damages. *See infra* paragraph 308), not as a type of damage.)

On the other hand, the immaterial damage is any loss that is not pecuniary (e.g., the sentimental loss resulting from destruction of the article left by deceased father). In contrast to some jurisdictions where compensation therefor is confined to the cases provided for by law (e.g., section 253, BGB), under Korean law, such a loss is, in principle, not excluded from the scope of damages. However, the Supreme Court is of the opinion that this damage shall in general be cured by compensation for the pecuniary damage (93Da59779). As a result, this damage constitutes the so-called special damages and is compensated only if the obligor had foreseen or could have foreseen special circumstances (Article 393, paragraph 2. *See infra* paragraph 304).

## III. Scope of Damages and Causation

### A. *Introduction*

*298.* The obligor shall be liable only for such loss as was caused by his/her failure in performance, and the victim (obligee) should be placed in the position where he/she would have been if such failure had not taken place. However, since it may be impossible as well as unjust if the loss suffered shall be fully compensated, the limitation of damages (especially for unforeseeable loss) shall be attempted in various ways, i.e., by operation of law or as *de lege lata* in case of the absence of provision concerned. In this context, Korean law adopted the former approach, but, the dominant view follows the latter.

*299.* With regard to causation, e.g., under German law, in order to prevent the liability for unforeseeable loss, a test of probability of damage is necessary (*Adäquanztheorie*). In other words, since the method and extent of damages pursuant to German law is the restoration, i.e., full compensation for all the losses on account of the failure to perform (section 249, paragraph 1 of BGB. *See infra* paragraph 305), the theory of "adequate causation" has been introduced in the stage of causation in order to mitigate the consequences of full compensation for all the losses caused, although this theory is currently replaced or supplemented by the theory of "range of protection." The adequate causation, as a "legal" causation, means that the obligor is liable only for probable consequences, not for highly unusual consequences of a failure in performance.

*300.* In Korea, the Supreme Court and the some (previously: most) scholars adhere to the theory of adequate causation (2010Da81315). However, under Article 393 which limits the scope of damages, the requirement of causation should be separate from the scope of compensation for damages (although the two are not divided precisely in practice, and the theory of adequate causation also takes foreseeability into account). The former is concerned with a causal link between a failure to perform and losses caused therefrom, while the latter is, based on the former, concerned with to what extent damages will be given.

Therefore, the concept of adequate causation is, in part, not necessary, and in part, not useful under Korean law, and the causation should be separated from the scope of damages.

*B. Causal Relation*

*301.* There should be a causal link between a failure to perform and losses occurred therefrom (i.e., a failure to perform should be the cause of loss(es) suffered by the obligee), and "*conditio sine qua non*" will suffice. In other words, this requirement itself shall be the relation that without failure to perform the loss would not have taken place (the "but-for" test).

On the other hand, the requirement of causation does not need that the failure to perform is the only cause of the damage, but it is sufficient that such failure is a relevant cause.

*C. Scope of Damages*

*302.* As to the scope of compensation for damages, Article 393 states that:

(1) The compensation for damages arising from the failure to perform an obligation shall be limited to ordinary damages.
(2) The obligor is responsible for compensation for damages which have arisen from any special circumstances, only if he/she had foreseen or could have foreseen such circumstances.

(This Article shall apply *mutatis mutandis* to torts claims. Article 763. However, there is a controversy over the reasonableness thereof.)

As just mentioned, the Supreme Court applies this Article in light of the German theory of "adequate causation." However, recent persuasive academic opinion is that this Article came from none other than an English case of *Hadley* v. *Baxendale* [1854] 9 Exch. 341.

*303.* In accordance with this Article, the scope of compensation for damages should be determined by the foreseeability (the so-called contemplation rule).

On the one hand, although this Article does not explicitly require the foreseeability as criteria concerning the ordinary (normal) loss, the foreseeability is an implied requirement therefor in my opinion. In other words, with regard to the ordinary loss, the foreseeability is determined by an objective criterion, i.e., from the point of view of not the very obligor but everyone, and therefore, the ordinary loss, as a loss foreseeable anyhow, should be compensated in any event. Classic examples of the ordinary loss are market price of the article destroyed and interest based on legal rate for nonperformance of monetary debt. However, in some cases, the line between the ordinary and special losses may be drawn with difficulty. In this case, in order to determine whether or not the loss is ordinary, various factors (such as whether the party was a merchant or not, and the purpose, type and nature of transaction) should be taken into account. For instance, in cases where the buyer lost profit of resale on account of a failure to perform on the part of the seller, the nature of the loss (the lost profit) is a matter of construction of the case in question (for instance, in a case where the buyer was a merchant and the article sold is a movable, the loss may belong to an ordinary loss).

*304.* On the other hand, as to the loss that has arisen on account of special circumstances (usually referred to as "special loss" for short), the (explicit) requirement of foreseeability is determined from the point of view of the very obligor. The occurrence itself and/or the extent of loss must be foreseeable. In this regard, the main and substantive issue is an evaluation of the foreseeability. This criterion is determined again by various factors such as whether the party was a merchant or not, and the purpose, type and nature of transaction. The burden of proof concerning foreseeability of special circumstances lies with the obligee. In addition, the Supreme Court ruled that the foreseeability of special circumstances is determined at the time of default, not at the time of the conclusion of contract (84DaKa1532). If the sphere of application of this Article is confined to the contractual obligations, the parties can be supposed to have entered into a contract taking into account foreseeable risks, and therefore, criterion of "at the time of the conclusion of the contract" (e.g., Article 74, CISG) may be justified. However, since Article 393 also covers losses, which do not result from the failure to perform "contractual" obligations, as well, the approach of the Supreme Court is generally accepted by the academic opinion. (On the other hand, in contrast to, e.g., Article 1231-3 of the French Civil Code, Article 393 apply also in case of a failure to perform "due to a gross or dishonest fault" (of course, including the case where such failure is deliberate).)

## IV. Method of Compensation for Damages

*305.* Compensation for damages may be provided by means of restitution in kind so as to restore the prior position. For instance, section 249, paragraph 1 of BGB states that "A person who is liable in damages must restore the position that would exist if the circumstance obliging him/her to pay damages had not occurred," although the obligee may demand the required monetary amount in lieu of restoration under paragraph 2.

In Korea, however, unless otherwise agreed upon between the parties, the damages shall be recovered in money (Article 394). This Article is not mandatory, and therefore, the parties may agree upon reparation of damage *in natura*.

This Article shall apply *mutatis mutandis* to torts claims (Article 763). For reference, under Article 764 the court may, upon application of the injured party, order the person who has impaired another's fame to take suitable measures to restore the injured party's fame, either in lieu of, or together with damages. The publication of apology in newspapers, etc., as "suitable measures" under this Article, is found in violation of the Constitution according to the decision of the Constitutional Court. 89HunMa160).

## V. Assessment of Damages

*306.* Damages should compensate the obligor for the loss suffered and the gain deprived, and the damages should be recovered in money as a rule. Therefore, the damages to be compensated should be assessed in money.

As to liquidated damages, *see supra* paragraphs 166 f. (For reference, Article 202-2, the Civil Procedure Act states that "Where it is admitted that damage has occurred, if it is considerably difficult to prove the specific amount of damages in light of the nature of the case, the court may fix as the amount of damages an amount that is deemed reasonable taking into consideration all circumstances based on the entire purport of pleadings and the results of examination of evidence.")

*307.* The amount of damages should be assessed on the basis of the actual loss suffered by the very victim (in case of a failure in performance: obligee), and the plaintiff should in principle allege and prove the fact that he/she has suffered damage and the amount of damage. In other words, damages should, as a rule, be assessed taking into account all the relevant circumstances (a concrete method of assessment). However, in cases where in spite of the fact that some losses have been incurred, the assessment of damages is impossible or very difficult, the court may find a considerable loss amount, in light of the purport of pleading and the results of evidence investigation.

On the other hand, the court may assess the damages in accordance with the objective standard (an abstract method of assessment), i.e., the supposed amount in money which a person in a similar position would generally suffer as a result of the failure to perform in question (e.g., difference between the price set forth by the contract and the market price in case of a failure to perform an obligation of the seller or difference between the agreed price and the cost of the replacement sale in a case where the seller has entered into a replacement sale due to a failure to perform an obligation of the buyer). In this respect, the abstract method guarantees a minimum amount of damages (*see* also *supra* paragraph 297 with regard to futile expenses). (On the other hand, in some cases, especially with regard to the violations of the intellectual property, benefit enjoyed by the liable person is presumed to be the amount of damages. E.g., Article 125, paragraph 1 of the Copyright Act lays down that "Where the holder of author's property right or other rights (excluding author's moral right and performer's moral right) protected pursuant to this Act ('holder of author's property right, etc.') claims compensation against a person who has infringed on such holder's rights intentionally or by negligence for damages sustained from the relevant infringement, if the infringing person has gained any profit by his/her infringement, the relevant amount of profit shall be presumed to be the amount of damages sustained by the holder of author's property right, etc.")

*308.* By contrast, with regard to damages of nonperformance of monetary debt, the obligee is not bound to prove the actual damages nor can the obligor set up the absence of negligence as a defense. (Article 397, paragraph 2. However, according to the ruling of the Supreme Court, the obligee should allege that he/she has suffered certain losses. 99Da49644) In such a case, damage shall be assessed at the agreed interest rate or the statutory interest rate in the absence of any agreement (The Supreme Court is of the opinion that special loss may be claimable, to which I assent. 91Da25369). With regard to the former rate, the Supreme Court ruled that in a case where the agreed interest rate is lower than the statutory rate, the damage owing to the delay shall be assessed at the statutory interest rate (2009Da85342), which is, in my opinion, contrary to the wording of proviso. (However, where there exists an agreed rate of interest which does not exceed the limitation by *lex scripta*, that agreed rate of interest shall prevail.)

*309.* With respect to assessment of damages, the Supreme Court found, in principle, that the moment at which the loss shall be assessed is the date of failure in performance. For instance, the compensatory damages (damages in lieu of performance) owing to the impossibility is assessed at the time of impossibility, and in case of the increase in price, the difference between the prices constitutes the so-called special damage (94Da61359,61366).

On the other hand, the obligee may claim compensation for damage which will arise in the future as a result of a failure in performance, and the future damages should be assessed at the time of a closure of pleadings on the basis of reasonable probability.

*310.* The court may order the obligor to pay a lump sum or to make periodical payments. With regard to the former, the intermediary interest should be deducted. As to the latter, Article 252, paragraph 1 of the Civil Procedure Act lays down that "Subsequent to a final and conclusive judgment ordering the payment of periodic payments, when a special situation occurs which greatly infringes on the equilibrium between the parties, as the situations forming the basis for computing such payments were significantly changed, the parties to such judgment may institute a lawsuit claiming to change the amount of periodic payments to be paid in the future."

*311.* On the other hand, the obligor shall *ipso iure* be bound to pay the legal interest on the amount to be paid as compensation for damages, and in particular, the amount of damages for nonperformance of monetary debt shall be determined by the legal rate of interest (Article 397, paragraph 1). In this context, the rate of interest of a claim bearing interest, unless otherwise provided for by *lex scripta* or agreed by the parties, shall be 5% per annum (Article 379. For obligations arising from commercial transactions, the rate is 6%. Article 54, the Commercial Code). The parties may agree upon different interest rates, but, this rate shall not exceed that set forth by the Interest Limitation Act (*see infra* paragraph 394).

## VI. Adjustment of Damages

### *A. Contributory Negligence*

*312.* The obligor should redress all the losses which his/her failure to perform has caused. However, the obligee often contributes to or aggravates the loss. In such a case, any negligence on the part of the obligee with regard to the failure to perform should be taken into account by the court in determining the liability for damages and/or assessing the amount thereof (Article 396), which is equivalent to the Anglo-American concept of "contributory negligence." As a result, usually the amount of damages shall be diminished in proportion to the degree in which the negligence of the obligee contributes to the loss. This Article may apply in cases where the liability of the obligor is based on risk. (According to the ruling of the Supreme Court, especially with regard to tort, in cases where circumstances which can be imputed to the obligor have contributed to the damage, the same rule shall apply. *See* 2009Da100920).

The contribution of the obligee may be concerned not merely with the occurrence of damage but also with its amount. In addition, the Supreme Court ruled that the obligee may be obliged to take the necessary measures to reduce damages in certain situations, and the damages caused by his/her negligence may be deducted (2003Da12083. In this case, by contrast, the reasonable costs for these measures may be claimed as damages.)

### *B. Offset of Profit and Loss*

*313.* The court approves the offset of profit and loss. In a case where one and the same failure to perform has caused the obligee losses as well as profits, profits arising from such failure should be deducted from the amount to be compensated. Whether the failure to perform has caused profits, should be answered by applying the same criteria for the causation as well as the scope of damages as discussed above (*see* also *supra* paragraphs 298 ff.).

In the same context, in cases where the obligee bears the risk of counter-performance, if the obligor has received any benefit by being relieved of his/her own obligation, he/she shall return such benefit to the obligee (Article 538, paragraph 2). In addition, in a case where an obligee has received by way of damages the full value of the thing or right which forms the subject of the claim, the obligor shall *ipso jure* be subrogated to the position of the obligee in respect of such thing or right (Article 399).

*314.* For reference, on the other hand, it is worth mentioning that with regard to tort-liability Article 765 grants the power to reduce the amount of damages to the court, saying that:

(1) The person liable to make compensation based on tort may petition the court for a reduction in the amount of compensation, if the damages were caused neither intentionally nor by gross negligence, and such payments of compensation shall be a severe hardship to his/her livelihood.
(2) The court may, if the petition mentioned in the preceding paragraph has been filed, reduce the amount of compensation after a study of the claimant's and obligor's respective property status and the cause giving rise to the damages.

# Part II. Specific Contracts

## Chapter 1. Agency

### §1. Overview

*315.* The effect of a contract shall bind only the parties thereto. However, similar to other jurisdictions, a juristic act (more exactly: declaration of intention) of one person (agent) may directly bind another person (principal). In other words, a juristic act can be effected by an agent.

The agency is one of the practically very important and theoretically very interesting institutions in private law. By means of agency, on the one hand, it is possible for a principal to expand the sphere of activity with respect to time and space, and to increase efficiency by using a professional or experienced agent. Thereby, agency has become an inevitable part of specialized modern society. On the other hand, since juristic acts of a person with limited capacity is, in principle, voidable (*supra* paragraph 89), the legal representative shall perform a juristic act on behalf of the person with limited capacity. In this regard, the agency by law usually serves to protect such a person. (In addition, with regard to the representation of a juristic person, provisions on agency shall apply *mutatis mutandis*. Article 59, paragraph 2).

Agency relationships consist of tripartite relations, i.e., relation between principal and agent, one between principal and third party, and one between agent and third party.

*316.* An agent is distinguished from messenger, in that an agent makes a declaration of his/her own intention (will) on behalf of the principal, while a messenger merely transmits the principal's declaration of intention. And an agent differs from the so-called indirect agent, in that for instance, a commission agent, as an indirect agent, makes it his/her business to effect sale and purchase of goods or securities using his/her own name for the account of another party (Article 101, the Commercial Code).

### §2. Relation Between Principal and Agent: Authority

#### I. Agency Authority

*317.* Agency shall be divided into two types: agency created by a juristic act and one created by law.

In case of the agency by law, agency may arise directly from provisions of *lex scripta*. For instance, the parent who exercises the parental authority shall become the agent by law of his/her minor child (Article 911). In addition, husband and wife shall exercise the authority of agency (power of representation) for each other on normal home affairs (Article 827). In some cases, the agent is appointed by the court. For instance, upon adjudication, an adult guardian shall be appointed ex officio by the Family Court, and the guardian shall become the legal representative of the ward (Articles 929, 936 and 938). The Civil Code also provides for agency by law of the administrator of property in cases where it is unknown whether an inheritor exists or not (Article 1053), the executor of a will if there exists no executor (Article 1096), and the administrator of a property of an absentee (Article 24), and they are appointed by the court.

It should be mentioned that the doctrine of agency of necessity is unknown in Korean law, although the institution of management of affairs of another without mandate (*negotiorum gestio*) allows an unauthorized person (manager) to intervene in affairs of another person (principal), where such intervention is in the interests of the principal (Articles 734 ff. *See infra* paragraph 442).

*318.* On the other hand, agency created by juristic acts shall be created by a unilateral act of the principal toward a prospective agent (i.e., not by an agreement between them). With regard to this type of agency, the relation between the principal and the agent varies according to circumstances concerned. Agency arises not merely from mandate but also from employment contract, contract for work or partnership contract. Most scholars separate underlying relations between the principal and the agent (which is denoted as "the caused juristic relations" in Article 128), such as mandate, employment and so on, from authorization as a unilateral act. However, the authority of agency created by juristic acts shall lapse upon termination of the caused juristic relations (Article 128). In this sense, the authorization should be considered as causal, as to which there is a controversy.

Specific form, such as a power of attorney, is not required to create agency, although such document is issued usually in practice. On the other hand, an agent need not be a person of full capacity (Article 117).

*319.* An authority of agency shall terminate upon: death of the principal, and death, commencement of adult guardianship, or bankruptcy on the part of the agent (Article 127). However, the agent's authority granted by a merchant with respect to his/her business shall not be extinguished by reason of death of the principal (Article 50, the Commercial Code). In addition, authority of agency created by juristic acts shall lapse upon termination of the caused juristic relations and in cases where the principal withdraws the delegation of authority before the caused juristic relations are terminated (Article 128).

## II. Scope of the Authority

*320.* In case of the agency created by juristic acts, the scope of agent's authority is specified by a unilateral act of the principal, while in case of the agency by law, the scope shall be determined by law. Since in the former case, the scope of the authority is not always obvious, Article 118 lays down that an agent whose authority is not specified has the authority to do only acts of preservation and acts of making use of or improving the thing or the right which is the subject of agency to the extent that the nature of such thing or right is not altered thereby. In addition, in order to facilitate business, the Commercial Code provides that a person entrusted with commercial activities may engage in activities which he/she has not been entrusted with to the extent that such activities are not contrary to the tenor of the entrustment (Article 49).

*321.* On the other hand, in order to protect the interests of the principal and/or to avoid conflicts of the interests, the agent's authority may be limited. Without the consent (as a rule: in advance. However, the *ex post facto* consent deserves to be a ratification) of the principal, an agent shall not perform a juristic act to which the agent himself/herself is the other party, or shall not become agent of both parties to one and the same juristic act (Article 124). Under this Article, self-contract or representation of both parties is restricted, but, the performance of an existing obligation is permitted, because in such a case the interests of the principal shall not be harmed. Other provisions which require appointment of a special representative, e.g., provisions on representatives of a juristic person (Article 64) and on the parental authority (Article 921), have the same purpose.

In addition, exercise of the agent's authority may be found to be contrary to the doctrine of bona fides, in a case where an agent with authority of agency acts apparently on behalf of the principal, however, in substance at a profit of himself/herself or a third person. In this case, according to the ruling of the Supreme Court, legal effects of such acts shall not bind the principal, if the third party was aware, or ought to have been aware, of the real intention of the agent (2000Da20694. by way of analogy of Article 107, paragraph 1).

## III. Subagent

*322.* A subagent shall represent the principal in respect of acts within the scope of his/her authority and has the same rights and duties as those of the agent toward the principal or third persons (Article 123).

An agent created by juristic acts may not appoint a subagent, except in cases where such an agent has obtained the consent (in substance: authorization) of his/her principal or an unavoidable reason exists (Article 120). If an agent appoints a subagent legitimately, the agent shall be responsible to the principal in respect of the appointment of and supervision over the subagent. In a case where an agent has appointed a subagent as designated by the principal, the agent shall incur no responsibility, unless he/she knew such subagent to be unsuitable or untrustworthy and failed to notify the principal thereof or to dismiss the subagent (Article 121).

By contrast, an agent by law may, in principle on his/her own responsibility, appoint a subagent (Article 122).

§3. Other Relations

## I. Relation Between Agent and Third Party

*323.* An agent is required to disclose that he/she is acting on behalf of a principal (Article 114, paragraph 1). A declaration of intention made by an agent without disclosing thereof shall be deemed to have been made on the agent's behalf, and therefore, the juristic acts of the agent have no effect upon the principal. However, this does not apply when the other party was aware, or ought to have been aware, that it was made on behalf of the principal (Article 115). In this regard, the doctrine of undisclosed principal is unknown in Korean law.

On the other hand, the Commercial Code furnishes an exception thereto for commercial transactions. A commercial activity of an agent shall be effective toward the principal, even if the agent does not disclose that he/she is acting on behalf of the principal. If the other party was not aware that the transaction was effected on behalf of the principal, he/she may demand performance as against the agent (Article 48).

*324.* In cases where the validity of a declaration of intention is to be affected by reason of the absence of intention, fraud or duress, or by reason of knowledge or negligent ignorance of particular circumstances, the existence or nonexistence of such reasons shall be determined with reference to the agent. However, in cases where an agent has been entrusted to perform a specific juristic act, if he/she has performed such an act in conformity with the principal's instructions, the principal may not set up the agent's ignorance of any circumstances of which the principal himself/herself was aware. The same shall apply if the principal was ignorant of such circumstances due to his/her own negligence (Article 116).

## II. Relation Between Principal and Third Party

*325.* When an agent is authorized by law or by a principal to perform a juristic acts on his/her behalf, legal effects of acts of the agent with a third party are attributed directly to the principal, not to the agent.

*326.* On the other hand, Article 13 of the Act on the Regulation of the Terms and Conditions states that: If a contract is entered into by the agent of a customer, and the customer fails to perform his/her obligations, any clause in standard terms of contract which imposes on the agent an obligation to carry out the customer's obligations in whole or in part shall be null and void.

§4. Representation Without Authority

## I. Effect in General

*327.* A declaration of intention made by an agent within the scope of his/her authority shall be effective directly in favor of and against the principal (Article 114, paragraph 1). In contrast, in cases where a person without authority of agency concludes a contract as an agent of another, such a contract shall not bind the putative principal (Article 130). In other words, if a person without authority acts on behalf of another person, the act has no effect on the latter as a rule.

*328.* The putative principal may ratify the act of a person without authority of agency. Ratification should, in principle, be addressed to the other party, not to the unauthorized agent. However, ratification addressed to the unauthorized agent may take effect, if the other party was aware thereof (Article 132). In the absence of any declaration of intention to the contrary, ratification shall be effective retroactively as from the time the contract was concluded; however, the right of a third person shall not be prejudiced thereby (Article 133).

On the other hand, the other party may give a peremptory notice to the principal demanding a definite answer on whether he/she ratifies the contract or not by specifying a reasonable period. If the principal does not send a definite answer within such period, he/she is deemed to have refused to ratify (Article 131). Until the principal ratifies the contract, the other party is entitled to withdraw a contract concluded by an unauthorized agent, unless the other party was aware that the agent had no authority of agency when the contract was entered (Article 134).

*329.* In cases where a person who has concluded a contract as an agent of another person can neither prove the authority of agency nor obtain the ratification of the principal, the unauthorized agent shall be liable to the other party, at the latter's choice, either for the performance of contractual obligations or for damages. However, this shall not apply if the other party was aware, or ought to have been aware, that the person who concluded a contract as an agent had no authority of the agency, or if such person was a person with limited capacity (Article 135). In this context, an unauthorized agent is liable, even without any cause for which he/she is responsible (especially in cases where he/she is bona fide and not at fault in believing that he/she was authorized).

## II. Apparent Authority

*330.* The existence and/or scope of the agent's authority is not always obvious from the outside, which may confuse other persons. Therefore, a contract concluded by a person purporting to be an agent without authority of agency may be effective against the putative (supposed) principal under certain circumstances, in order to protect those who mistakenly believed that an agent was acting within his/her authority. This (referred to as apparent/ostensible authority) can be justified on the ground that the putative principal has contributed anyhow to such an appearance, although there is nothing to correspond to the doctrine of *estoppel* of the Common law.

*331.* The Civil Code furnishes three types of apparent authority

First, a person who has expressed to a third person that the former has conferred certain authority of agency to other person(s) shall be liable for any juristic act performed by such other person(s) with the third person within the scope of such authority, unless the third person was aware, or ought to have been aware, that such other person had no authority of agency (Article 125). For instance, the putative principal (A) who expressed to a third person (B) that A granted certain authority to the other person (C) may not deny effects of the act performed by C (unauthorized agent), if B is bona fide and not negligent in believing that C was authorized.

On the other hand, in a case where a person (X) has permitted another person (Y) to use X's name or trade name in commercial transactions, e.g., in order to increase Y's credibility, under Article 24 of the Commercial Code, X shall be jointly and severally liable with Y in respect of any obligations arising from a transaction in favor of a third party, which has effected such transaction in belief that Y is the business owner.

*332*. The second and most important type of apparent authority is concerned with the act exceeding the scope of authority. In cases where an agent has performed a juristic act exceeding his/her authority, and the opposing party had justifiable/reasonable reasons for believing that the agent had authority to perform such an act, the principal shall be liable for the act (Article 126). Since the scope of the agent's authority is not always obvious from the outside, this type is not seldom in practice.

In this type, it is necessary that certain authority of agency has actually been granted to the person who has performed a juristic act. In this regard, agency created by a juristic act causes no problem. By contrast, whether this Article shall apply to agency by law or not is an issue of controversy. The Supreme Court found that such an agency suffices also (97Da3828), about which the recent influential opinions raise doubts especially with regard to an agency for a person with limited capacity (however, they also are in general of the opinion that the authority of agency between husband and wife for normal home affairs may suffice). On the other hand, an issuance of a blank power of attorney may be construed as a grant of authority. As a result, in the case where the person obtaining such a letter legitimately abuses it, this is a matter under this Article. (By contrast, in case where the unauthorized holder of such a letter uses it, Article 125 shall apply.) In addition, the requirement of "justifiable/reasonable reasons" is very important in practice. The Supreme Court found that this requirement is complied with if the opposing party is bona fide and not negligent in believing that the agent has been authorized for the act performed by him/her as a whole (97Da3828. In my opinion, with regard to this requirement, attribution of the principal to the appearance of authority should also be taken into account). This requirement is discussed mainly concerning act of disposal, issuance of promissory notes, surety, and so on.

*333*. The third type of apparent authority is related to termination of the authority of agency. Termination of authority (*supra* paragraph 319) may not be set up against a third person acting in good faith, unless such third person was negligent in not knowing such termination (Article 129). Therefore, in a case where the "former" agent acted as though he/she is still authorized, such an act may be binding the "former" principal. In order to prevent this result, the principal has to let it be known that the authority of agency has terminated.

## §5. Commercial Agency

*334.* Agency under the Civil Code should be distinguished from one which is set forth by the Commercial Code (commercial agency), although to a relation to the other party, provisions in the Civil Code shall apply with the exception of authority of a commercial agent to receive notification laid down in Article 90 of the Commercial Code.

A commercial agent is a person who engages in the business of acting on behalf of a particular merchant (principal), not as a commercial employee of any person but as agent or broker in transactions falling within the same line of business as such merchant (Article 87, the preceding Code).

In addition to the duty of care and due diligence set forth by the Civil Code regarding mandate (Article 681), a commercial agent owes duty of notification and duty to keep trade secrets (Articles 88 and 92-3, the Commercial Code). Moreover, without a permission of the principal, a commercial agent shall not make, for his/her own account or for a third party, any transaction in the same line of business as the principal, or serve as an unlimited liability member or a director of a company whose purpose is to engage in the same kind of business of the principal (Article 89, paragraph 1, the preceding Code), and in cases where a commercial agent has made a transaction in contravention thereof, and such transaction has been made on his/her own account, the principal may regard such transaction as having been done on his/her own account, and if it has been made for the account of a third party, the principal may request the agent to transfer the profit accrued from such transaction to the principal (Article 89, paragraph 2, Article 17. paragraph 2, the preceding Code).

On the other hand, a commercial agent as a merchant may demand reasonable remuneration in respect of an act on behalf of the principal (Article 61, the preceding Code), and may retain goods or securities which he/she holds in his/her possession on behalf of the principal, in respect of the obligations which have arisen from his/her agency or brokerage in transactions and which have become due, until he/she receives repayment of such obligations, unless there exists any agreement to the contrary between the parties (Article 91, the preceding Code). In addition, a commercial agent shall be entitled to goodwill compensation. If a principal obtains new customers or his/her business transactions increase substantially by way of the activities of his/her commercial agent, and the principal thereby gains profits even after the contract is terminated, the agent may request reasonable compensation from the principal, except in cases where the contract is terminated by any cause attributable to the agent (Article 92-2, paragraph 1, the preceding Code). In this case, a claim for compensation shall be extinguished after six months has elapsed from the time of termination of contract (*ibid.*, paragraph 3).

A commercial agency terminates after the expiry of the period for which the contract was concluded. In addition, if the parties have not the specified duration of the contract, either of them may terminate the contract by giving two months' notice thereof (Article 92, paragraph 1, the preceding Code).

# Chapter 2. Bailment

## §1. Introduction

*335.* A bailment (referred to also as deposit, but a bailment as a safekeeping contract should be distinguished from a deposit as a ground for extinction of a claim. As to the latter *see supra* paragraph 224) shall become effective when one of the parties (bailor; depositor) has committed to the other party (bailee; depositary) the custody of money, securities or any other things, and the bailee has consented thereto (Article 693). In contrast to the French legal family, a bailment is a consensual contract (i.e., not a real contract), and therefore, the handing over of the thing is not its constitutive element: This contract comes into existence when an agreement thereto is made. On the other hand, remuneration is also not a constitutive element: In the absence of any agreement to the contrary, a bailee may not demand remuneration from the bailor (Article 701, Article 686, paragraph 1). However, in cases where the bailee is a merchant, he/she may demand reasonable remuneration in respect of bailment (Article 61, the Commercial Code).

To the warehousing as a specialized business for bailment, Articles 155 ff. of the Commercial Code shall apply.

## §2. Obligations of the Bailor

*336.* As just mentioned, in principle, remuneration is not due. However, the bailor owes remuneration to the bailee, in cases where an agreement thereto is made or where a bailee is a merchant. If a bailment terminates due to any cause not attributable to the bailee, he/she is entitled to remuneration in proportion to the custody already made by him/her (Article 701, Article 686, paragraph 3). In addition, the bailor should reimburse the expenses borne by the bailee, regardless of owing remuneration (Article 701, Article 688, paragraphs 1 and 2).

On the other hand, a bailor shall indemnify the bailee for damages suffered on account of the nature of or any defect in the bailed articles, unless the bailee was aware of such defects (Article 697).

## §3. Obligations of the Bailee

*337.* The primary obligation of the bailee is to have custody over and return the articles bailed. In this regard, a gratuitous bailee shall exercise the same degree of care in the custody of the articles bailed as he/she exercises for his/her own property (Article 695). By contrast, a merchant who has accepted bailment of articles within the scope of his/her business, even though he/she does not receive any remuneration therefor, shall exercise the due care of a good manager (Article 62, the Commercial Code). On the other hand, a bailee may not allow any third person to custody the articles bailed without obtaining the consent of the bailor or any inevitable reason (Article 701, Article 682, paragraph 1)

A bailee may not use the articles bailed (including allowing third persons to do so) without obtaining the consent of the bailor (Article 694). However, in some cases using the article bailed is required to keep the article in a good state (e.g., a racehorse should be exercised periodically). In addition, a bailee shall be obliged to deliver the fruits arising from the articles bailed (Articles 701 and 684).

If a third person asserting rights over the articles bailed has brought a lawsuit against the bailee or levied an attachment thereon, the bailee must notify the bailor thereof without delay (Article 696).

## §4. Termination

*338.* If a period was specified for a bailment, a bailee may not, in the absence of any inevitable reason, rescind a contract of bailment for the future, prior to the due date. On the contrary, the bailor may rescind the contract for the future at any time (Article 698). In this sense, the period is set forth for the benefit of the bailor. If no period was specified, either party may rescind a contract of bailment for the future at any time (Article 699).

Upon termination of bailment, the bailee should return the articles bailed in the state of its receipt. The articles bailed shall be returned at the place where they have been kept. However, if the bailee has on any justifiable/reasonable grounds removed it to another place, he/she may return it at the place where the articles actually exist (Article 700).

## §5. Bailment for Consumption

*339.* In a case where the bailee is, pursuant to the contract, allowed to consume the articles bailed, provisions on loans for consumption shall apply *mutatis mutandis*. In such a case, the bailee shall not be obliged to return the articles bailed itself, but may return the same amount of articles of the same kind. If no time for its return has been specified by the parties, the bailor may at any time demand its return (Article 702).

*340.* Contract of deposit account belongs to this type of bailment (according to the ruling of the Supreme Court and the dominant view, a contract of deposit account is a real contract. 97Da34822). With regard to this contract, the question about who is the party to the contract in cases where a depositor differs from a nominal account holder may arise, and it is a problem of interpretation. In this regard, previously, the genuine intentions of the parties (i.e., depositor and depositary) were of importance, as in other types of contract, according to which the party was determined first of all on the basis of their common intention, otherwise objectively (2001Da32120). However, after enforcement of the Act on Real Name Financial Transactions and Confidentiality, this is no longer the case. Financial companies, etc., shall perform financial transactions with customers under their real names, and financial assets held in the account that is identified under the real name of the account owner shall be presumed to be owned by the account owner (Article 3, this Act), and the Supreme Court denies de facto any exception thereto (2008Da45828).

## §6. Liability of Hospitality Business Operator

*341.* Unless a hospitality business operator (i.e., a person who engages in the business of making transactions by theaters, hotels, restaurants or other facilities used by the public) proves the fact that he/she has not been negligent in giving due care in the custody of articles deposited from his/her guests, such operator shall be liable to compensate damages resulting from the loss of or damage to the articles kept in his/her custody (Article 152, paragraph 1, the Commercial Code). A hospitality business operator shall be liable for damages for the loss of or damage to portable goods brought into his/her establishments, even if not particularly deposited by the guest, when it is due to the lack of due care of the business operator or any of his/her employees (*ibid.*, paragraph 2). No hospitality business operator shall be exonerated from this liability, even if he/she has informed that he/she is not liable for the loss of or damage to the portable goods of guests (*ibid.*, paragraph 3). On the other hand, with respect to money, securities and other valuables, no hospitality business operator shall be liable for damages resulting from the loss of or damage to such articles, unless the guest deposits them to the business operator by expressly stating the description and value thereof (Article 153, the preceding Code).

These liabilities shall be extinguished by prescription if six months have elapsed since a hospitality business operator returned the articles deposited to the relevant guest, or the portables were recovered by the guest (Article 154, paragraph 1, the preceding Code). This period shall be computed from the date the guest left the establishment, if the articles were totally lost (*ibid.*, paragraph 2). However, this limitation of liability shall not apply where a hospitality business operator or any of his/her employee has acted in bad faith (*ibid.*, paragraph 3).

# Chapter 3. The Aleatory Contract

## §1. Introduction

*342.* The effects of contract, with regard to advantage or prejudice, for one or each of the parties, may depend upon some future uncertain events. This contract may be denoted as aleatory (a chance contract). The aleatory contract shall bring about advantage or prejudice to at least one of the contracting parties. In this sense, a contract of sale with a speculative character (e.g., sale of next year's crop at so much per ton) is not aleatory.

Insurance and life annuity are lawful examples thereof, while a wager (gambling) is the simplest form of an aleatory contract, but it shall in most cases be contrary to social order (Article 103. *See* 72Da2249), and therefore, the winner may not claim performance; however, in cases where the loser has performed voluntarily, he/she may not claim restitution (Article 746. In addition, it may constitute a crime. Article 246, the Criminal Code).

## §2. Life Annuity

*343.* A contract of life annuity shall become effective when one of the parties has promised to the other party to deliver monies or other things to the other party or to a third person periodically until death of the first party, the other party, or the third person (Article 725).

This contract may be onerous or gratuitous. In case of a gratuitous contract, provisions on gift may apply. On the other hand, to the onerous contract of life annuity, provisions on sale shall apply. In this case, however, the disproportion between the performances owed by each of the parties is of no importance, because what the obligor has to pay depends upon how long the obligee lives.

If an obligor in a life annuity neglects to pay the periodical payment or fails to perform any of his/her other duties after he/she has received the principal of the annuity, the obligee may demand a return of such principal and claim damages. In such cases, the obligee should return to the obligor the balance, after interest on the principal sum has been deducted from periodical payments already received by him/her (Article 727). On the other hand, if a death of the person above mentioned occurs due to any cause attributable to the obligor, the court may, upon application of the obligee or his/her successor, declare that the obligation shall continue to exist for a reasonable period (Article 729).

# Chapter 4. Sale of Goods

## §1. Overview

*344.* There are a series of contracts in which one of the parties promises to transfer certain real right(s) to the other party.

First, a contract of sale is the most important and usual type. In this contract, certain real right(s) and the purchase-money shall be exchanged concurrently. In this sense, this contract is an archetype of an synallagmatic as well as onerous contract. In this regard, provisions on this contract shall in principle apply *mutatis mutandis* to other contracts for value (Article 567).

Second, a contract of gift shall become effective when one of the parties declares an intention to transfer a certain property of his/her own gratuitously to the other party, and the other party agrees thereto (Article 553). This contract differs from a contract of sale in that the former is a gratuitous contract (*see supra* paragraph 33). As a result, the binding force of a gift is weakened in some respects: A contract of gift may be rescinded in cases of not in writing (by either party. Article 555), ingratitude acts of the donee (Article 556. e.g., commitment of a crime against the donor, his/her spouse or lineal relatives by blood, or failure to perform an obligation to support the donor) and significant change in the donor's property status (Article 557). In each case, however, rescission shall not have any effect in respect of portion for which performance has been completed (Article 558). In addition, a donor shall, in principle, not be liable for any defect in or absence of the thing or right which forms the subject of gift. However, in cases where he/she was aware of such defect or deficiency and has nevertheless failed to inform the donee thereof, the donor will be liable for such a defect or deficiency (Article 559).

Third, a contract of exchange becomes effective when the parties agree to exchange any property right other than the ownership of money (Article 596). If one of the parties has promised to transfer the property rights together with the ownership of money (supplementary money), provisions on purchase-money for sale contracts shall apply *mutatis mutandis* with respect to that money (Article 597).

## §2. Formation and Effects of Contract of Sale

### I. Formation of Contract of Sale

*345.* As a consensual contract, a sale shall become effective, when one of the parties (seller) promises to transfer a property right to the other party (buyer), and the buyer promises to pay the purchase money to the seller (Article 563).

Objects of sale may be either things or rights, insofar as these are suitable to be transferred. Things or rights which will exist in the future may be the object of a sale if determinable at the time of the conclusion of contract. On the other hand, the price (purchase-money) is a constitutive element of a sale. In cases where the price is not explicitly agreed upon by the parties, the price shall be determined by way of interpretation in which the court shall take into account preengagement, de facto custom (Article 106) and reasonable price including market price, etc. (*see supra* paragraphs 150 and 151).

For reference, the expenses relating to a contract of sale shall be borne equally by both parties (Article 566), but this Article is not mandatory.

## II. Effects of Contract of Sale

*346.* In a contract of sale, the seller shall transfer a right (ownership) of the object of a sale to the buyer, and the buyer shall pay the purchase-money to the seller (Article 568, paragraph 1). These duties of both parties (including, in principle, the duty of the seller to hand possession of the object sold over to the buyer) shall, unless there exists any agreement or custom to the contrary, be performed concurrently by both parties (*ibid.*, paragraph 2; for example, the buyer may refuse to pay the purchase-money to the extent of amount secured by hypothec, until the hypothec is cancelled), and in a case where a due date has been specified for the performance of duties of one party, it shall be presumed that the same due date has been assigned for the other party's performance of duties (Article 585). In addition, Article 587 lays down that "If the object of a sale which has not yet been delivered produces fruits after a contract of sale has been entered, such fruits shall vest in the seller. The buyer shall pay interest on the purchase-price from the day of delivery, unless a due date has been specified for the payment of the purchase-price."

In a case where a third person asserts a right over the object of sale, and consequently, there is a danger of the buyer's losing what he/she has bought in whole or in part, he/she may refuse to pay the purchase-money to the extent of such danger, unless the seller furnishes reasonable security (Article 588), and in this case, the seller may demand the buyer to deposit the purchase-money (Article 589).

*347.* The contract of sale creates only an "obligation" of the seller to transfer an ownership, and this obligation shall be fulfilled when the buyer has become the owner. In this sense, the conclusion of a valid contract of sale does not result in the change in the ownership of the object sold per se, in contrast with the French legal family. To the problem of if and when the ownership passes to the buyer, provisions of Part Two (Real Rights) shall apply: The ownership of an immovable is transferred upon its registration (Article 186), and that of movables by its delivery, which includes summary assignment, agreement on possession, and assignment of claim for return of object (Articles 188–190). As to the relation between the validity of contract of sale and the transfer of ownership, *see supra* paragraph 21.

On the other hand, the obligation of the seller shall be fulfilled when the buyer has become the owner. In this regard, it should be mentioned that if a person who is in good faith and without negligence commences the possession of a "movable" peaceably and openly by an act of transaction, he/she shall acquire its ownership immediately even if the assigner is not an owner (Article 249). In such a case, the obligation of the seller is regarded as fulfilled. (However, the original owner may claim damages (usually in tort) against the seller. On the other hand, a bona fide acquisition of an immovable is impossible.)

In addition, the seller should deliver and transfer the thing sold to the buyer free of physical or legal defects (including any claims of third parties), in the absence of any stipulation to the contrary. If the seller does not fulfill this obligation, the seller's liability for warranty shall arise (*see supra* paragraphs 263 ff.).

*348.* In some cases, in addition to the transfer of ownership, the seller obliged to deliver the thing sold to the buyer. In such a case, the obligation shall be fulfilled by the assignment of possession, i.e., when the buyer has de facto control over the thing sold. Although, as just mentioned, delivery of movables is a condition for the transfer of ownership of "movables," delivery may be independent from the transfer of ownership of movables. For instance, in case of a conditional sale under reservation of the ownership, despite delivery of the thing sold the seller is still the owner of the thing (*see infra* paragraph 356).

*349.* For reference, the seller may assume product liability: Where the manufacturer of a product cannot be identified, a person who supplies it by means of sale, lease, or other form of transaction for profit shall compensate for the damage to the life, body or property of a person caused by a defect of a product; however, the foregoing shall not apply if such person informs the injured person or his/her legal representative of the identity of the manufacturer or the supplier within a reasonable period upon request from the injured person or his/her legal representative (Article 3, paragraph 3, the Product Liability Act).

## §3. Redemption

*350.* If a seller reserves the right of redemption at the time of conclusion of the contract of sale, he/she may redeem the object sold by refunding the purchase-money received and the expenses relating to such a sale borne by the buyer. In a case where any special agreement concerning the redemption-money has been made between the parties, such agreement shall apply. In the absence of any agreement to the contrary, the fruits of the object of sale and the interest on the purchase-price shall be deemed to have been setoff against each other (Article 590).

Pursuant to the redemption, the seller may compel the buyer to comply with certain conditions imposed by the seller in that if the buyer fails to meet such conditions, the seller may redeem. Furthermore, redemption may be used as a security for the buyer (obligee). A buy-back option is also a means of security, but is not subject to the restriction concerning redemption (e.g., on simultaneity of the agreement or time limit).

*351.* The period for redemption may not exceed five years in case of immovables and three years in case of movables. If any period specially agreed upon between the parties exceeds such period, the period shall be reduced to the period just mentioned. This period may not subsequently be extended. If no period for redemption has been specified, the period shall be deemed to be five years in case of immovables and three years in case of movables (Article 591).

The seller shall lose the right of redemption, unless he/she tenders the purchase-money he/she received and the expenses relating to the sale to the buyer within the period for redemption (Article 594, paragraph 1). If the buyer or any subsequent purchaser has disbursed expenses in respect of the object of a sale, the seller shall reimburse the same amount, but with respect to useful expenses the court may, upon application of the seller, allow him/her a reasonable period for reimbursement (*ibid.*, paragraph 2).

In cases where the object of a sale is an immovable, if reservation of the right of redemption has been registered simultaneously with the registration of a sale, such registration shall be effective against the third persons (Article 592). As a result, even if the ownership of object of a sale was conveyed to a third person, the seller may exercise the right of redemption against the new owner.

## §4. Special Types of Sale

### I. Consumer Sale

*352.* The term “consumers” in this context means those who use goods and services (including facilities) provided by enterpriser for their daily lives as consumers or for their production activities (Article 2, Nr. 1, the Framework Act on Consumers).

In recent years, significant modifications to the principle of the freedom of contract have been made in the interests of consumers against abuses by means of the large scale of modern commerce including fraudulent businesses such as pyramid business schemes. In this regard, similar to other jurisdictions, an innovation is the “cooling-off” period (together with the duty of the seller to give certain information and to explain. *See supra* paragraph 81), which is designed to strengthen the position of consumers who rashly make an unnecessary purchase due to unfair persuasion or undue influence of the seller. As a result, the buyer may withdraw his/her offer without any compensation. (Withdrawal of offer corresponds in substance to rescission.) In this regard, three Acts should be mentioned. (These Acts are mandatory.)

*353.* First, the Installment Transactions Act is to protect consumers’ rights and interests, enhance market confidence and contribute to the sound development of the national economy by ensuring fairness in transactions based on installment contracts and prepaid installment contracts (Article 1). Pursuant to this Act, before concluding an installment contract, an installment business operator shall disclose relevant terms of sale, such as cash price, the price payable by installments, terms of payment and the actual annual rate of an installment commission, so that consumers may understand the standard terms of installment contract (Articles 5 and 23). An installment business operator shall conclude an installment contract in written form (including an electronic document) which indicates relevant terms of sale, such as (in addition to those aforementioned) names and addresses of the installment business operator, the consumer and the credit provider, matters concerning the title retention of the goods, matters concerning the period to withdraw an offer, method of the exercise and effect of withdrawal (Articles 6 and 23). On the other hand, a consumer may withdraw an offer of an installment contract, by a written statement, within seven days from the date, e.g., on which he/she received a contract document (Article 8, paragraphs 1 through 4. In cases of prepaid installment contracts, within fourteen days: Article 24, paragraph 1). In addition, Article 12, paragraph 1 of the preceding Act lays down that: The amount of damages that an installment business operator or a credit provider may demand of a consumer due to the consumer's failure to meet the obligations of making installment payments may not exceed damages for delay equivalent to the amount calculated by multiplying the amount of overdue installment payments by the rate set forth by the Presidential Decree within the maximum limit of the interest prescribed by the Interest Limitation Act.

*354.* Second, the Door-to-Door Sales, etc. Act is to protect the rights and interests of consumers and raise the credibility of markets by providing for matters regarding fair transactions of goods and services through door-to-door sales, telemarketing, multilevel marketing, recurring transactions, transactions for soliciting business, etc., thereby contributing to robust development of the national economy (Article 1). This Act requires reporting or registration of business operator (Articles 5 and 13), and lays down duty to provide certain information (Articles 7, 16 and 30), revocation of subscription (within fourteen days: Articles 8 and 17. In case of a contract for recurring transactions or transactions for soliciting business, at any time during the contract period: Article 31), restrictions on claims for damages (Articles 10, 19 and 32), and prohibited acts (Articles 11, 23 and 34).

*355.* Third, the Act on the Consumer Protection in Electronic Commerce, etc. is to protect the rights and interests of consumers by providing for matters relating to the fair trade of goods or services by means of electronic commerce transaction, mail order, etc. (Article 1). A business operator (a person who manufactures (including processing or packaging), imports or sells goods, or provides services) shall prepare procedures necessary for confirmation and correction of contents, before the time of imposition of transaction amount or the placement of an order by a consumer, in order to prevent loss caused by discrepancies, etc., in the declaration of intention due to consumer's error in manipulation, etc., in the electronic commerce transaction (Article 7), and a mail-order distributor shall promptly notify the consumer of the information regarding confirmation of receipt of the declaration of intention of order, and possibility of sale, if he/she takes an order from a consumer regarding the transaction of goods, etc. (Article 14). In addition, this Act provides for reporting (Article 12), duty to provide information on identity and terms of transaction (Article 13), cancellation of orders (Article 17), restriction on amount of compensation for damage (Article 19), and prohibited acts (Article 21).

## II. Conditional Sale under Reservation of the Ownership

*356.* In a sale of a movable, the seller shall transfer the ownership of the thing sold to the buyer (Article 568, paragraph 1), and the ownership of movable passes, in principle, when the seller has handed the thing over to the buyer (Article 188, paragraph 1). In some cases (especially in sales in installments), however, the parties agree that the ownership of the thing sold shall only pass on payment of the last installment. In this case, despite delivery of the thing sold, the seller is still the owner of the thing. Thereby, the seller may exercise the right to repossess in the event of the buyer's bankruptcy (Articles 70, 407 ff., the Debtor Rehabilitation and Bankruptcy Act). By contrast, at the time of delivery, the risk with regard to the counter-performance shall pass to the buyer, and therefore, in case of the accidental destruction or deterioration of the thing sold the purchase-price is still owed. On the other hand, on payment of the last installment, the buyer becomes the owner of the thing per se.

In practice, such a conditional sale under reservation of the ownership is not rare (however, not available concerning the object be registered, such as immovables). In this case, reservation of the ownership is to secure the payment (unless a bona fide third person acquires the ownership of object under Article 249), and therefore, the reserved ownership of the seller should be treated as a right of security.

## III. Special Types under the Commercial Code

*357.* Provisions on the so-called factoring agreement are inserted into the Commercial Code in 2010. Article 168-11 of this Code lays down that "A person who engages in the business of purchasing and recovering business bonds acquired or to be acquired by another person through the sale of goods or securities, provision of services, etc., is called a bonds purchasing business entity." and Article 168-12 states that "When a debtor of business bonds fails to settle his/her debt, a bonds purchasing business entity may require the debtor under a bonds purchasing agreement to redeem the amount of the business bonds. However, this shall not apply if separately set forth by the bonds purchasing agreement." The debtor under a bonds purchasing agreement is usually a businessman, and he/she sells business bonds to the bonds purchasing business entity by way of a global cession. In this case, the businessman may receive immediate cash payment, and in practice, usually (and in contrast to the just cited Article) the bonds purchasing business entity bears the risk that the debtor of business bonds will be unable to pay.

## IV. International Sale

*358.* To contracts of sale of goods between parties whose places of business are in different countries, CISG shall apply. As mentioned above (*supra* paragraph 52), in 2005 CISG had entered into force in Korea.

# Chapter 5. Contract to Supply Services

## §1. Overview

*359.* There are a series of contracts in which one of the parties promises to supply services.

First, a contract of employment shall become effective when one of the parties (employee) promises to render services to the other party (employer), and the employer promises to pay remuneration therefor to the employee (Article 655). In this contract, the employee is obliged to supply labor service as such, and is not interested in the attainment of any particular goal (i.e., beyond his/her reach). On the other hand, especially the Labor Standards Act provides for the minimum standards for employment which modify the principle and provisions of the Civil Code in order to protect workers (e.g., restriction on dismissal (Articles 23 ff.), preferential payment for claims for wages (Article 38)).

Second, a contract for work shall become effective when one of the parties (contractor) has promised to complete a certain job, and the other party has promised to pay remuneration for the outcome of such work (Article 664). In this contract, not the work itself, but the successful attainment of a particular job as an outcome of the work is of crucial significance. This contract will be discussed later.

Third, provisions on package tour contract are inserted into the Civil Code in 2015. A package tour contract shall take effect when it is agreed upon between the parties that one of the parties (package tour organizer) provides the other party (consumer) with a combination of transport, accommodation, sightseeing or other tour-related services, and the other party promises to pay the price therefor (Article 674-2). The Civil Code provides especially for rescission of contract before departure (Article 674-3), rescission of contract due to extenuating circumstances (Article 674-4) and package tour organizer's liability for warranty (Articles 674-6 ff.).

Fourth, an advertisement offering prizes shall become effective when an advertiser has expressed his/her intention to give a certain reward to any person who performs a certain act, and a contestant has accomplished such an act as has been specified in the advertisement (Article 675). The advertisement is a real contract, and belongs to *contractus nominati* (*supra* paragraph 30), although some scholars are of the opinion that it is a unilateral act.

Fifth, a mandate shall become effective when one of the parties (mandator) has entrusted the other party (mandatary) with the management of certain affairs, and the other party has consented thereto (Article 680). In contrast to a contract for work, in this contract, not an outcome of work, but the work (more precisely: the management of affairs with due care) itself is of great significance. Mandate is a consensual contract which does not require any special form. This contract will also be discussed later.

§2. CONTRACTS FOR WORK

## I. Introduction

*360.* The contractor is obliged to complete a certain job. In this sense, obligation(s) arising from a contract for work belongs to obligation of result (*supra* paragraph 147). The job may be tangible (e.g., construction of a building) as well as intangible (e.g., carriage of a passenger somewhere). This contract is consensual, i.e., does not require any special form, although in practice a contract in writing is not seldom.

*361.* There is a controversy surrounding the legal nature of contract for supply of goods in which one of the parties undertakes to manufacture certain goods with materials to be provided by himself/herself, as this contract has characteristics of a contract of sale as well as of a contract for work. The Supreme Court is of the opinion that whether the completed subject matter is fungible (generic) or not is decisive (94Da42976). According to this approach, in a case where the completed subject matter is a fungible, provisions on the contract of sale shall apply, while in cases of not fungible, provisions on the contract for work shall apply.

## II. Effects of Contract for Work

*362.* The primary obligation of a contractor is to complete a certain job and, if necessary, to deliver the completed subject matter of the work to the party ordering the work.

In this respect, the question about to whom the ownership of the completed subject matter belongs is one of the controversial issues. In cases where the party ordering the work provided all or most of materials, the completed thing belongs to him/her, of course. On the other hand, with regard to cases where the contractor provided all or most of materials, the Supreme Court found that the ownership belongs to the contractor regardless of e.g., the name in the registration, unless otherwise agreed upon between the parties (98Du16675. For reference, under Article 259, paragraph 1, if the value added by the contractor considerably exceeds that of the "movables" provided by the party ordering the work, the contractor shall acquire the ownership of the thing completed), about which most scholars raise doubts. Nevertheless, in practice, an agreement to the contrary is not seldom, and, what is more, the agreement does not need to be explicit.

On the other hand, the standardized agreement for construction contains usually a penalty clause, i.e., clause under which the party ordering the work may deduct a certain proportion or amount of remuneration if the construction has not been completed in time (*see* also *supra* paragraphs 164 ff.).

*363.* Unless otherwise agreed upon between the parties or the nature of work ordered does not so allow, the contractor may make performance by a third person, because in this contract, as mentioned above, an outcome of the work is of great significance (In such case, the contractor remains responsible for acts of such a third person. Article 391). In this regard, the subcontract of construction works is regulated by the Framework Act on the Construction Industry. For instance, no constructor shall subcontract all of the construction works contracted to him/her or most of the major portions set forth by the Presidential Decree of such construction works to any third constructor (Article 29, paragraph 1). On the other hand, each subcontractor shall assume the same obligation to the project owner as the contractor does with respect to any construction works he/she has subcontracted (Article 32, paragraph 1), and under certain circumstances, a project owner may or shall make a direct payment of the subcontract price to a subcontractor for the portion of works performed by a subcontractor (Article 35, paragraphs 1 and 2).

*364.* The Civil Code contains specific provisions on the contractor's liability for warranty. As a result, in spite of Article 567 (*see supra* paragraphs 33 and 344), provisions on the seller's liability for warranty shall not apply *mutatis mutandis* to this contract. Nevertheless, the approach of the Supreme Court as to the relation between provisions on the seller's liability for warranty and those on the failure to perform obligations remains unaltered concerning the contractor's liability (2001Da70337. *See supra* paragraphs 271 and 272). In addition, contributory negligence of the party ordering the work shall be reflected in assessing the damage (2001Da70337).

In cases where there is any defect in the completed subject matter of a work or in a certain part of the subject matter of a work which has been completed before completion of all the work, the party ordering the work may demand the contractor to repair/rectify such defect within a specified period. However, this shall not apply if a defect is not significant/material, and excessive costs are required for repair (Article 667, paragraph 1. In such a case, the contractor shall not be compelled to repair). The party ordering the work may claim damages in lieu of, or together with, repair of defect (*ibid.*, paragraph 2. e.g., in case of a damage in lieu of repair, the difference between the market values of the completed work with and without defect), and may refuse to pay remuneration to the extent of loss caused by defect (*ibid.*, paragraph 3). In addition, if the purpose of the contract cannot be achieved because of defect(s) in the completed subject matter of the work, the party ordering the work may rescind the contract. However, this shall not apply to a building or any other structure on land (Article 668).

These provisions shall not apply if the defect in the completed subject matter of the work has arisen on account of the nature of materials supplied by the party ordering the work or by reason of instructions given by him/her, unless the contractor, with knowledge of the impropriety of the materials or instructions, has failed to notify the party ordering the work thereof (Article 669).

*365.* Demand for repair of defect(s), claim for damages or rescission of contract just mentioned shall be made within one year from the day of delivery of the subject matter of the work. In cases where delivery is not required, this period shall commence to run from the day on which the work was completed (Article 670). However, a contractor with respect to land, a building or any other structure shall be liable for any defects in the subject matter of the work or in its foundations for a period of five years after delivery, and in cases where the subject matter of the work is made of stone, limestone, brick, metal or any other similar material, this period shall be ten years (Article 671).

On the other hand, even where there was a special agreement between the parties that the contractor shall not be bound by warranty liabilities, he/she may not be relieved of liabilities with respect to defects in workmanship or materials of which he/she was aware and nevertheless failed to give notice thereof (Article 672).

*366.* The main obligation of the party ordering the work is to pay remuneration for completion of the contracted work. Payment of remuneration shall be made simultaneously with delivery of the completed subject matter of the work, and in cases where delivery is not required, remuneration shall be paid without delay after the work has been performed (Article 665). In this regard, the contractor of an immovable may demand of the party ordering the work to create mortgage on the immovable in order to secure the contractor's claim in relation to his/her remuneration (Article 666). In addition, the contractor may exercise the right of retention (Article 320) over the thing completed until remuneration is paid.

However, this provision is not mandatory, and in practice, payment in installments is customary, especially in contracts for construction of a building. On the other hand, with regard to the contract of construction works an advance payment is usually agreed upon in order to enable the contractor to prepare construction (e.g., to purchase materials). In cases where an advance was paid, the amount in the proportion of the completed stage shall be set off.

*367.* The Civil Code contains specific provisions on rescission of the contract for work. (Both parties are, pursuant to the general rule, entitled to rescind the contract in case of the other party's failure to perform of course.) Before completion of the contracted work, the party ordering the work may rescind the contract at any time, but shall be liable for damages (actual costs spent and the profit expected) (Article 673). If the party ordering the contracted work has been declared bankrupt, the contractor or the bankruptcy trustee may rescind the contract. In such a case, the contractor may claim in the distribution of the bankrupt estate remuneration for the part of work already completed and for any other expenses which are not included in such remuneration. In such cases, neither party may demand from the other party compensation for any losses which have arisen from rescission of the contract (Article 674).

On the other hand, in cases where the completed work is destroyed before delivery or contractor's notification of completion, the contractor bears the risk, unless otherwise agreed upon between the parties (Upon completion and delivery of the contracted work, the risk passes to the party ordering the work). In such a case, the party ordering the work shall be relieved of the obligation to pay remuneration.

§3. MANDATE

## I. Introduction

*368.* In contrast to a contract for work, an obligation arising from a mandate belongs to obligation of means (*supra* paragraph 147). In other words, the obligation of the mandatary is to carry out the affairs, not to bring about a certain result(s). Therefore, a mandatary shall carry out the affairs entrusted to him/her with the care of a good manager in accordance with the tenor of mandate (Article 681). Especially in cases where the mandatary is a professional expert, he/she should provide competent advice concerning consequences of the mandated/entrusted business. In addition, owing to the trust (fiduciary) relationship between the parties, a mandatary may not allow any third person to carry out the mandated affairs on the behalf of the mandatary without obtaining the consent of the mandator or any inevitable reasons (Article 682, paragraph 1).

The mandated business consists of not only legal affairs but also factual or non-economic affairs (i.e., the management of affairs is not confined to juristic acts).

## II. Effects of Mandate

*369.* The primary obligation of mandatary is to carry out the mandated business with the care just mentioned and due diligence. This duty is based on the trust relationship between the parties, and therefore is required even in cases where a mandate is gratuitous. In addition, even in case of a refusal to pay remuneration agreed upon, this duty is required until termination of the mandate. (This duty shall apply *mutatis mutandis* to the partner (Article 707), the administrator for the property of the absentee (Article 24), the director (Article 382, the Commercial Code) and so on.)

A mandatary is also obliged to report (Article 683), and to deliver and transfer all the money and any other things acquired, and the fruits collected therefrom (Article 684). In addition, he/she shall be liable for pecuniary consumption of money (Article 685).

On the other hand, granting authority of agency is not an essential effect of the mandate. However, agency usually arises from a mandate especially with regard to carrying out legal affairs.

*370.* Payment of remuneration is not a constitutive element of a mandate, and therefore, a mandate, as a rule, is gratuitous: In the absence of any agreement to the contrary, a mandatary may not demand remuneration from the mandator (Article 686). However, such agreement shall be usual and normal in practice and may be implicit. (In addition, if a mandatary is a merchant, he/she can demand reasonable remuneration under Article 61 of the Commercial Code.) In case of an agreement to the contrary, a mandatary may not demand it until the entrusted affairs have been completely performed, and if remuneration has been fixed by periods, he/she may demand it after expiration of the period (Article 686, paragraph 2). If a mandate terminates in the course of the performance of the entrusted affairs by the mandatary due to any cause not attributable to him/her, he/she is entitled to demand remuneration in proportion to the affairs already managed by him/her (*ibid.*, paragraph 3).

On the other hand, a mandator should reimburse the necessary expenses of the mandatary (including interest thereon from the day they were paid) (Article 688, paragraph 1). Even if the expenses turn out to be unnecessary, the mandator should reimburse the expenses so long as the mandatary reasonably believes that they were necessary. If a mandatary has assumed a debt necessary in the course of carrying out the mandated business, he/she may request the mandator to repay the debt on behalf of the mandatary, and, in case where the debt is not due, to furnish adequate security (*ibid.*, paragraph 2). If any expense is required for carrying out the mandated business, the mandator shall, upon demand by the mandatary, pay such expense in advance (Article 687). In addition, if a mandatary, without any negligence on his/her part, sustains a loss in the course of carrying out the mandated business, he/she may demand compensation therefor from the mandator (Article 688, paragraph 3).

*371.* The Civil Code contains some specific provisions on rescission of mandate which reflects the trust relationship between the parties. As a rule, either party may at any time rescind a mandate for the future (termination). However, if one of the parties terminates a mandate without any inevitable reasons when it would be unfavorable to the other party, the former shall compensate the latter for any damages occasioned by such rescission (Article 689). In this case, the ground for damages is concerned with the timing of rescission, not with termination itself. And a mandate shall terminate upon death or bankruptcy of either party. The same shall apply where the Family Court adjudicates on commencement of adult guardianship for the mandatary (Article 690).

On the other hand, if, upon termination of the mandate, the circumstances are of an urgent nature requiring the continuous management, the mandatary, his/her successor or his/her agent by law shall continue to manage the mandated affairs until the mandator, his/her successor, or his/her agent by law becomes in a position to take over management of the affairs. In this case, the continuous management after termination of mandate shall be deemed to have the same effect as the original mandate (Article 691). No termination of mandate may, whether the ground therefor exists on the part of the mandator or of the mandatary, be set up against the other party, unless the other party is given notice thereof or he/she is otherwise aware thereof (Article 692).

# Chapter 6. Lease and Loan

## §1. LEASE UNDER THE CIVIL CODE

### I. Introduction

*372.* Lease is of great significance in our everyday lives. A lease shall become effective when one of the parties (lessor) has promised to allow the other party (lessee) to use and take profits from a certain object, and the lessor has promised to pay the rent for it (Article 618). The object of a lease is, in general, the things including immovables.

Lease is a consensual contract which does not require any special form. Even in cases where the object leased belongs to the person other than the lessor, the contract of lease as an act of obligation is, in principle, valid. (Although there is no explicit provision such as Article 569 (*supra* paragraph 263), Article 619 premises the validity of such a lease.) In such a case, the lessee may not rescind the lease for the future on the ground of only that reason, and should pay the rent for duration of lease and return the benefit equivalent to the rent after termination of lease, until the property leased is returned or using of and taking profits from the property is prevented (The owner may exercise *rei vindicatio* and claim restitution against the lessor and/or the lessee).

*373.* Similar to other jurisdictions, sometimes the (security) deposit money is handed over to the lessor. This money shall, after all, be allocated to the unpaid rent and compensation for loss (It is at the lessor's disposal whether this money shall be allocated to any sum owed to the lessor, which becomes due before termination of lease), and if there is any surplus, the lessor shall return it to the lessee. According to the ruling of the Supreme Court, at the time when a lease terminates, the lessee's duty for *restitutio in integrum* and the lessor's duty to return the deposit money left should be performed concurrently (77Da1241,1242).

*374.* On the other hand, in case of the assignment or creation of the lease of commercial building, the premium is often handed over to the assigner or lessor. In contrast to the deposit money, the premium represents normally the commercial value for the assignment or creation of the lease including goodwill, and therefore is, in principle, not an object of restoration on termination of lease. The lessee who paid the premium shall, in principle, acquire merely a guaranty for duration of lease for a certain period (including the right to assign the lease or to sublease) and/or a claim for reimbursement of useful expenses. In this context, recently, the Commercial Building Lease Protection Act has been revised to guarantee possibility to recover the premium (*see infra* paragraph 390).

### II. Effects of Lease

*375.* The primary obligation of the lessor is to deliver the object to the lessee and to maintain conditions necessary for using of and taking profits from the leased object while the lease is in force (Article 623). As a result, the lessor must effect all necessary repairs therefor, even in cases where the lessee caused the condition to be repaired (in such a case, he/she shall be liable for the loss if it was due to his/her fault). If the lessor fails to do so, the lessee is entitled to claim damages or to rescind the lease for the future. In addition, the lessee may refuse to pay the rent to the extent that using of and taking profits from the object are restricted. However, in practice, it is not seldom that the lessee undertakes a task of maintenance at his/her own expense in accordance with the special agreement or custom.

In addition, the lessor must himself/herself refrain from disturbing use of the lessee and is liable for all the defects that hinder using of or taking profits from the object. Therefore, the lessor should recover possession of the object leased if a third person intruded thereupon. In this respect, the lessee is entitled to exercise those rights belonging to the lessor-owner to the disturbance (*see supra* paragraph 198). On the other hand, provisions on the seller's liability for warranty shall apply *mutatis mutandis* to the lease. As to the duty of the lessor to take necessary steps to protect the life and health of another person, *see supra* paragraph 257.

*376.* The lessee's primary obligation is to pay the agreed upon rent. As to the time to pay the rent, Article 633 provides for a payment in arrears as a rule; however, in practice, payment in advance is usual. In addition, in Korea, with regard to lease of immovables (especially buildings), a large amount of money is handed over to the lessor as a deposit money, and the interest thereon shall be allocated to the rent in whole or in part, which is a special form of "lease" concerning payment of the rent. On the basis of a rent claim, the lessee may acquire a pledge for accessories, fruits, etc., on leased land, a mortgage on building on leased land and a pledge for accessories attached to leased building, etc., all of which are recognized by law (Articles 648–650).

In cases of lease of a building or any other structure, if the amount of the rent in arrears reaches the rent for two terms, the lessor may rescind the contract for the future (Article 640). If the lessee assigns his/her rights with the consent of the lessor, in order to rescind the contract for the future, the new lessee's default of the rent should amount to the required sum.

On the other hand, if any part of a leased object is lost and thereby has become unusable or impossible to take profit therefrom due to any cause not attributable to the negligence of the lessee, the lessee may demand a reduction of the rent in proportion to the value of the lost part, and in cases where the remaining part of the object is not sufficient to enable the lessee to attain the objective of the lease, the lessee may rescind the contract for the future (Article 627).

It should be added that if the rent previously agreed upon by the parties has become unreasonable due to the increase or decrease of the public impost imposed upon the object leased or any other change in the economic situation, either party may demand of the other party to raise or reduce the rent for the future (Article 628). Since this Article is mandatory unilaterally for the lessee (Article 652), an agreement not to reduce the rent shall be void.

*377.* Duration of a lease is usually agreed upon between the parties. On the one hand, the Civil Code stipulated, at the beginning, that duration of a lease may not exceed twenty years in Article 651, paragraph 1. However, on account of the ruling of the Constitutional Court in 2013 which found this Article unconstitutional (2011HunBa234), this Article was deleted in 2016. On the other hand, the Civil Code contains no provision on the minimum term of lease (as to lease in special Acts, *see infra* paragraphs 385 and 390).

Article 619 provides for a short-term lease made by a person with limited capacity or with no authority to dispose of property. This term may be renewed pursuant to Article 620. In addition, Article 639 provides for an implicit renewal: "If the lessee continues to use the object leased or takes profits therefrom after expiration of the term of lease, and the lessor fails to raise any objection thereto within a reasonable period, it shall be deemed to have created a new lease on the same terms and conditions as those of the previous one. In this case, either party may give notice to the other party to rescind the lease for the future in accordance with provisions on the rescission of lease for the future without specified term."

On the other hand, in cases where no term for a lease has been specified, either party may give notice to the other party at any time to rescind the lease for the future. This rescission shall be effective upon expiration of periods which depend upon circumstances concerned (Article 635).

## III. The Right of Lessee

*378.* A lessee may assign his/her rights of lease or sublease the object leased with the consent (in substance: approval) of the lessor. If the lessee assigns or subleases without obtaining the consent of the lessor, the lessor may rescind the contract for the future (Article 629. This Article is not mandatory. On the other hand, to the successful bidder of the object leased, this Article shall apply, and therefore, in such a case the consent of the lessor is required too. 92Da24950). However, the Supreme Court ruled, based on the doctrine of bona fides, that the lessor may not rescind a lease for the future if assignment or sublease does not amount to a breach of faith (e.g., in a case where the lessee assigns, upon divorce, his rights to his ex-wife who lived with him until then. 92Da45308). In case of a legitimate assignment, the assignee becomes the new lessee, but the existing liabilities remain in principle with the assignor. In case of a legitimate sublease, the sub-lessee assumes the obligations (e.g., to pay the rent) directly to the lessor (Article 630). In this case, an advance payment of the rent to the sub-lessor may not be set up against the lessor (2006Da45459).

*379.* On the other hand, the lease has, in principle, effect only between the parties thereto and not against a third person (e.g., the person who acquired ownership of the leased object) (*supra* paragraph 177). However, similar to most other jurisdictions, *lex scripta* regarding the lease aims to protect especially the lessee of immovables. For instance, an increase of the rent is limited and duration of the lease is guaranteed for a certain period. Any agreement entered into by the parties in contravention of provisions aimed to protect the lessee which is unfavorable to either the lessee or sub-lessee shall be void (Article 652). Particularly in this context, the rule of "lease has priority over sale" shall be accepted under certain circumstances.

The lessee of an immovable may, unless there exists any agreement to the contrary between the parties, request the lessor to cooperate in effecting necessary formalities for the registration of the lease, and the lease, if registered, shall be effective against third persons from the time the registration has been effected (Article 621). In addition, in cases where the purpose of a lease of land is to own a building, if a building on such land has been registered by the lessee, the lease of land shall be effective against a third person even if such a lease of land has not been registered, but if a building has been destroyed or has become dilapidated from use prior to expiration of the term, it shall lose this effect (Article 622). In these cases, if the leased thing is sold, the original lessor shall be replaced by the seller (*see* also *supra* paragraph 40), and therefore, the new owner/lessor shall be liable to return the deposit money (of course, with the necessary deduction). For reference, under Article 3-4 of the Housing Lease Protection Act, the housing lessee may obtain the preferential repayment right (*see infra* paragraph 387).

## IV. Termination of Lease and Its Effects

*380.* Lease terminates by expiration of the term or rescission for the future with or without notice. As to the deposit money, *see supra* paragraph 373.

Upon termination of the lease, the lessee shall restore the object leased to its original condition (Articles 654 and 615. In this regard, the lessee is obliged to preserve the object with the care of a good manager until it is returned (Article 374), and shall be liable for any loss, unless he/she proves the absence of his/her intention or negligence. Article 390). According to the ruling of the Supreme Court, an agreement of the parties that maintenance shall be at the lessee's expenses should be construed that the duty to restore and the claim for reimbursement of necessary (not useful) expenses are waived simultaneously (2002Da38828).

On the other hand, upon termination of the lease, the lessee may remove any thing which he/she has annexed thereto. Under Article 256, the owner of an immovable acquires the ownership of anything affixed thereto, but this shall not affect the rights of another person who has attached such item as its accessory and retained the title thereto, and the right of the leasee constitutes such rights. (In cases where the object affixed can no longer be separated, the object becomes part of the main thing, and therefore, the lessee may not remove it, but can merely claim reimbursement of useful expenses.) In this respect, if the lessee of a building or any other structure has attached an article to such a building, etc., as its accessory with the consent of the lessor for the benefit of the lessee's use, the lessee may demand the lessor to purchase such accessories at the time when contract of lease terminates (Article 646). In such a case the lessee may exercise *exceptio non adimpleti contractus*. However, since this put-option of the lessee is a privilege for the faithful lessee, if the lease was terminated due to any cause attributable to the lessee, he/she may not exercise this option.

*381.* Under Article 626, the lessor is obliged to reimburse the expenses: (1) If a lessee has borne necessary expenses relating to the preservation of the object leased (e.g., to repair or to discharge burdens affecting the object), he/she may demand reimbursement thereof from the lessor. The reimbursement should be done upon demand (even before termination of the lease), and the lessee may exercise the right of retention over the object leased. (2) If the lessee has borne useful (beneficial) expenses relating to the object, the lessor shall reimburse the lessee, to the extent that the increase in value remains subsisting at the time when the lease terminates, (at the lessor's choice) the amount disbursed by the lessee or the amount by which the value of the object has been increased. In such a case, the court may, upon application of the lessor, allow him/her reasonable period for reimbursement. Except in case of the allowance of such period, the lessee may, upon termination of the lease, claim reimbursement and exercise the right of retention over the object. However, in cases where the lessee is obliged to restore, he/she may not claim reimbursement of useful expenses. On the other hand, the claim for reimbursement should be made within six months from the date of return of the object leased to the lessor (Articles 654, 617). In addition, the lessee may not resort to Article 203, which applies only to the reimbursement of expenses without any contractual ground (2001Da64752).

*382.* Article 643 (via Article 283) provides for the lessee's right to demand a renewal of the contract and to demand purchase of building, etc. In case where the objective of the lease of land is to own a building or any other structure, or is for planting, collecting salt and stock farming, if buildings, trees or any other facilities on land remains after expiration of the term of lease, the lessee may demand a renewal of the contract, and, if the lessor does not want to renew the contract, the lessee may demand of the lessor to purchase the structures or trees at a reasonable price. The Supreme Court held that in a case where a part of the building is on an adjoining land that is not leased, the lessee's put-option may be exercised only when the part which is on the land leased is capable of being owned as a separate property (93Da42634).

## §2. Lease under Special Acts

### I. Lease under the Commercial Code

*383.* Provisions on the financial lease business have been inserted into the Commercial Code in 2010. Article 168-2 of the this Code lays down that "A person who engages in the business of acquiring and borrowing machinery, facilities and other property ('article under financial lease') selected by a financial lessee from any third party ('supplier'), and then making financial lessees use such machinery, facilities and other property is called a financial lease business operator." However, this activity is a financing method rather than a lease in the proper sense. In this respect, Article 2, Number 10 of the Specialized Credit Finance Business Act states that: "Facilities leasing" means a financing method whereby goods provided for by the Presidential Decree, newly purchased or leased are leased to others for use for a certain period against payment therefor receivable periodically in installments. The disposal of the goods at the end of that period shall be decided by an agreement between the parties concerned.

## II. Housing Lease

*384.* The Housing Lease Protection Act was enacted in 1981. The purpose of this Act is to secure stability in the residential life of national citizens, by providing for exceptions to the Civil Code, with respect to the lease of buildings for residence (Article 1). With regard to the housing lease, some remarks should be made.

First, this Act shall apply to a lease of the whole or part of buildings for residence including cases where a part of a leased house is used for any purpose other than residence (Article 2).

*385.* Second, with respect to a lease whose duration (term) is not specified or is specified for less than two years, the duration of such lease shall be deemed to be two years. However, the lessee may assert that the duration specified for less than two years shall be valid. Even though the period for lease has expired, the lease shall be deemed to continue until a deposit money is repaid to the lessee (Article 4). On the other hand, if the lessor fails to notify the lessee of a refusal of renewal, or to give notification to the lessee to the effect that the lessor would not renew the contract without any change in the condition, six months to one month before the duration of lease expires, the lease shall be deemed to have been renewed under the same conditions as the former one at the time the duration expires. The same shall apply in cases where the lessee has not notified by one month before the duration of lease expires. In this case, the duration of the lease shall be deemed to be two years (although the lessee may notify at any time the lessor of termination of contract. Article 6-2, paragraph 1). However, with respect to a lessee who has failed to pay the rent up to two installments thereof, or who seriously violates obligations pursuant to the lease contract, the just mentioned shall not apply (Article 6).

*386.* Third, even if not registered, in cases where the lessee has completed the delivery of a house and the resident registration, the lease shall take effect against any third person from the following day thereof (Article 3, paragraph 1: opposing power or counterforce). In this case, the transferee (including any person who has succeeded to the right to lease) of a leased house shall be deemed to have succeeded to the status of the lessor (*ibid.*, paragraph 4). In addition, if no deposit money is refunded after termination of the lease, the lessee may file an application for a leasehold registration order with the court having jurisdiction over location of the leased house (Article 3-3, paragraph 1). If the lessee completes the registration of a leasehold following the execution of the leasehold registration order, he/she shall obtain the opposing power just mentioned and the preferential repayment right (*ibid.*, paragraph 5. This paragraph shall apply *mutatis mutandis* to the house lease registration pursuant to Article 621 of the Civil Code. Article 3-4, paragraph 1, the preceding Act).

*387.* Fourth, the recovery of deposit money shall be of great significance for most lessees. In this respect, any lessee who has met the requirements for opposing power just mentioned and obtained the fixed date on the lease contract document, shall be entitled to receive the repayment of the deposit money from the converted price of the leased house (including the site thereof), in preference to any junior obligees and other creditors, at the time of an official auction conducted under the Civil Execution Act and a public sale under the National Tax Collection Act (Article 3-2, paragraph 2. the Housing Lease Protection Act: preferential repayment right).

In addition, some lessees shall be entitled to receive a repayment to the extent of a specified amount of the deposit money in preference to the other persons holding the security rights in the leased house (including the creditor who has priority to the lessee). In such cases, the lessee shall comply with requirements for the opposing power before application for official auction of the house is registered (Article 8, paragraph 1). The extent and standard of a specified amount of the deposit money, and a lessee who is entitled to receive a preferential repayment shall be set forth by the Presidential Decree (Article 8, paragraphs 1 and 3).

*388.* Fifth, if the rent or deposit money agreed upon becomes unreasonable due to an increase or decrease of taxes, public dues and other charges on the leased house, or a change in economic circumstances, the party concerned may demand any increase or decrease thereof prospectively (Article 7, paragraph 1. No request for increase in the rent or deposit money shall exceed the amount equivalent to 1/20 of any agreed upon rent, etc., and no request for increase shall be made within one year after a lease contract is concluded or the agreed upon rent, etc., is increased. Article 8, the Enforcement Decree of the Housing Lease Act).

In addition, the preceding Act provides for succession of the right of lease (Article 9).

## III. Commercial Building Lease

*389.* The Commercial Building Lease Protection Act was enacted in 2002 to guarantee stability of the economic life of people by providing for exceptions to the Civil Code concerning the lease of commercial buildings (Article 1). This Act shall apply to the lease of commercial buildings. However, in cases where the amount of security deposit money exceeds that laid down by the Presidential Decree, this shall not apply (Article 2, paragraph 1. with some exceptions mainly regarding deposit money and premium).

In substance, this Act resembles the Housing Lease Protection Act; however, the former replaces the resident registration as a requirement of the opposing power with the business registration (Article 3).

*390.* On the other hand, Article 10 provides for the lessee's right to request a renewal of the contract. Where a lessee requests for a renewal of the contract between six months and one month before expiration of the duration of lease, a lessor shall not refuse it without justifiable grounds set forth by the Act (*ibid.*, paragraph 1. e.g., where the lessee has been in arrears with an amount equivalent to three periods of the rent or where he/she has subleased all or part of the leased building without obtaining the consent of the landlord). The grounds set forth by the Act are limitative as well as mandatory. Where a lessor has failed to notify a lessee of the denial to renew or of modification of terms and conditions within the period, the lease under the same terms and conditions as those of previous lease shall be deemed to have been made when such period expires. In such cases, the period during which such lease continues to exist shall be deemed to be one year (*ibid.*, paragraph 4). This right to request a renewal may be exercised within the extent that the whole period of the lease including the period of the initial lease does not exceed ten years (*ibid.*, paragraph 2).

In addition, Article 10-4 prohibits any act of the lessor, which impedes the possibility of the lessee to recover the premium by a means of an assignment of his/her status of the lessee to a third person (including the sublease), for six months before the expiration of the duration of lease, unless there are justifiable grounds to refuse a renewal of contract (e.g., where the proposed lessee is incapable of paying the deposit money or rent, or where he/she is likely not to fulfill terms of the lessee). In cases where the lessor violates this duty, the lessee may claim damages.

## IV. Farmland Lease

*391.* In the past, leasing of farmland was prohibited under Article 17 of the Farmland Reform Act (abolished), in compliance with the purpose of which farmland should be owned and used by a person who uses or will use it for his/her own agricultural management. However, at present under Article 23 of the Farmland Act, farmland may be leased or borrowed gratuitously under some restricted circumstances (e.g., if leased or borrowed gratuitously by a person who has not been engaged temporarily in agricultural management on grounds of disease, conscription, school attendance, taking public office by election or other inevitable reasons set forth by the Presidential Decree).

Each contract of lease or of gratuitous borrowing (limited to those intending to be engaged in agricultural management) shall in principle be entered into in writing (Article 24, paragraph 1). Each contract of lease shall, despite the nonexistence of its registration, begin to take effect in relation to a third person from the date following the date on which the lessee obtains the confirmation from the head of a local government having jurisdiction over the seat of farmland and takes delivery of the farmland (*ibid.*, paragraph 2). On the other hand, a transferee of the leased farmland shall be deemed to be succeeded to the legal status of the lessor of the farmland pursuant to this Act (Article 26).

The duration of the lease shall in principle be for at least three years (Article 24-2, paragraph 1), and when the duration of the lease is not specified or is shorter than three years, the lease shall be deemed to be agreed to remain valid for three years (*ibid.*, paragraph 2). Where the lessor fails to give the lessee a notice of his/her intention that he/she will not renew the lease or will change terms and conditions of the lease by no later than three months before the lease ends, the lease shall be deemed to be renewed under the same terms and conditions as the previous one at the time the validity of lease has been terminated (Article 25). On the other hand, in cases where the contracting parties to a lease fails to reach a mutual agreement on the lease contract in terms of the duration of lease, rents, etc., they may apply for mediation to the head of a local government having jurisdiction over the seat of farmland (Article 24-3, paragraph 1).

Any contract in contravention of this Act and to the disadvantage of the lessee shall be nullified (Article 26-2).

## §3. Loan for Use

*392.* In contrast to leases, a loan for use is a gratuitous contract. A loan for use becomes effective when one of the parties (lender) promises to deliver an object to the other party (borrower) for his/her gratuitous using thereof and taking profits therefrom, and the borrower promises to return such object after having used thereof and taken profits therefrom (Article 609).

## §4. Loan for Consumption

*393.* A loan for consumption becomes effective when one of the parties (borrower) promises to transfer the ownership of money or any other substitute to the other party (lender), and the lender promises to return the same amount of money or the same in kind, quality and quantity of any substitute therefor (Article 598). In contrast to leases or loans for use, the borrower receives money or other substitute for his/her use and consumption. Loan for consumption is a consensual contract that does not require money or other substitute to be delivered (*supra* paragraph 31).

Regarding cases where the object of loan is defective, Article 602 provides for the lender's liability for warranty.

*394.* The payment of interest is not a constitutive element for loans for consumption. However, a loan for consumption bearing interest is normal and usual in practice (a synallagmatic contract). In this case, the interest rate may be agreed upon by the parties, and, in the absence of such agreement and relevant Acts, shall be 5% per annum (Article 379). On the other hand, when a merchant has loaned money to another person in respect of his/her business, the merchant may request for the payment of statutory interest thereon, and if a merchant has made substituted donation for another person within the scope of his/her business, the merchant may request for statutory interest thereon from the date of the substituted donation (Article 55, the Commercial Code). The statutory interest rate on obligations arising out of commercial activities shall be 6% per annum (Article 54, the preceding Code). If an order (including judgment) to perform a monetary debt is adjudicated, a special statutory rate constituting standards for computing the amount of indemnification for damages resulting from the default of monetary debt within the extent of 40/100 per year (for the present: 15% per annum) of interest applies from the date next to the day a written complaint or a document corresponding thereto was served on the obligor. However, where it is deemed to be reasonable for an obligor to contest whether he/she is responsible for performance of obligations or the extent thereof not later than a ruling that the obligor is responsible for performance of such obligations at a fact-finding proceeding is adjudicated, the statutory rate just mentioned shall not apply to the reasonable extent (Article 3, the Act on Special Cases concerning Expedition, etc., of Legal Proceedings).

The interest rate agreed upon by the parties should not exceed the limit set forth by the Interest Limitation Act. (On the other hand, the Supreme Court found that the excessively high rate of interest may be void under Article 103. 2004Da50426) In this context, it is necessary as well as useful to introduce the Interest Limitation Act. The purpose of this Act is to realize economic justice by prescribing appropriate limits to interest rates (Article 1). This Act regulates interest by way of the maximum interest rate control: the maximum interest rate pursuant to a loan contract shall be stipulated by the Presidential Decree within the extent that does not exceed 25% per annum (Article 2, paragraph 1, for the present: 24% per annum), and any amount exceeding the maximum interest rate just mentioned as the interest rate set forth by the contract shall be void (*ibid.*, paragraph 3). If an obligor has arbitrarily paid interest exceeding the maximum interest rate, the amount overpaid shall be allocated to the payment of the principal and the obligor may request for the refund thereof, if no principal remains outstanding (*ibid.*, paragraph 4). In addition, Article 8 of the Act on Registration of Credit Business, etc., and Protection of Finance Users regulates the interest rates of credit service providers.

*395.* In cases where no time for the return of an object borrowed has been agreed upon by the parties, the lender may demand a return of the object specifying a reasonable period, by contrast the borrower may return the object borrowed at any time (Article 603, paragraph 2). On the other hand, either party to a (prospective) loan for consumption bearing no interest may rescind the contract at any time before the object thereof has been delivered to the borrower, and, if damages have been caused to the other party due to the rescission of a contract, the rescinding party shall be liable to compensate for such damages (Article 601).

*396.* In order to protect the borrower, the Civil Code prohibits some agreements. At first, in the case of pecuniary loans, if the borrower accepts delivery of negotiable instruments or any other thing in lieu of the agreed sum of money, the amount of the loan shall be the current price of the object at the time of such delivery to the borrower (not the agreed repayment amount. Article 606). Second, if the borrower has promised to transfer any of his/her property right in lieu of the borrowed object, the value of the substituted property at the time of the promise shall not exceed the aggregate of the original amount borrowed plus the interest thereon (Article 607). This Article shall apply only in the case where (1) the obligation arises from a loan for consumption or quasi-loan for consumption, (2) the agreement was made prior to due date, and (3) the value of the substitute at the time of the promise exceeds the amount of the principal and interest thereon. As to the cases where the substitute is immovables, *see supra* paragraph 223.

Any agreement which is in violation of these provisions and is prejudicial to the borrower is not valid even if claimed as a redemption or as any other legal remedy (Article 608). This Article is regarded as a form of concretization of Article 104 (*supra* paragraph 123). However, in cases where the substitute is immovables, since the promise to return by substitute is usually combined with the provisional registration and compromise before instituting a lawsuit (Articles 385 ff. the Civil Procedure Act), and such a compromise has res judicata, in spite of Article 608, the obligee may acquire ownership of the substitute. In this context, the Supreme Court construes the promise to return by substitute as a security contract and has held that the obligee should return the surplus to the obligor (81Da254). Furthermore, with regard to the return of any borrowed object, the Provisional Registration Security Act was enacted.

## Chapter 7. Compromise

*397.* A compromise (settlement) shall become effective when the parties to a dispute have agreed to terminate a dispute through reciprocal concessions (Article 731). The dispute as a subject of comprise may be a dispute in the field of the property law or the law of inheritance, but not one under the family law, because legal relationship in this field is not at the free disposal of the parties. The dispute (e.g., regarding the existence or the amount of the obligation) may be concerned with the existing uncertainties as well as with the future uncertainties.

The primary effect of compromise is self-binding of the parties with regard to the dispute, and in this sense, the contract has a dispositive effect. The parties leave the old situation aside and create a new situation, which will be sustained even if it would later appear that the assumed situation does not correspond to the situation which really existed. In this respect, a contract of compromise shall have the effect that the rights conceded by one of the parties is thereby extinguished, and the other party will, in turn, acquire the pertinent rights by the virtue of the compromise (Article 732). This Article is not mandatory.

*398.* As just mentioned, the parties have taken the risk that the real situation may differ from the assumed situation. As a result, a contract of compromise may, in principle, not be voided on the ground of a mistake. However, this shall not be the case where such a mistake is concerned with the matters relating to the qualification of either party of a compromise or any matters other than those which are pertinent to the dispute subject to the compromise (Article 733. By contrast, a contract of compromise may be voided on the ground of fraud or duress). The second instance of exceptions means matters which were not objects of reciprocal concessions by the parties when the dispute was settled.

In this regard, there is a controversy about to the extent of which an unexpected aftereffect may affect the effect of the contract of compromise in which especially the parties to an accident have agreed to waive the claim for damages for the future. The Supreme Court is in part of the opinion that a contract of comprise may be voided on the ground of a mistake (71Da399), and takes in part the view that the unexpected aftereffect was not objects of reciprocal concessions when the contract was made, and therefore, the damages which are beyond the amount expected by the aggrieved party when the dispute was settled are not covered by the contract of compromise (97Da423).

*399.* It is worth mentioning that when a compromise is entered in the protocol of pleadings or that of the preparatory date for pleadings, such protocol shall have the same effect as a final and conclusive judgment (Article 220, the Civil Procedure Act). In this respect, as for a civil dispute, a party may file a motion for compromise with the district court in the place where the general forum of the other party is located, by specifying the gist and counts of a motion and the situations of the dispute (Article 385, paragraph 1, the preceding Act: compromise before instituting a lawsuit).

# Chapter 8. Suretyship

## §1. Introduction

*400.* The suretyship constitutes a personal security and plays an important role in the credit system. However, in contrast to, e.g., BGB, which provides for a suretyship as one of named contracts (sections 765 ff.), the Civil Code lays down suretyship as a kind of obligations with multiple parties (i.e., as guarantee obligation). Therefore, this chapter begins with claims/obligations with multiple parties and deals with the suretyship thereafter.

## §2. Claims/Obligations with Multiple Parties

*401.* Under the Civil Code, besides suretyship, there are three types of claim/obligation with multiple parties: divisible claim/obligation, indivisible claim/obligation, and joint and several obligation.

*402.* As a rule, in cases where there are more than one obligee or obligor, each obligee or obligor shall, in the absence of any agreement to the contrary, have rights or assume duties in equal proportions (Article 408).

This rule of divisible obligation reflects the ideological basis of the Civil Code, i.e., liberalism as well as individualism; however, it may be contrary to the interests and expectations of the parties, and the Korean conventional practice. Especially, the obligee should bear the risk of insolvency on the part of obligors, because any of the obligors who performed his/her proportion of the obligation shall be discharged, regardless of whether the remaining obligors perform their proportion. Therefore, it is generally accepted to limit the applicability of this rule. For instance, if the obligors' joint property status was taken into account at the time when the contract was made, an obligation arising therefrom is presumed as a joint and several obligation. In addition, Article 57, paragraph 1 of the Commercial Code lays down that "If more than two persons assume obligations arising out of transactions that are commercial activities in respect of one or all of them, they shall be jointly and severally liable for the obligations."

*403.* The second type is indivisible obligations. In cases where the subject of a claim is indivisible by its nature or owing to the declarations of intention of the parties involved and there are more than one obligee, each obligee may demand performance for the benefit of all the obligees, and the relevant obligor may effect performance to any one of the obligees for the benefit of all the obligees (Article 409). In this case, each obligee may demand performance in whole against any or all of the obligors. Among the obligees, an act done by or any fact concerning any one of the obligees shall have no effect upon the other obligees, except the fact which has an effect upon all the obligees, such as performance or demand therefor (Article 410, paragraph 1). Where a novation or a release has been effected between one indivisible obligee and the obligor, other indivisible obligees who have received performance in whole must reimburse the obligor that which would have been allocated to such obligee if he/she had not lost his/her right (*ibid.*, paragraph 2).

*404.* The third type of obligation with multiple obligors is a joint and several obligation. If each of the several obligors shall be responsible for performance in whole and performance by one of the obligors discharges the other's obligation, the obligation shall be a joint and several obligation (Article 413). In this case, the obligee may demand performance of obligation in whole or in part, against any or all of the joint and several obligors, simultaneously or successively (Article 414).

In case of joint and several obligations, claims against each obligor are independent and do not influence each other. In other words, any fact relating to one of the obligors shall not be effective on the other obligor(s) (Article 423: the principle of relative effect). However, in spite of this principle, there are broad exceptions: demand for performance, novation, setoff, release, merger, completion of extinctive prescription and *mora creditoris* with respect to one of the obligors shall affect other obligors in whole or in part (Articles 416–422). As a result, a joint and several obligation under the Civil Code is less advantageous to the obligee than under e.g., BGB. Therefore, to strengthen the position of the obligee, scholarly opinions have introduced the concept of "untrue" joint and several obligations in which any fact which arises with respect to one of the obligors, except performance and its equivalent, does not affect other obligors, which the Supreme Court approved (*see* 98Da5777).

*405.* In cases where one joint and several obligor has acquired any common discharge by performance of the obligation or otherwise at his/her own expense, he/she shall be entitled to obtain reimbursement from other joint and several obligor(s) to the extent of the respective portion of the obligations which is borne by each of other obligors. The amount of reimbursement shall include the compensation of the legal interest from the day of discharge, any unavoidable expenses and other damages (Article 425). On the other hand, notices before and after common discharge by performance or its equivalent are a requirement for reimbursement (Article 426). In addition, in a case where one joint and several obligor is insolvent, the part which he/she is unable to pay shall be borne by the person demanding reimbursement and other solvent obligor(s) in proportion to their respective portion (Article 427). The joint and several obligor who may demand reimbursement shall be subrogated to the rights of the obligee (Article 482, paragraph 1, *supra* paragraph 218).

## §3. Suretyship

### I. Introduction

*406.* A surety (guarantor) promises against the obligee to perform the obligation of a third person (principal obligor) in the event of a failure in performance of the latter, and therefore is liable to perform the obligation upon which the principal obligor has defaulted (Article 428, paragraph 1). Suretyship arises usually from a contract between the obligee and the surety, regardless of the consent or knowledge of the principal obligor, although in practice a tripartite contract between obligee, (principal) obligor and surety is not rare. The suretyship can be entered into for future obligations of the principal obligor, to the extent that they are sufficiently determinable.

*407.* The Civil Code did not require a contract of suretyship to be in writing at the beginning. However, as a result of the revision in 2015 (Enforcement date: February 4, 2016), which adopts relevant provisions of the Special Act on the Protection of Guarantors, a suretyship takes effect only where the intention to provide it is indicated in writing, affixing the surety's name and seal thereon or signed by the surety (Article 428-2, paragraph 1). This provision aims to protect the surety against making hasty promises and to clarify the existence and/or scope of liability. (In this regard, it should be added that in a case where the intention to provide a suretyship is indicated in an electronic form, the surety is not valid pursuant to proviso to *ibid.*; however, Article 4, paragraph 2 of the Framework Act on Electronic Documents and Transactions makes exception thereto, stating that "An electronic document showing the intent of guaranty which has been drawn up by the guarantor for the purpose of his/her business or project shall, notwithstanding the proviso toArticle 428-2 (1) of the Civil Code, be deemed a document under the main sentence of the same paragraph.") This shall also apply if a surety obligation is changed disadvantageously to the surety (Article 428-2, paragraph 2). However, a surety who has already fulfilled his/her surety obligation may not assert the invalidation of the suretyship to the extent of such fulfillment due to any defect in the methods just mentioned (*ibid.*, paragraph 3). (Provisions on the formal requirements have another implication for proof. *See supra* paragraph 72) In addition, in case of a suretyship provided for a multiple undetermined obligations (floating suretyship. *See infra* paragraphs 416 f.), the upper limit of the amount of obligations for which the suretyship is provided shall be specified in writing (Article 428-3, paragraph 1). In such a case, a suretyship agreement becomes void, unless the upper limit of the amount of obligations is specified in writing (*ibid.*, paragraph 2).

*408.* On the other hand, the suretyship is, in essence, a legal means for satisfaction of the obligee's claim, and the interest of the obligee conflicts usually with that of the surety. However, since a surety, especially so-called goodwill surety, enters usually into a contract of suretyship, without prudent consideration of the effect thereof, a need to protect him/her should be taken into account *de lege lata* and *de lege ferenda*. In this regard, Article 436-2, inserted in 2015, lays down the obligee's duty to provide certain information and to give written notice. Where an obligee has or is aware of, at the time of concluding a suretyship agreement, any credit information concerning the principal obligor's obligations which may affect decision on whether to conclude a suretyship agreement or any terms and conditions thereof, the obligee shall notify the surety of such credit information. The same shall also apply where a suretyship agreement is renewed (*ibid.*, paragraph 1). Every obligee shall give written notice to the surety upon occurrence of some events (e.g., where the principal obligor fails to pay to the principal, interest, etc., incidental to the principal obligation for at least three months or where the obligee becomes aware that a significant change has been made to the credit information concerning the principal obligor's obligations) after concluding a suretyship agreement (*ibid.*, paragraph 2). Where an obligee inflicts losses on the surety on account of a violation of any of duties of the obligee above mentioned, the court may grant reduction of or exemption from the surety obligations, depending on the details, degree, etc., of the relevant violation (*ibid.*, paragraph 4).

## II. Legal Nature of the Suretyship

*409.* At first, a contract of suretyship is a contract which should be distinguished from the contract from which principal obligations arise. Therefore, a surety may stipulate in advance the amount of penalty or damages with regard to his/her own surety obligation (Article 429, paragraph 2).

*410.* Second, nevertheless, a contract of suretyship is accessory to a contract between the obligee and the principal obligor. In other words, the suretyship is dependent upon the contract from which principal obligations arise. As a result, in a case where the principal obligation is extinguished, the suretyship extinguishes as well, which is referred to as "appendant nature." In addition, if burden of a surety is more onerous than that of the principal obligor as to either its subject or its terms, it shall be reduced to the extent of the principal obligation (Article 430). On the other hand, a surety may avail himself/herself of any defense against the obligee which the principal obligor has against the obligee (Article 433, paragraph 1), and, what is more, may avail himself/herself of any claim which the principal obligor has against the obligee as a setoff against the latter (Article 434). Besides, so far as the principal obligor has against the obligee the right of avoidance, rescission, or rescission for the future, the surety may refuse to perform obligations against the obligee (Article 435), which aims to protect the surety in situations which otherwise might lead to unreasonable results.

On the other hand, in a case where the principal obligation is assigned by the obligee, the suretyship shall be accompanied, and an interruption of prescription against the principal obligor shall also be effective as against the surety (Article 440).

*411.* Third, in a case where an obligee has demanded performance of the obligation from the surety, the surety may, upon proving that the principal obligor has sufficient means to effect performance and that the execution on the property of the principal obligor would be easily performed, enter a plea as a defense that the obligee must demand performance of the principal obligor first (defense of demand/peremptory notice) and that he/she must first levy execution on the property of the principal obligor (defense of reference/inquiry) (Article 437). In spite of legitimate pleading of such defense, if the obligee has, owing to his/her laches, been unable to obtain partial or full performance from the principal obligor, the surety shall be relieved of the liability to the extent that the obligee would have received performance, if he/she had not been negligent (Article 438).

This defense of demand and reference is derived from the subsidiary/supplementary nature of suretyship. Owing to the disadvantage of this defense from the viewpoint of the obligee, the joint and several suretyship is more usual type than an ordinary suretyship, because this defense is not allowed when the surety has assumed an obligation jointly and severally liable with the principal obligor.

## III. Scope of Surety Obligation

*412.* The surety obligation shall include interest, penalty, and compensation of damages with regard to the principal obligation, and all the other charges incidental to such obligation (Article 429, paragraph 1). In cases where the contract between the principal obligor and the obligee is rescinded, the suretyship secures the obligor's duty to recover the *status quo ante*.

## IV. Right to Demand Reimbursement

*413.* In cases where a surety has performed the obligation or has otherwise procured the discharge of the principal obligor at the former's own expense, the principal obligor shall be liable to reimburse the surety. As requirement for reimbursement, a surety should notify the principal obligor before and after performance or procurement. If the surety fails to do so, the reimbursement shall be restricted (Article 445). In addition, a surety shall be by operation of law subrogated to the rights of the obligee by effecting performance (Article 481). As to subrogation, *see supra* paragraphs 216 ff.

*414.* The scope and method of reimbursement depend upon the existence of request and/or the will of the principal obligor.

At first, in case of a surety at the request of the principal obligor (referred to as "entrusted surety"), the right to demand reimbursement shall include compensation of the legal interest from the day of discharge, any unavoidable expenses and other damages (Articles 441 and 425). Under certain circumstances (e.g., where a surety has, without his/her negligence, had a judgment ordering him/her to perform the obligation to the obligee, where five years have elapsed after conclusion of the contract of suretyship, or where the time for performance of the obligation is uncertain and even its maximum duration is unascertainable), an entrusted surety may exercise in advance his/her right to demand reimbursement against the principal obligor (Article 442). In such a case, the principal obligor may demand the surety to obtain the discharge of the principal obligor or to provide security (Article 443). In addition, in cases where the principal obligor has not notified the entrusted surety that the principal obligor has obtained a discharge by his/her own act, and the surety has in good faith effected performance to the obligee or otherwise has procured a discharge for value, the surety may treat his/her act of discharge as effective (Article 446). In a case where both the principal obligor and the surety have effected performance without notice, the Supreme Court found that the right to demand reimbursement shall arise from the performance which precedes (95Da46265. In such a case, the later performance should be returned from the obligee.)

*415.* On the other hand, the principal obligor is liable to reimburse the surety without request of the principal obligor to the extent that he/she was enriched at the time of discharge (Article 444, paragraph 1), and in case of a surety against the will of the principal obligor, the scope of reimbursement is restricted to the extent that the principal obligor is still being enriched (*ibid.*, paragraph 2: equivalent to the scope of the restitution in bad faith under Article 748, paragraph 2. *See infra* paragraph 452). In addition, the duty of notice of the principal obligor should not apply to the not entrusted surety.

## V. Floating Suretyship

*416.* In practice, the floating/continuing suretyship is not rare. In a continuing relationship (e.g., between a wholesaler and a manufacturer or between a bank and an obligor), it is necessary to secure unspecified obligations, the amount of which varies. In contrast to the floating sum mortgage (Article 357. although with only one Article), there was no provision on this kind of suretyship in the Civil Code at the beginning, and the judge-made law has been developed. Since such a suretyship may be too severe on the surety, in cases where important changes occur in circumstances which form the basis of contract (e.g., when the principal obligor's property status rapidly deteriorates, or a director of a company who stood surety for the company resigned his/her position as director), the surety may rescind the contract of suretyship for the future and be released from the "further" (not existing) obligation. In addition, in assessing the amount of the surety obligation, the court may take into account the contribution of the obligee as to expansion of the principal obligation and other relevant circumstances, which include the duty to notify a significant worsening of the obligor's property status. This case-law is inserted into the Civil Code (through the Revision in 2015). For instance, the Civil Code provides for the floating surety (Article 428-3. although only concerning the upper limit of the amount for the suretyship) and the obligee's duty to notify (Article 436-2), which is not confined to a floating surety.

*417.* On the other hand, it is not seldom for Korean companies to require a surety when employing an individual. With regard to the contract for fidelity guarantee, i.e., the contract agreeing to bear liability for compensation for relevant damage in cases where an employee inflicts loss on his/her employer due to any cause attributable to the former in the course of performing his/her duties, the Fidelity Guarantee Act was enacted in 1957, which was totally revised in 2002. This Act provides for duration of the contract (Article 3), the employer's duty to notify (Article 4), the guarantor's right to rescind the contract (Article 5), and responsibility of the fidelity guarantor (Article 6).

# Chapter 9. Real Securities over Movables

## §1. Introduction to Real Securities

*418.* The purpose of security rights (including suretyship) is to provide security for the obligee in the event that the obligor does not fulfill his/her obligations voluntarily.

Real securities are provided for in Part Two of the Civil Code, and there are three types of real securities: right of retention, pledge, and mortgage (hypothec). Various statutes, for instance, the Factory and Mining Assets Mortgage Act, the Act on Mortgage on Motor Vehicles and other Specific Movables and the Standing Timber Act, also provide for real securities. In addition, there are atypical real securities which have been developed in practice and approved by the court. These atypical securities include proprietary security ("transfer mortgage") and retention of title. In order to regulate these securities, some special statutes, e.g., the Provisional Registration Security Act and the Act on Security over Movable Property, Claims, etc., are enacted.

The Civil Code does not provide for a preferential right (i.e., statutory lien) as real security. However, for instance, Article 38, paragraph 2 of the Labor Standards Act lays down that claims for the wages of the last three months and worker's accident compensations shall be paid in preference to any claim secured by pledges, mortgages or the security rights pursuant to the Act on Security over Movable Property, Claims, etc. (including claim for taxes or public charges) on the whole property of the employer (*see* also *supra* paragraph 188).

*419.* In Korea, the most common and important security right is a mortgage. A mortgagee is entitled to obtain satisfaction of his/her claim prior to other obligees out of the immovable(s), which has been furnished as security by the obligor or a third person without transferring its possession (Article 356). Since a mortgage may be created as a rule over immovables, let's skip this topic. However, it should be mentioned, in this regard, that the Civil Code does not provide for a type of security, such as *Grundschuld* of BGB. which is not dependent on the existence of the claim secured, and therefore, if the claim secured becomes extinct by prescription or by any other reason, the mortgage shall also lapse with it (appendant nature. Article 369). In addition, any person having *chonsegwon* (right of registered lease on deposit money base, which is unique to Korean law) is also entitled to obtain the repayment of deposit money in preference to persons having the junior right or other obligees, with respect to the whole real property (Article 303, paragraph 1).

*420.* As to the right of retention. If a possessor of a thing or securities belonging to another person has any claim which has been arisen in respect of such thing or securities, and if payment of the claim has become due, the possessor may retain possession of the thing or securities until the claim is satisfied (Article 320, paragraph 1). The object of retention need not be a movable.

The requirement of "in respect of" is of great importance in practice, especially in the interests of the owner of the object, because the holder of such right may retain possession of the thing even if its owner is one other than the obligor. According to the ruling of the Supreme Court, this requirement is complied with in case of a claim in direct connection with the object itself (e.g., claim for reimbursement of useful expenses) and a claim for damages on account of the very object (*see* 2005Da16942). By contrast, this requirement does not matter concerning mercantile liens provided for by the Commercial Code, as the object of retention should belong to the obligor. (Article 58 of this Code states that "If a claim which has arisen from a commercial activity between merchants has become due, the obligee may, until he/she obtains performance thereof, retain things or securities belonging to the obligor which have come into the possession of the obligee through a commercial activity with the obligor, unless there is any specific agreement between the parties.")

The right of retention shall not be extinguished by the official auction (civil execution), and a successful bidder shall be responsible for reimbursing to the holder of such right the claims that are secured by such right (Article 91, paragraph 5, the Civil Execution Act). In this context, the person having a right of retention is granted a de facto preferential authority.

## §2. Pledge of Movables

*421.* In contrast to the right of retention, pledge (as well as mortgage) is, in principle, created by agreement between the parties. A pledgee of movables is entitled to hold possession of the movables which he/she has received from the obligor or a third person as security for the claim, and to obtain satisfaction of pledgee's claim out of the movables prior to other creditors (Article 329). In order to establish the right of pledge, the pledger should have the right to dispose of the object of the pledge. However, provisions on a bona fide acquisition (Articles 249 ff.) shall apply *mutatis mutandis* in case of the pledge of movables.

On the other hand, the Civil Code provides for pledge recognized by law to secure claims based on the lease of land or building etc. (Articles 648 and 650. *supra* paragraph 376).

*422.* Unless otherwise set forth in an agreement, a pledge shall secure the principal, interest, penalty, expenses to exercise the pledge, expenses to preserve the pledged article and the losses arising from a failure to perform an obligation secured or from latent defects in the pledged article (Article 334). A pledgee may retain the pledged article until he/she obtains satisfaction of his/her claim, unless there is any obligee who has priority to the pledgee (Article 335), and may sell the pledged article by official auction to obtain satisfaction of his/her claim (Article 338, paragraph 1). In addition, a pledgee may request from the court immediate allocation of the pledged article to the satisfaction of the debt in accordance with the evaluation of an appraiser, if there is a justifiable reason for doing so. In such a case, the pledgee must notify the obligor and the pledger of the request in advance (*ibid.*, paragraph 2). In this case, if the value of the pledged article exceeds the amount of the debt above mentioned, the pledgee must pay the balance (difference) to the pledger. On the other hand, a pledgee may obtain satisfaction of his/her claim out of other property of the obligor only in respect to the portion which has not been satisfied out of the pledged article (Article 340, paragraph 1). A pledge may also be exercised against money or other things which the pledger is entitled to receive by reason of the loss of or damage to the pledged article. In such case, an attachment should be levied thereon prior to their payment or delivery of the money or other things (Article 342).

On the other hand, a pledger may, by a contract made prior to the due date for performance (including an act to create pledge), not allow nor promise to allow the pledgee, by means of satisfaction of his/her claim, to acquire the ownership of the pledged article or to dispose of it otherwise than in the manner provided for by law (Article 339), which is to prevent the pledgee from obtaining excessive profit from the pledged article. However, this Article shall not apply to security pledges established for the purpose of collateral for claims arising out of commercial activities (Article 59, the Commercial Code). Therefore, the so-called forfeited pledge is not prohibited in commercial transactions.

In a case where a person, who has pledged his/her own property to secure a debt of another, discharges the debt or loses the ownership of the pledged article in consequence of exercise of the pledge, the former is entitled to be indemnified by the obligor pursuant to provisions on surety obligations (Article 341).

*423.* In contrast to mortgage, a pledge of movables shall become effective upon delivery of the object of pledge to the obligee (Article 330), and a pledgee may not allow the pledger to possess the pledged article on the behalf of the pledgee (Article 332). Since possession of the property is transferred to the pledgee, the pledger cannot use the pledged article, and the pledgee should keep the pledged article with the care of a good manager (cf. Article 374). In addition, the procedure to exercise the pledge is inconvenient and often disproportionately costly. In this context, a pledge is usually not a desirable form of real securities, and therefore in practice, atypical real securities, especially proprietary securities, have been developed, and this practice has been approved as well as regulated by the court. Furthermore, to remove the risk and such inconvenience and to facilitate the borrowing of funds and safety, the Act on Security over Movable property, Claims, etc. recognizes "security interest in movable property" (*see infra* paragraph 428). This security interest is, in substance, mortgage over movables.

## §3. Pledge of Rights

*424.* Pledges are confined to the object other than registered property, and the usual object of pledge is a movable. However, a pledge may be created over a property right; but, the right to use and take profits from the immovable may not be the object of a pledge (Article 345). (In addition, *lex scripta* provides for various types of pledge. E.g., pledge of intellectual property rights, Article 121 of the Patent Act, Article 62 of the Trademark Act, Article 47 of the Copyright Act; pledge of registered shares, Articles 338–340 of the Commercial Code).

*425.* Unless otherwise set forth by law, a pledge of rights shall be created in accordance with the method regarding the transfer of such rights (Article 346). In a case where a nominative claim has been made the object of a pledge, the creation of pledge may not be set up against third persons including the original obligor, unless notice thereof has been given to the original obligor, or the original obligor has given his/her consent thereto under Article 450 (Article 349. *See* also *supra* paragraph 186). In this regard, a notice (in practice, the consent hardly matters) as requirement for setting up the pledge over a nominative claim against a third person should be put in writing with a certified fixed date (Article 450, paragraph 2), and it is bothersome to the pledgee.

Therefore, an atypical real security over property right, i.e., proprietary security, has been developed in practice and endorsed by the court. In addition, to remove the risk and such inconvenience, the Act on Security over Movable property, Claims, etc. (*see* also *infra* paragraph 428) recognizes "security interest in a claim," i.e., a registered security interest in a nominative claim (including more than two claims or a prospective claim) for the payment of money pursuant to a security agreement. Under Article 35 of the preceding Act, any acquisition, loss or alteration of a security interest in a claim by an agreement shall be a valid defense against a third party other than the obligor of a nominative obligation ("third-party obligor"), only when the acquisition, loss or alteration is registered in the collateral security register (*ibid.*, paragraph 1). A secured party or a person who has created a security interest (referring to an assigner or assignee, if a security interest in a claim is assigned) shall not have a valid defense against a third-party obligor, unless he/she notifies the third-party obligor of the registration by delivering the certificate of registration, or the third-party obligor accepts it (*ibid.*, paragraph 2. *See* also *supra* paragraph 188).

## §4. Atypical Real Securities over Movables and the Act on Security over Movable Property, Claims, Etc.

*426.* As mentioned above, the pledger shall be deprived of possession of the collateral and thereby cannot use and take the profit from the pledged property, in contrast to the mortgagor who continues to use and take the profit from the mortgaged property. On the other hand, a pledgee shall be bound to preserve the pledged article with the care of a good manager (cf. Article 374). In this sense, a pledge is impractical especially for commercial transactions. In order to remove such an inconvenience, the need for mortgage over a movable or group of movables has increased. However, movables may, in principle, not be object of mortgage, because a mortgage over movables cannot be publicized by means of registration.

In this context, in order to remove demerit of the pledge over movables and at the same time to meet requirement of publicity, some Acts, e.g., the Factory and Mining Assets Mortgage Act, the Act on Mortgage on Motor Vehicles and other Specific Movables, have been enacted.

*427.* On the other hand, atypical real security rights over movables have been developed in practice and endorsed by the court. For instance, the obligor sells an article to the obligee, who promises to allow the obligor to repurchase the article sold, once he/she repays the debt. (In addition, the parties usually agree that in case of a failure to perform, the obligee may, for satisfaction of his/her claim, demand delivery of the article (before the failure to perform, the seller is usually entitled to possess, as well as to use and take the profit from the article pursuant to the agreement creating atypical real security rights), or sell the article and collect his/her claim from the proceeds therefrom. In this case Article 339 shall not apply).

However, this type of atypical securities also have shortcomings. At first, since the obligee is legally an owner in spite of the transfer of ownership merely for the purpose to secure a debt, there is a risk of abuse of the ownership, if value of the property is much higher than the amounts of debt. The Supreme Court ruled that the difference between the amount of debt and price of the property should be returned to the obligor (96Da31116. *See* also Arts 607 and 608), but it is insufficient to protect the obligor in that he/she shall obtain claim for restitution instead of real property lost. (For reference, with regard to the atypical real securities over immovables, the Provisional Registration Security Act has been enacted to protect the obligee.) Second, the obligor cannot establish the second security.

*428.* In this context, the Act on Security over Movable Property, Claims, etc. has been enacted in 2010. The purpose of this Act is to facilitate the borrowing of funds and safety in financial transactions by providing for matters regarding security interest in movable property, obligations and intellectual property rights, and registration or record thereof (Article 1). Pursuant to this Act, a corporation or a person with its trade name registered in accordance with the Commercial Registration Act may file for registration of collateral security, when it provides movable property as security in accordance with a security agreement (Article 3, paragraph 1, Act on Security over Movable Property, Claims, etc.) In cases where more than two movable assets (including movable assets expected to be acquired in the future) are provided as security, if it is possible to specify the assets by the types, places for storage and quantity of the assets or in any similar manner, such assets may be registered as collateral for a security interest (*ibid.*, paragraph 2). A security interest in movable property may be created by setting only the maximum amount of the claim secured by collateral and by fixing its amount later in the future. In such cases, any claim discharged or transferred before such claim is finally fixed shall not affect the security interest already created in movable property (Article 5, paragraph 1, the preceding Act).

*429.* A secured party shall be entitled to collect his/her claim, prior to other obligees, from the collateral provided by an obligor, etc., or a third party (Article 8, the preceding Act). In this context, the preceding Act lays down the priority between rights. Any acquisition of, loss of or alteration to a security interest in movable property by an agreement shall become effective when such acquisition, loss or alteration is registered in the collateral security register (Article 7, paragraph 1, the preceding Act). The order of priority between security interests in one and the same movable property shall be determined by the order of registration (*ibid.*, paragraph 2). Except as otherwise provided for by *lex scripta*, if registration in the collateral security register pursuant to this Act and delivery as requirement for proprietary securities (including summary delivery, agreement on possession and assignment of a claim to return subject matter as set forth by the Civil Code. *supra* paragraph 29) have been completed with respect to one and the same movable property, the order of priority vis-a-vis the interests and rights in such cases shall be determined by the order of such events (Article 7, paragraph 3, Act on Security over Movable Property, Claims, etc. In this sense, the priority of security interest pursuant to this Act over conventionally used atypical real security rights (i.e., proprietary securities) was not adopted, over which there was a severe controversy in the legislative process.

*430.* It should be added that similar to other jurisdictions, retention of ownership (*supra* paragraph 356) is also used in order to secure payment of the installment sales of goods.

# Chapter 10. Contracts with the Government and Other Public Administrations

*431.* In cases where the government or other public administration enters into a civil contract, general rules of the contract law shall apply; however, the freedom of contract may be restricted owing to the public interests concerned (especially with regard to the choice of the contracting party to and/or contents of the contract). In addition, to promote smooth administration of contracts by providing for basic matters regarding contracts to which the state or a local government is a party, the Act on Contracts to which the State is a Party or the Act on Contracts to which a Local Government is a Party shall apply. Since both Acts resemble each other in contents, only the former will be introduced here.

This Act shall apply to the contract to which the State is a party, including government procurement contract entered into through international tendering procedures and contract entered into between the State as a party and a national of the Republic of Korea as the counterparty (Article 2).

*432.* A contract shall be concluded by agreement of the parties thereto on equal footings, and the parties shall perform terms and conditions of the contract in good faith (Article 5, paragraph 1. Paragraph 2 provides for the principle of reciprocity regarding the government procurement contracts made through international tendering procedures). In addition, in order to improve transparency and fairness, the head or contracting officer of a central government agency shall require a tenderer or contractor to promise that he/she will not offer or receive money, goods, entertainment or any other benefit, directly or indirectly, in the course of making or accepting a tender or signing or performing a contract (even after the completion of the relevant project or delivery of goods) and make an agreement ("integrity agreement") on condition that the relevant tender or tender acceptance may be revoked, or the relevant contract may be rescinded or rescinded for the future, if the tenderer or contractor does not keep such promise (Article 5-2, paragraph 1). If a tenderer or contractor does not comply with the integrity agreement, the head or contracting officer of the competent central government agency shall, in principle, revoke the relevant tendering procedure or acceptance of the relevant tender or shall rescind or rescind for the future the relevant contract (Article 5-3).

Where the head or contracting officer of a central government agency intends to make a contract, he/she shall call for open tenders for contract. However, if it is deemed to be necessary in light of the purposes, nature, size, etc., of the contract, he/she may place restrictions on the qualification for participants or designate participants to invite competitive tenders or may execute a negotiated contract, as set forth by the Presidential Decree (Article 7, paragraph 1). In a competitive tendering procedure that becomes a source of revenue, a person who tenders the highest price shall, in principle, be determined as the successful tenderer (Article 10, paragraph 1).

When the head or contracting officer of a central government agency executes a contract, he/she shall, in principle, prepare a written contract document, clearly specifying certain matters (e.g., purposes and the amount of the contract, period of performance, burden of risk, or penalty of delay) therein (Article 11, paragraph 1).

*433.* In case of a contract for construction works, manufacturing, purchasing or services, or any other contract that imposes a burden on the National Treasury, the head or contracting officer of a central government agency shall, in principle, pay the price therefor after conducting an inspection or making an inspection record (Article 15, paragraph 1). Except as otherwise provided for expressly in any other *lex scripta*, he/she shall require to pay the price in advance toward the counterparty to a contract of sale or lease of an asset or for the supply of services, or any other contract that becomes a source of revenue (Article 16). When it is necessary to adjust the contract amount due to price fluctuation, a design modification or an amendment to terms and conditions of contract after a contract for construction works, manufacturing or services or any other contract that imposes a burden on the National Treasury is concluded, the head or contracting officer of the competent central government agency shall adjust the contract amount, as set forth by the Presidential Decree (Article 19).

# Chapter 11. Contract of Partnership

## §1. Introduction

*434.* A partnership contract shall become effective when more than two persons have agreed to carry on a joint undertaking by making mutual contributions thereto. The contribution may be made in cash or in kind such as other property (e.g., good will or even undertaking not to engage in a certain business), or labor service(s) (Article 703).

A partnership contract creates merely "contractual" obligations among partners. Therefore, the entity (e.g., contractor's consortium), which operates on the basis of the very contract ("partnership relation"), should be distinguished from the partnership company in that the latter has the juristic personality (i.e., legal capacity. *See supra* paragraph 98).

Each partner owes obligations (including the duty to make a contribution) against all the other partners. In a case where one of the partners is unable to make the contribution agreed upon, he/she will be excluded from the partnership relation, which has, in principle, no impact on the validity of the partnership contract. On the other hand, all the partners should partake in the profit from the joint undertaking; however, they may agree that some of them do not bear the loss therefrom.

To the partnership contract, neither provisions on synallagmatic contract (Articles 536 ff.) nor those on sale as archetype of contract for value (especially on the liability for warranty. *See* Article 567) shall apply.

## §2. Method of Managing Partnership Affairs

*435.* The management of the partnership affairs shall be determined by majority of the partners (not by majority of shares) (Article 706, paragraph 2). Nevertheless, in cases where more than one partner has been delegated to manage the partnership affairs under the partnership contract or elected with an affirmative vote of not less than two-thirds of all the partners (*ibid.*, paragraph 1), he/she (hereafter "operating partner") shall take charge of the affairs of partnership. If several operating partners are appointed, the management of the affairs shall be determined by majority of such partners (*ibid.*, paragraph 2). These notwithstanding, the ordinary affairs of partnership may be managed by each partner or each operating partner individually; however, he/she shall immediately suspend these acts, if other partners or other operating partners raise an objection to such acts before the completion thereof (Article 706, paragraph 3). (As a result, paragraph 2 shall, in principle, apply to the special affairs of partnership.) In addition, each partner may, at any time, inspect the condition of affairs and property of partnership (Article 710). On the other hand, each partner or operating partner managing the partnership affairs shall be presumed to have the authority of agency to manage the partnership affairs (Article 709), and provisions on mandate (especially on duty of care and due diligence. *See supra* paragraphs 369 ff.) shall apply *mutatis mutandis* to such partner(s) (Article 707).

An operating partner may not be allowed to resign without justifiable reasons and may be dismissed by the unanimous consent of the other partners (Article 708).

## §3. Patrimonial Aspect of Partnership

*436.* The contribution made by each partner and other property of the partnership (e.g., items acquired in the course of the joint undertaking) shall belong to all the partners jointly (Article 704. partnership assets). For instance, with regard to the obligation to make contribution, each partner, in the absence of operating partner, may claim performance against the defaulting partner, but this claim is not personal in nature (i.e., the obligee of a partner claiming performance may not attach this claim). On the other hand, the claim for compensation for loss incurred to the partnership property also belongs to all the partners jointly, not to individual partners.

If a property is owned by several persons through a partnership relationship under the statutory provisions or pursuant to the contract, the partnership assets shall belong to partnership-ownership. The rights of persons having partnership-ownership shall reach the whole of the property in partnership-ownership (Article 271, paragraph 1). None of the persons having partnership-ownership of a piece of partnership assets may dispose of or make alterations to the property without obtaining the consent of all the other persons having partnership-ownership; however, each person is entitled to do any act of preservation (Article 272).

Any partner shall not dispose of his/her shares in partnership assets as well as in the individual items that are part of partnership assets without obtaining the consent of all the other partners, and he/she cannot demand partition (division) of the property (Article 273. By contrast, the co-owners are entitled to dispose of their own shares, and each co-owner may demand partition of the article jointly owned pursuant to Articles 263 and 268). The obligee of a partner may attach the share of the latter, but such attachment is effective only to the distribution of assets upon dissolution.

The partnership-ownership of property shall terminate by dissolution of the partnership or assignment of the property. With regard to partition of the property in partnership-ownership upon termination of the partnership-ownership of property, provisions on the partition of the property jointly owned shall apply *mutatis mutandis* (Article 274).

*437.* On the other hand, all the partners bear the partnership liabilities in proportion to the ratio of loss. As a result, an obligee of the partnership may either execute the partnership assets or the assets of each partner up to his/her apportioned amount of liability (unlimited liability. As to the claim arising from a commercial activity *see* also Article 57, paragraph 1, the Commercial Code and *supra* paragraph 402).

In the absence of any agreement among the partners concerning the ratio of distribution of profits and/or losses, it shall be determined in proportion to the value of contribution of each partner, and if the ratio has been specified solely with respect to either profits or losses, such ratio shall be presumed to apply both to profits and losses (Article 711). However, an obligee of the partnership, who was not aware of the ratio of distribution of losses among the partners at the time when the claim came into existence, may exercise his/her right against each partner in equal distributions (Article 712). Attachment of a partner's distribution shall be effective against the partner's right to future dividends and return of the distribution (Article 714).

If any partner does not have sufficient means to discharge his/her obligations (i.e., in insolvency), his/her portion shall be equally divided among other partners (Article 713). An obligor of the partnership may not set off his/her obligation against his/her claim against a partner (Article 715).

## §4. Status of Partner

*438.* An entry in or retirement from the partnership relation does not affect the partnership relation itself. With regard to retirement, the Civil Code provides for voluntary retirement (Article 716) and nonvoluntary retirement (Article 717. As to expulsion, *see* Article 718).

The accounts between an ex-partner and remaining partners shall be settled according to the condition of the partnership assets at the time when the former ceased to be a partner and the share of an ex-partner may be refunded in money, irrespective of the kind of his/her original contribution. In case of any matter not yet completed at the time when a partner ceases to be such, the account may be settled after such matters have been completed (Article 719).

## §5. Dissolve and Liquidation

*439.* Any partner may demand a dissolution of the partnership if any unavoidable reason therefor (e.g., breakdown of the relationship of trust) exists (Article 720). In case of a partnership relation composed of only two partners, a demand for division of the partnership assets may be construed as a demand for dissolution. If a partnership relation is dissolved, the liquidation shall be conducted jointly by all the partners or by a person appointed by them (Article 721, paragraph 1). Provisions on liquidation of the juristic person shall apply *mutatis mutandis* to the duties and powers of the liquidator (Article 724, paragraph 1). The residual assets shall be distributed among the partners in proportion to the value of their contributions (*ibid.*, paragraph 2). In contrast to the liquidation of the juristic person, provisions on liquidation of the partnership are not mandatory.

# Chapter 12. Quasi-Contracts

## §1. *Negotiorum Gestio*

### I. Overview of Quasi-Contracts

*440.* Part Three of the Civil Code provides also for obligations arising from other sources than contracts. There are three categories: management of affairs of another without mandate, unjust enrichment, and tort. Among them, first two categories may be equivalent to quasi-contracts in the French classification of the sources of obligations (*see supra* paragraph 38).

### II. Management of Affairs of Another Without Mandate

*441.* A management of affairs of another without mandate (*negotiorum gestio*) occurs where a person (manager) commences the management of affairs for another person (principal) without any obligation (and authority) to do so pursuant to a juristic act or by law. A typical example is a repair of the roof of the house of a neighbor, who is away on vacation, or care of a pet dog in the owner's absence. The management may consist of a juristic act as well as a real act (e.g., repair of a thing). The affairs should be of another person, but may be at the same time of manager himself/herself (e.g., repair of the thing jointly owned by the manager and the principal). In this context, it is not necessary that the manager should know who the principal is (i.e., a mistake as to identity of the principal does not matter). By contrast, in cases where a person manages affairs of another believing that they are the manager's own, not provisions on *negotiorum gestio*, but those on unjust enrichment shall apply.

*442.* A management is subject to restraint in order to protect the interests of principal from an "unwanted" intervention. Therefore, upon commencement of the management, certain obligations are imposed by law.

At first, a manager must manage affairs in the manner most advantageous to the principal in compliance with the nature of such affairs. In addition, the management may be justified even if it is in fact not in accordance with the actual intention of the principal; however, if a manager knows or should have known the intention of the principal, the manager must engage in management in conformity with the (presumed) intention of the principal, unless it is contrary to public policy. In a case where a manager has managed the affairs in violation thereof, he/she shall be liable for the losses caused thereby even if he/she was not guilty of negligence. However, if the manager's act of management conforms to the public interests, he/she shall not be liable for damages, unless he/she was grossly negligent (Article 734. As to the urgent management, *see* Article 735).

On the other hand, a manager shall give a notice thereof to the principal without delay (Article 736) and continue the management until the principal, his/her successor or his/her agent by law can undertake it (Article 737). A manager owes duties to report and to deliver and transfer things acquired, and is liable for pecuniary consumption (Articles 738, 683 through 685). On the other hand, since a manager does not have to sustain any loss, he/she is entitled to claim for reimbursement of all necessary and useful expenses (Article 739, paragraph 1. In cases where the management is against the (presumed) intention of the principal, expenses shall be reimbursed under provisions on unjust enrichment, which limit the scope of reimbursement to the extent of the actual benefit of the principal. *Ibid.*, paragraph 3) and to claim for indemnification suffered without negligence (Article 740).

*443.* A management of affairs of another without mandate is regarded as a necessitous intervention, and therefore precludes wrongfulness. Since, however, a manager may not gain from the management, he/she may, in principle, not claim rewards. In this regard, the Supreme Court found recently, in a case where a merchant (M) has managed affairs on behalf of another person (P) without mandate within the scope of M's business, that M may demand reasonable remunerations for such activities (2007Da55477). In this case, money in question is not a reward, but a remuneration for a merchant who has performed any act on behalf of another person within the scope of business (Article 61, the Commercial Code).

## III. False Management of Affairs of Another Without a Mandate

*444.* It is not seldom that a person manages affairs of another person as the former's own, with the knowledge that he/she is not entitled to do so. For instance, in a case where a person who has infringed the author's property right intentionally has gained certain profits therefrom, the infringing person lacks an intention to manage on behalf of another person (i.e., the author). Since, on the other hand, there is no provision which lays down that provisions on *negotiorum gestio* may apply in such situation (such as section 687 of BGB), the wrongdoer shall, in principle, be liable for damages and/or restitution (pursuant to general principles of liability in tort as well as unjust enrichment) against the injured party.

*445.* In this regard, it is one of the controversial issues whether provisions on *negotiorum gestio* may apply (even by way of analogy) in such a case, because a claim for damages as well as restitution is limited to the loss actually suffered, and therefore, in a case where the profit gained exceeds the loss suffered, the wrongdoer may unlawfully hold and enjoy the difference. Some scholars are of the opinion that in order to protect the victim by depriving of such profit, provisions on *negotiorum gestio* (under which any benefit derived from the management may be deprived of) should apply in this case by way of analogy.

In my opinion, however, this approach is not acceptable from the perspective of the entire legal system. For instance, Article 125, paragraph 1 of the Copyright Act states that "Where the holder of author's property right or other rights protected pursuant to this Act ('holder of author's property right, etc.') claims compensation against a person who has infringed on author's property rights intentionally or by negligence for damages sustained from the relevant infringement, if the infringing person has gained any profit by his/her infringement, the relevant amount of profit shall be presumed to be the amount of damages sustained by the holder of author's property right, etc." (As to the practical implication of this provision, *see* also *supra* paragraph 307) This Article implies on the one hand that in case above mentioned provisions on *negotiorum gestio* shall not apply, and on the other hand that the profit exceeding the loss may exceptionally be deprived of pursuant to *lex scripta*. The Supreme Court is presumably of the same opinion.

## §2. Unjust Enrichment

### I. Introduction

*446.* Any person shall not enrich himself/herself at the cost of another person without any legitimate ground therefor. Therefore, a person (beneficiary) who without any legal ground has derived a benefit from the property or services of another and thereby caused a loss to the latter shall be bound to return that benefit (Article 741).

In other words, the unjust enrichment is a benefit caused at the expense of another without any legal ground therefor, and the benefit may take form of the acquisition of some rights or possession (with use of a thing) or the discharge from an obligation.

*447.* The Civil Code provides for unjust enrichment in a coherent system based on fairness and equilibrium, to which many (in the past: most) scholars assent. However, at least two types of unjust enrichment, i.e., enrichment as a result of performance of another person and one by other means should be differentiated. (In this regard, there is an influential view that unjust enrichment may and should be categorized into 3 or 4 types in accordance with the cause of occurrence, which I assent.)

The first type of unjust enrichment is a benefit resulting from performance of a putative obligation. Typical examples are a benefit derived from performance of the void, voided or rescinded contract and the second performance of an obligation already discharged. This type may be denoted as "a performance *condictio*." Even in cases where the thing sold and delivered does not belong to the seller, the seller may demand a return of the thing if the sale turns out to be invalid (except in cases where the buyer has already returned the thing to the owner). In addition, since the validity of transfer of the ownership is dependent upon the validity of the contract creating the obligation to transfer the ownership (*supra* paragraph 21), in a case where a sale of an immovable property is void or voided, the seller may exercise claim for restitution as well as for claim for return of the article owned (Article 213. *rei vindicatio*).

In this type, since the enrichment takes place as a result of performance of a (putative) obligation, the person who has effected performance should allege and prove the lack of legal ground, i.e., the absence of or the discharge from the obligation owed (2017Da37324).

*448.* The second type is made up of various causes of occurrence. Among them, enrichment by way of intervention in the sphere of another person is of great significance. Some examples for this type are cases where a person other than the owner has derived benefit from disposal of the ownership of a thing without having an authority to do so (If the thing sold is a movable, the bona fide assignee may acquire the ownership. Article 249. Otherwise, the owner may exercise the claim for return of the thing. Article 213. *rei vindicatio*), where a seller of a house leased took the rent from the lessee after transfer of the ownership (*see supra* paragraph 372), and where performance was made to a person who is not entitled to receive it and thereby the true obligee loses his/her claim (*see supra* paragraph 208). This type may be denoted as "an intervention *condictio*." An intervention may also take place without any act of the person enriched himself/herself, e.g., in a case where cows of the beneficiary eat grass in meadows which are close to the farm.

In this type, in contrast to the performance *condictio*, enrichment is derived by the beneficiary himself/herself or equivalent thereto from the thing or right which belongs exclusively to the other person even without deliberation, and therefore, the legal ground constitutes the defense of the beneficiary. As a result, at first, the claimant should allege and prove his/her exclusive entitlement and the infringement thereon by the beneficiary or equivalent thereto. Then, the beneficiary may show a legal ground for the benefit obtained (e.g., completion of the period for acquiring ownership of immovables by possession. Article 245, paragraph 1) as a defense (2017Da37324). In this context, statutory provisions which entitle the beneficiary to enjoy benefit (e.g., discharge from an obligation by way of completion of the period of extinctive prescription, or bona fide acquisition) and a final and conclusive judgment constitute a legal ground, and therefore, the claim for restitution shall, in principle, be denied. By contrast, as the only exception thereto, Article 261 lays down that a person who has sustained a loss by reason of provisions of annexing may request compensation based on the ground of unjust enrichment. According to the ruling of the Supreme Court, in this case, the requirements of unjust enrichment should be complied with (2009Da15602).

*449.* In addition, enrichment may occur by way of performance of a person other than the obligor (e.g., a third person or a surety), as a result of which the obligor is discharged from his/her obligations (Article 469). In such case, the reimbursement corresponds in substance to a recourse *condictio*. To this type of enrichment, special provisions (e.g., Articles 441 and 444 regarding suretyship) shall apply.

On the other hand, enrichment may take place owing to expenses for improvement paid on the article belonging to another person, e.g., performance of useful/beneficial act, such as renovation of a building of the beneficiary (*condictio* for expense on improvements). As to this type of enrichment, there are some special provisions, e.g., Articles 203 (claim of possessor for reimbursement) and 626 (lessee's right to obtain reimbursement).

*450.* With regard to restitution, the *actio de in rem verso* is one of the most controversial issues. For instance, X (contractor) and L concluded a contract for repairing a building. The building is owned by Y, and L is a lessee. As a result of the repairing, the value of the building increased, but L became bankrupt in the meantime. In this case, may X demand Y a restitution for the value increased instead of the claim for remuneration against L? The Supreme Court ruled that X may claim only against L, i.e., the counterpart of the contract, not against Y (99Da66564,66571). If X can demand Y for restitution, the risk allocation (The risk accompanied with contract should, in principle, be borne by the parties thereto.) may be distorted, and X would be given de facto preferential treatment over other obligees of L. (In this case, L has a right to demand Y for reimbursement, and X can exercise A's right against Y. Article 626, paragraph 2 and Article 404, paragraph 1).

In this regard, the unjust enrichment is subsidiary in nature.

## II. Method and Scope of Restitution

*451.* The benefit may be an ownership or possession of a thing, or an assigned right (including anything which he/she acquires in compensation for destruction, damage or deprivation of the object obtained), and the beneficiary is liable to return the benefit itself, e.g., the object itself which he/she has actually received. In cases where restitution *in natura* is not possible (e.g., benefit consisted of the performance of work), he/she shall return the value of the object received (Article 747, paragraph 1). In such case, a third party acting in bad faith, who has obtained the object or the benefits gratuitously from the beneficiary, shall be liable to return such objects (*ibid.*, paragraph 2).

*452.* With respect to the amount of benefits to be returned, the Civil Code draws the line between the beneficiaries in good faith and those in bad faith. In this regard, if the beneficiary becomes aware of the fact that no legal ground therefor had ever existed after he/she had received such benefit, he/she shall be a beneficiary in bad faith from the time of his/her awareness of such fact, and the beneficiary in good faith shall, if defeated in a lawsuit, be deemed to be a beneficiary in bad faith from the time such action was filed (Article 749).

The beneficiary in good faith shall be liable to return the benefit to the extent that he/she is still enriched thereby (Article 748, paragraph 1). Under this provision, which aims to protect reliance of the beneficiary in good faith, a decrease in the benefit during the interim period need not be returned. In this case, the claimant should prove the fact that the beneficiary has unconsumed benefit still (however, according to the ruling of the Supreme Court, in cases where the benefit received was money or its equivalent, the benefit is presumed to exist. 96Da32881).

On the other hand, a beneficiary in bad faith shall return the benefits received together with interest on the money received (or profit gained from using the thing or exercising the right), and if there has been any loss, he/she shall be bound also to make compensation therefor (*ibid.*, paragraph 2). Articles 141 and 548 constitute exceptions thereto (*see supra* paragraphs 89 and 284).

*453.* Whether the so-called operating profit (i.e., benefit gained from operating the object received e.g., by way of using the thing or exercising the right) is the object of restitution or not, is one of the controversial issues. The situation goes worse with regard to the surplus profit, i.e., profit which exceeds the profit expected (usually the ordinary profit), as a result of contribution of the beneficiary. The Supreme Court found that the operating profit should, in principle, be returned and the restitution shall be limited to the ordinary profit, and therefore, the surplus profit is not the object of restitution (94Da25551). In the same context, if the loss which a beneficiary suffers from operating the object, it should be borne by himself/herself (96Da47568).

## III. Restrictions on Restitution

*454.* There are some exceptions to the claim for restitution (concerning the performance *condictio*).

First, in cases where a person has discharged an obligation with knowledge that such obligation did not exist, he/she may not demand a return of the subject matter (Article 742). However, in case of the performance under pressure (e.g., threatened with compulsory execution), he/she may claim restitution.

Second, in the event that a person, not liable to an obligation, has discharged such obligation by mistake and such discharge conforms to a sense of morality, he/she may not demand a return of the subject matter (Article 744). For instance, in a case where a person contributes to the maintenance of a relative whom the former is not legally obliged to support, he/she may not claim restitution.

Third, in cases where a person other than the obligor has discharged an obligation by mistake, the former may, as a rule, demand a return of his/her performance. However, if the obligee has in good faith destroyed evidentiary documents, waived any security, or lost his/her claim by prescription, the person who has performed the obligation may not demand return of his/her performance. In this case, such person may exercise his/her right of subrogation against the obligor (Article 745). This case should be distinguished from performance by third persons under Article 469 (*see supra* paragraph 205).

*455.* Finally, in the event where a person granted property or rendered service for an illegal cause, he/she may not demand a return of benefits resulting therefrom (Article 746). Any person may invoke his/her own wrongdoing to the extent that he/she can allege nullity of the contract. However, he/she may not be entitled to claim restitution of his/her own performance (equivalent to the clean hands doctrine of Anglo-American law). According to the ruling of the Supreme Court, the "illegal cause" means only a violation of social order under Article 103 (i.e., excluding simple illicit causes. 2001Da1782). For instance, the person who has performed the obligation arising from gambling may not claim restitution (gambling is, in principle, evaluated as contrary to social order in Korea. *See supra* paragraph 342).

On the other hand, under proviso to Article 746, if such illegal cause exists solely on the part of the beneficiary, the person who has performed the obligation may demand return of the benefits. Since, however, in case of the violation of Article 103, the parties usually share illegal causes, the party to an executory contract, who alone has performed, will be in a very disadvantageous position. Taking this unjust result into account, the Supreme Court found that in a case where the illegitimacy on the part of the beneficiary overwhelmingly preponderates over that on the other part, claim for restitution is possible (93Da12947). (In other words, the party claiming restitution may succeed if his/her illegitimacy is conspicuously less reprehensible than that of the other party.)

## IV. Payment but Not Due

*456.* Under Article 743, in a case where an obligor has discharged an obligation, which has not yet fallen due, he/she may not demand a return of the subject matter. However, if the obligor discharges such obligation by mistake, the obligee shall return the benefit gained therefrom (not the subject matter itself). In this regard, besides the payment in money, the performance of any act, which constitutes the object of an obligation, may also deserve of the discharge.

# Table of Korean Cases

*All references are to paragraph numbers.*

## Table of Korean Cases

**Table of Korean Cases**

# Index

*The numbers here refer to paragraph numbers.*

**Index**

www.ingramcontent.com/pod-product-compliance
Ingram Content Group UK Ltd.
Pitfield, Milton Keynes, MK11 3LW, UK
UKHW020142290926
15471UKWH00004B/645

9 789403 511436